JANIE HIBLER

# THE BERRY BIBLE

WITH 175 RECIPES USING CULTIVATED and WILD, FRESH and FROZEN BERRIES

Printed in the United States of America



Published by AmazonEncore
P.O. Box 400818
Las Vegas, NV 89140

ISBN10: 1935597124
ISBN13: 9781935597124

*This book is dedicated to all the people in the berry industry,*

*from the farmers and their harvest crews, to the world's berry horticulturalists,*

*whose hard work brings such infinite pleasures to our tables.*

# CONTENTS

# ACKNOWLEDGMENTS

A special thank you to the following people, without whose help this book could not have been written:

My husband, Gary Hibler, for his invaluable help with proofreading, moral support, and unending patience; my editor, Harriet Bell, whose friendship I value as much as her top-notch editing; and my agent, Judith Weber, for believing in me and this project.

Dr. Chad Finn, for being an inspiration, mentor, and scientific adviser for this book, and to the following for their guidance: Dr. Dan Barney, Dr. Jim Hancock, Dr. Kim Hummer, Dr. Jim Joseph, Steven McKay, Dr. Tom Sjulin, Dr. Gary Stoner, Dr. David Yarborough, Dr. Harlene Hatterman-Valenti, Dr. Jerry Parsons, Dr. Carlos Fear, Vern Nelson, and Dr. Maxine Thompson.

My longtime friend and chief recipe tester, Betty Shenberger, and assistant recipe tester, Shannon Robbins, as well as Susan Franklin, Nancy Smith, Judy Lakin, Karen Pierce, and Kathy Kurtz.

Ed Gowans, who built the "berry box" and patiently used it to beautifully photograph every berry I brought him.

Chris Benton, copy editor; Ann Cahn, production editor; Karen Lumley, production manager; Roberto de Vicq de Cumptich, jacket art director; and Leah Carlson-Stanisic, interior art director—a dream team every author should be lucky enough to have.

The following organizations for their help: the Oregon Raspberry and Blackberry Commission, the Washington Red Raspberry Commission, the British Columbia Blueberry Council, the California Strawberry Commission, the Cape Cod Cranberry Growers' Association, the Wild Blueberry Association of North America, the Ontario Berry Growers' Association, the International Ribes Association, the Florida Strawberry Growers' Association, CanolaInfo, and the Porto Wine Institute.

And to all the others who contributed in one way or another to this book: Carol Adams, Kathy Allcock, Jeff Allen, Claire Archibald, Sonja Atkinson, Beatrice Bentley, Carolyn Bentley, Ed and Aggie Bostrom, Jerry Boucock, Philippe Boulot, Flo Braker, John and Mary Brewer, Julia Child, Chris Christensen, Lois Cochran, Bill and Linda Coonrod, Kerry De Buser, Daphne Dervin, Brooke Dojny, Barbara Durbin, Rick Edwards, Jennifer Flanagan, Jay and Terry Franke, Kassie Franke, Evelyn Franz, Pat Fusco, Darra Goldstein, Jane Hergenhan, Audrey, Emma, Gretchen, and Kelly Hibler, Kristin Hibler, Lynette Hibler, Ross and Betty Hibler, Ross and Jeanne Hibler, Trish Hibler, Betty Lou Hutchens, Joan Ida, Joy Jinks, Rob Kasper, Dan and Betty Kelner, Jim Keyser, Paula Lambert, Anna Tasca Lanza, Dorothy Long, Jude Lutge, Sharon Maasdam, Ed Mashburn, Rick McClure, Ellen McFarland, Cat McKenzie, Janet Mendel, Anne Messelink, Lorinda Moholt, Jeffery Neumeier, Patrick O'Connell, Beatrice Ojakangas, Marlene Parrish, Janet and Linda Pendergrass, Pete Peterson, Karen Pierce, Dennis and Rachael Pleasant, Delphine Polon, Molly Schaefer-Priest, Gerald and Jane Rainey, Don Reeser, Marcus Samuelsson, Adam Sappington, Kari Schaefer, Sally Schneider, Eric Schramn, Jan-Marie Schroeder, Jo Seagar, Karen Sehon, Jim Shenberger, Marie Simmons, Jennie and Lee Simpson, Stu Stein, Mary Stewart, Zanne Stewart, Hakan Swahn, Gail Timmons, Tommie van de Kamp, Ed Walker, Doug Walta, Lucia Watson, Patricia Wells, Cathy Whims, Linda Wisner, Catherine Woesthoff, Susan VandeKerk, and Mike Zobel.

*"The intention of every other piece of prose may be discussed and even mistrusted; but the purpose of a cookery book is one and unmistakable. Its object can conceivably be no other than to increase the happiness of mankind."*

—JOSEPH CONRAD

# INTRODUCTION

I have wanted to write a berry cookbook since 1983, when I completed *Dungeness Crabs and Blackberry Cobblers*. Although that book was about the culinary history of the Pacific Northwest, I was unable to adequately cover the local berry industry, which produces the greatest diversity of cultivated berries in the world, a fact largely unknown outside the region. *The Berry Bible* includes a wide range of wild and cultivated berries and fruits—the product of those 20 years of cogitation. It was a story waiting to be told.

Blueberries, cranberries, and Concord grapes are commonly said to be America's only three native fruits, but that simply isn't so. Muscadine grapes, blackberries, and black raspberries are 100 percent North American, and lingonberries and red raspberries are both derived from species that are native to the Northern Hemisphere. The first cultivated red raspberries and lingonberries were from European species, but they are the same species that grow in the northern United States and Canada. And strawberries are half North American (*Fragaria virginiana*) and half South American (*Fragaria chiloensis*).

As I was growing up in Arcata, California, 90 miles south of the Oregon border, picking wild berries was one of the highlights of summer. We gathered thimbleberries and salmonberries from the banks of the creek that bordered our property and wild blackberries and coastal huckleberries down by our barn. Going berry picking with the neighborhood kids was a special part of our summer.

As young adults, my husband and I moved to Portland, Oregon, in 1972. We enjoyed hiking in the Cascades and picking many of the same varieties of berries we had grown up with, and we were introduced to the plethora of cultivated berries growing in the fertile Willamette Valley. With our infant daughter in my backpack and our young son equipped with his own bucket, we'd spend summer mornings picking berries and the afternoons putting them up. I learned how to make preserves from my German grandmother, and my aunt, who grows blackberries commercially, taught me the secrets of making berry syrups. Stocking my freezer with berries and my pantry with jams, syrups, and fruit leathers was all part of existing on a minimal graduate student's budget.

When the children were older, I bribed them and neighborhood kids into helping me pick berries by offering to bake them each a pie of their very own. I could always get a few extra hands that way.

While running a Portland cooking school, one of my greatest pleasures was taking visiting chefs and cooking teachers from other parts of the United States and Europe on drives: I could have them at the nearest berry fields in less than 20 minutes.

It was those rich, fertile soils of the Willamette Valley that attracted pioneers to Oregon in the mid-1800s. With their first plantings they found ideal growing conditions for small fruit crops. The long springs, from the beginning of March to the end of June, gave the fruit time to develop exceptional flavor; the lengthy summer days with little rain and cool nights slowed down the crops' growth and made the fruit sweet, while the coastal breezes kept the fruit from rotting.

Numerous members of Oregon's berry industry are second- and third-generation families, like the Kerrs, who produce fruit juice concentrates for the wholesale trade and are directly related to the old Portland Kerr family, manufactures of the Kerr canning jar. The infrastructure for Oregon's berry industry is built on the foundation laid by previous generations of plant breeders, berry farmers, and processors.

But the birth of America's commercial berry industry began much earlier on the East Coast. By the early 1800s, strawberries, raspberries, gooseberries, and currants were being grown commercially in Boston, New York, Philadelphia, and Baltimore from European stock brought to this country by the settlers. Cultivated cranberries were shipped out of Boston to Europe, and by the 1840s wild blueberries were being harvested commercially. By the middle of the nineteenth century, a variety of America's wild berries were domesticated and crossed with the European berries. Our raspberries, currants, and gooseberries are all a mixture of North American and European stock.

The American berry industry has greatly benefited from public (USDA and university) and private breeding programs. The most obvious results are the improved fresh market cultivars for each region that have enabled growers to extend berry seasons with early-, middle-, and late-ripening berries.

Many universities and private breeding programs, such as Driscoll Strawberry Associates, develop their own cultivars, which they patent. An assortment of the berries developed in the United States is now being grown throughout the world. It is interesting to note that it takes at least six years from the time a strawberry cultivar is developed to reach the consumer, seven to eight years for raspberries, and 12 to 15 years for blueberries.

With our global economy and a wide range of berry cultivars extending the berry seasons, fresh berries are available at our markets almost year-round, but unfortunately, they are not always premier fruit. This is in part because 12 corporations own 50 percent of the nation's grocery stores, and their suppliers buy large quantities of berries for their produce departments. They want a steady supply of fruit that can, as inexpensively as possible, fill the produce tables. To meet the demands of long-distance shipping and storage, some growers pick fruit when it is very firm but unripe. The berries will eventually become fully colored, but they will never be sweet or develop that berry flavor had they field ripened.

According to Dr. Chad Finn, USDA small plant breeder, "The companies that are involved in supplying berries to consumers are responsive to the consumer's demands. As long as the consumer is primarily demanding an attractive fruit in the grocery store year-round, and at an inexpensive price, then that is what they will provide. If flavor and great eating quality are demanded by the consumer, and they are willing to pay what it would cost to bring that to their grocery store, the companies will very quickly adjust their practices. For this to happen, consumers need to let their local grocer know that they are satisfied or dissatisfied with what is available and why."

When buying berries, ask for the cultivar name so you know what you are getting. Dr. Tom Sjulin, director of strawberry research at Driscoll's, says, "It's not the time of the year that's important when buying berries; it's the cultivar." So, when you find a berry you like, keep asking for it, and take bad berries back. Nothing is going to change until consumers start demanding it.

During the time it has taken me to write this book, I have traveled extensively to learn about the berries from other regions. I spent a week in scenic Washington County, Maine, the heart of the state's wild blueberry industry, visiting the barrens, growers, and processing facilities. I traveled to Saskatoon, in Saskatchewan, Canada, where the tall Saskatoon (we call them *Juneberries*) shrubs line the meandering Saskatchewan River, which flows through the center of this prairie town. At the weekly farmers' market, I bought fresh berries and drank Saskatoon lemonade while looking over the local vendors' tables loaded with Saskatoon pies, turnovers, jams, jellies, and other locally made berry products. I relished the beauty of Massachusetts's brilliant crimson-colored cranberry bogs during harvest, and I picked wild blueberries in Tangle Lakes, Alaska, with Aggie Bostrom, an Inuit Indian. In Carlsbad, California, I sampled berries from a roadside stand next to strawberry fields surrounded by a rainbow of fragrant stock and ranunculus. Farther up the coast, at Driscoll's Strawberry

Associates in Watsonville, fields of artichokes lined the road as I drove north to the center of the strawberry fields. During a stay near Carpentras, the strawberry capital of France, I sampled three different strawberry cultivars and Ardèche raspberries, sold at the weekly farmers' market at Beaumes-de-Venise. And in the Netherlands, I ate bowls of strawberries grown in the lowlands in plastic tunnels. In my own backyard in Oregon, I've watched marionberries being picked at the peak of harvest and taken directly to the processor, where they were washed and frozen in a matter of minutes for the IQF (individually quick frozen) market.

I eventually settled down and wrote this book. I start with the latest word on the health benefits of berries and why it is so advantageous to include them in your diet. (At last there is something we all love that is actually good for us to eat.) Next is an A-to-Z resource that profiles important culinary berries and berrylike fruits. I have also included several newcomers—the blue honeysuckle berry and the sea buckthorn—that will likely play a significant role in the near future.

In "Berry Basics," I guide you through important information such as how to create your own purees and sugar syrup—steps that you can do ahead of time that will make cooking with berries an easy, satisfying experience.

The other sections feature 175 of my favorite berry dishes. Over the years I have collected an entire file drawer full of berry recipes. Some are my own creations; others have come from my travels, family, friends, chefs, and neighbors. I picked out only the best for this book, and they have all been retested by me and then again by a group of testers. Like all recipes, these are meant to inspire you in the kitchen and bring immeasurable pleasure to your table. Enjoy!

# GOOD HEALTH AND BERRIES

"Eat five to eight helpings of fruits and vegetables a day, but include berries three to four times a week," says Dr. Gary Stoner, director of the Laboratory of Cancer Chemoprevention and Etiology at Ohio State University. Berries contain an abundance of plant chemicals—scientifically called *phytochemicals*—micronutrients found in plants that help our bodies fight disease. Out of the 900 known phytochemicals, scientists have studied only a handful, but berry researchers around the world unanimously agree on the potency of their protective powers in keeping not only plants healthy but humans, too.

Phytochemicals are found in vegetables, fruits, grains, legumes, seeds, licorice root, soy, green tea, and wine. Tufts University researchers measured 50 fruits and vegetables and ranked berries as having the highest levels of anthocyanins, one of the most important groups of phytochemicals. These water-soluble plant pigments are responsible for making a raspberry red, a blueberry blue, and staining your shirt if you are not careful. While it's true that 90 percent of berries are water, don't be fooled: that colorful juice is loaded with powerful antioxidants and other disease-fighting chemicals that give berries a vital role in helping us maintain our good health. And remember—the darker colored the berry, the greater the anthocyanin level and consequently the greater the protection.

How do anthocyanins work? There are multiple sites on a DNA molecule where free radicals can attach and send the wrong signals to our bodies, just as a virus attacks your computer. Anthocyanins act as our body's antivirus software by scavenging for those free radicals that attach to our DNA, as well as to proteins and lipids, and enabling our bodies to prevent disease before it starts. To date, researchers have linked anthocyanins to antiviral and anticancer activity, reducing coronary heart disease, controlling diabetes, slowing the effects of aging, and improving vision.

Berries also contain significant amounts of phenolic acids, another important phytochemical. One of the most powerful is ellagic acid, which is especially high in boysenberries, black raspberries, and cranberries. This phytochemical works together with the anthocyanins, similar to the way our computer's maintenance software keeps our computer running smoothly. Ellagic acid helps prevent disease by stimulating enzymes to rid the body of harmful toxins, which helps in protecting the digestive system against esophageal and colon cancer.

Tannins, found in high concentrations in cranberries and many other berry types, are also members of the polyphenolic family. These phytochemicals are helpful in preventing urinary tract infections, gum disease, and some types of ulcers by stopping harmful bacteria from attaching to our cells' walls.

Scientists are clear in pointing out that it is a combination of all the phytochemicals and nutrients in berries—anthocyanins, phenolic acids, fiber, tannins, vitamins, and minerals, to name a few—working together that help prevent disease. They advise eating a variety of berries three to four times a week if you can. But what about eating cooked berries? Studies have shown that ellagic acid and anthocyanin levels in caneberry jam and juice remain stable during processing with high heat. While a portion of the nutraceutical qualities may be diminished in other berries, the consensus is that it's better than not eating any berries at all. Although some phytochemicals won't be as powerful once the berries are heated, they will still contain a significant amount of health-benefiting properties.

# THE A-TO-Z BERRY ENCYCLOPEDIA

As English developed from the Germanic language, *ber*, an Old Norse word, evolved into Old English as *berie*, which ultimately became *berry*.

Today *Merriam-Webster's Collegiate Dictionary*, eleventh edition, lists berry as

**1 a:** a pulpy and usu. edible fruit (as a strawberry, raspberry, or checkerberry) of small size irrespective of its structure
**b:** a simple fruit (as a grape, blueberry, tomato, or cucumber) with a pulpy or fleshy pericarp
**c:** the dry seed of some plants (as wheat)

**2:** an egg of a fish or lobster

All of the berries listed in the following pages fit into either the first or second categories. Most of them are native to North America, which has an abundance of wild berries. I have included all of the important culinary berries and a few fruits, like the mayhaw and chokecherry, which cooks use as berries but actually are a small apple and cherry, respectively. The sea buckthorn berry, the blue honeysuckle berry, and the hardy kiwi are all recent arrivals to America, but they will most likely play a significant role in the North American berry industry, as either a food or a nutraceutical, in the near future.

While berries often have a variety of colloquial names, as a help to travelers I have listed the most common, as well as their name in the language of the countries where they grow and are popular culinary berries.

The word *cultivar* is used extensively in this section of the book. It is a contraction of *cultivated variety* and is commonly used in the fruit horticultural world to describe an asexually propagated improved plant, like the 'Marion', 'Boysen', etcetera. In the vegetable world, *variety* is used more commonly.

# ARBUTUS

**Common names** • madrone, madroña, strawberry tree, corbézzolo (Italy), Erdbeerebaum (Germany), arbousier (France).

**Scientific classification** • *Arbutus* is a genus of trees and shrubs in the heath family (Ericaceae) that is closely related to the manzanita tree and the blueberry. Included in this genus are the madrone (*Arbutus menziesii*) and strawberry tree (*Arbutus unedo*). Their names are derived from the original name given them by Pliny in the first century—*Arbutus unedo* is Latin for "I eat one," referring to the sour taste of the fruit of the strawberry tree—one berry is all you will want. *Menziesii* is in honor of Archibald Menzies (1754–1842), a British naval surgeon and botanist.

**Habitat and distribution** • There are 15 species in the *Arbutus* genus, five in North America and at least 10 in Europe and western Asia. The madrone, native to North America, where four different species grow in the western and southwestern coastal states, is a lovely broad-leaf evergreen tree that is identified by its reddish paper-thin bark, which peels off the tree in curls. Madrones reach an average height of 30 to 70 feet but can be as tall as 100 feet. They prefer dry bluffs and often grow at graceful angles along the slopes. Their clusters of bright red and yellow berries ripen in the fall and provide a welcome food source for neighboring wildlife.

The strawberry tree is a native of southern Europe, but it can be found in other areas, too, where it thrives on rocky coastal slopes and in immature oak woods. This slow-growing evergreen tree, with its characteristic flaky bark, only reaches a height of 15 to 25 feet, and produces dime- to quarter-sized, strawberry-red fruit that ripens in the fall.

**History** • Native Americans ate madrone berries and carved eating utensils from the tree's bulbous roots. The Salish of Vancouver Island boiled the bark of the Pacific madrone with camas bulbs to color the bulbs pink, while the neighboring Saanich steeped the arbutus bark and leaves for colds and stomach remedies. In the Southwest, the caballeros prized the hard and handsomely colored reddish brown madrone wood for making their spurs.

**Where they are grown commercially** • Madrones and strawberry trees are prized by landscapers and are widely grown in the United States and Europe for ornamental gardens.

**How to pick** • Leave the madrone berries for the birds. The scarlet fruit of the strawberry tree ripen in the fall and are easy to pick as they hang on stems, like cherries, but they are larger.

**How to buy** • Not available commercially.

**How to store** • If you wait until the strawberry tree fruit ripens completely in the fall—it will be deep red, soft, and fall to the ground—gather the berries as soon as you can and store in an open container in the refrigerator. Eat the fruit within 24 hours as they decay rapidly. Younger fruit that have turned red but are still slightly hard can be stored in an open container in the refrigerator for two to three days until they soften.

**Notes for the cook** • Madrone berries are edible and are beautiful to look at but not very tasty. The strawberry tree is different. In southern Italy and Sardinia, where the tree grows wild, its sour fruit is stewed for jam, and the bitter honey made by bees that gather nectar from the strawberry tree flower is highly prized and sold commercially. Try the jam on biscuits or scones and the bitter honey drizzled over a wedge of blue cheese as an appetizer with crackers. You can order both from A. G. Ferrari, 688 Mission Street, San Francisco, CA 94105; 415-344-0644; www.agferrari.com.

## ARCTIC RASPBERRY

**Common names** • Arctic bramble, nagoonberry, dwarf raspberry, crimson bramble, Ackerbeere (Germany), lampóne àrtico (Italy), framboise Arctique (France), åkcrbär (Sweden), mesimarja (Finland).

**Scientific classification** • *Rubus arcticus* are members of the rose family (Rosaceae) and are related to blackberries and raspberries.

**Habitat and distribution** • Arctic raspberries are dwarf raspberries (there is also a dwarf blackberry subspecies) that bear flowers on annual shoots from underground rhizomes. These globe-shaped berries range in color from pale yellow to wine red to purple, depending on where they grow. They are highly regarded for their intense raspberry aroma. In the Northern Hemisphere, three subspecies of Arctic brambles flourish in low-elevation bogs and meadows and at higher elevations in streamside thickets from the Arctic to the northern United States. In Europe the berries are found primarily in the northern parts of Sweden, Finland, and Russia.

**History** • Local inhabitants have cherished the rare Arctic raspberries in their diet for centuries. In North America these prized berries are traditionally added to Eskimo ice cream, eaten fresh with milk and sugar, or cooked down into an intensely flavored jam; in Europe they are made into jam, liqueur, parfaits, and various other desserts.

**Where they are grown commercially** • Arctic brambles have been domesticated only recently and are cultivated in just two places: Sweden, where a cross between the Alaskan and Nordic Arctic bramble is grown, and Finland, where clones of the country's indigenous berry are being raised. The majority of Arctic brambles in Finland are used by distilleries to make a liqueur called mesimarja.

**How to pick** • Perfectly ripe fruit will be full colored with its characteristic fruity flavor and aroma, and the soft berries will fall easily from the stalk. Like blackberries, though, they stay attached to the receptacle and sepals when they are picked.

**How to buy** • Not available commercially. Related hybrid (*R. stellarcticus*) is commonly sold as plants.

**How to store** • The delicate Arctic brambles have a shelf life of only two to three days. Store the berries unwashed and uncovered in the refrigerator in a shallow container on a paper towel to absorb moisture that can cause molding. Wash the berries just before using.

To freeze, first rinse the berries (see page 69) and drain thoroughly, then transfer to a baking sheet lined with paper towels and pat dry. Discard immature and overripe berries. Put the lined baking sheet in the freezer until the berries are frozen. Pour the individually frozen berries into self-sealing plastic freezer bags and freeze for up to two years.

Frozen berries should be used frozen and folded into batters just prior to baking. (The exception is pancake batter, which cooks quickly and doesn't allow the fruit time to thaw.) Thaw the berries on a plate lined with a paper towel for 20 minutes at room temperature.

**Notes for the cook** • Arctic brambles have the sepal and receptacle still attached when they are picked, making it time consuming to remove them from the berries. Instead, grind the fruit whole, including the sepals and receptacles, in a food processor before using them.

## ARONIA (*BLACK CHOKEBERRY*)

**Common names** • chokeberry, black chokeberry, aronia (Germany and Italy), melanocarpa (France). The name is derived from the bitter-tasting berries produced by some of the members of the *Aronia* genus. Do not confuse the black chokeberry with the chokecherry (*Prunus virginiana*), a wild cherry.

**Scientific classification** • Aronias, members of the rose family (Rosaceae), include three chokeberries: the black chokeberry (*Aronia melanocarpa*), the red chokeberry (*A. arbutifolia*), and the purple chokeberry (*A. atropurpurea*). *Aronia melanocarpa* is derived from modification of the Greek word *aria,* referring to *Sorbus aria* (mountain ash, which also produces berries in clusters), and *melano,* Greek for "dark/black," and *carpa* for "fruit." They are closely enough related to the mountain ash that hybrids between aronia and ash have been developed that have the dark fruit of aronia and the plant habit of the ash.

**Habitat and distribution** • Aronias are native to the eastern half of the Northern Hemisphere, growing from Nova Scotia to Michigan to northern Florida. These deciduous shrubs, which often grow to nine feet tall and just as wide, prefer wet swampy areas, where they flourish as thickets. They produce clusters of dark berries that ripen in late summer.

**History** • The Native Americans dried black chokeberries and used them in combination with other local berries for sustenance. The root and leaves were used for a variety of ailments.

**Where they are grown commercially** • While widely ignored in the U.S., Soviet plant breeders obtained seeds around 1900 that were of eastern U.S. origin. A concerted development program commenced, leading to large plantings after World War II. Today aronias are commonly grown in the former Soviet Union (especially Siberia), eastern Europe, and Denmark, where they are known as healing plants and their fruit is processed into juice. There are now some small plantings in the Pacific Northwest and the Midwest and test gardens in Indiana and Michigan.

**How to pick** • Harvest the berry clusters in late August or early September, when the foliage turns crimson to reddish orange and the berries are black.

**How to buy** • The berries are not available commercially. Aronia juice from fruit grown in the Masurian Lakeland region of Poland is now being sold in supermarkets in the United States. Named varieties are available at nurseries.

**How to store** • Keep the berries unwashed and uncovered in the refrigerator in a shallow container on a paper towel to absorb moisture that can cause molding. They will keep for two to four days. Wash just before using.

To freeze, first rinse the berries (see page 69) and drain thoroughly, then transfer to a baking sheet lined with paper towels and pat dry. Discard immature and overripe berries. Put the lined baking sheet in the freezer until the berries are frozen. Pour the individually frozen berries into self-sealing plastic freezer bags and freeze for up to one year.

**Notes for the cook** • Aronia berries are pea size, violet-black with brilliant red flesh. Wild berries are too bitter to be eaten raw, but they have a good flavor when cooked and are most often made into syrup, jam or jelly, or juice. Some commercial varieties are edible raw.

## BARBERRY

**Common names** • Oregon grape, Cascade barberry, Rocky Mountain grape, California barberry, hollyleaved barberry, trailing mahonia, Beale's barberry, shining netvein barberry, red barberry, Texas barberry, algerita, and épine vinette (France).

**Scientific classification** • Barberry is the English name for *Berberis,* derived from Arabic. These plants are members of the huge international barberry family (Berberidaceae). In North America scientists cannot seem to agree on the classification of the Oregon grape, and it has been variously listed as a species of *Mahonia* or of *Berberis.*

**Habitat and distribution** • Members of the barberry family are native to Asia, Europe, North America, and the tropical mountains of South America. Altogether there are about 450 species of these shrubs, which can be evergreen or deciduous and grow in a variety of climates from the tropics to shady forests. Eleven varieties grow throughout much of the United States.

**History** • An Arabic writer of medicine mentioned barberries as early as the twelfth century. One of the first recipes using barberries comes from the British, who made Barberry Drops, a type of candy made from the berry clusters. In North America, all of the Pacific Northwest Native Americans prized the root of the Oregon grape. It was boiled fresh for stomach problems and itchy eyes and used as a yellow basket dye. The sour berries were mashed, boiled, and mixed with other berries before they were dried.

**Where they are grown commercially** • Barberries are cultivated as ornamental garden plants only.

**How to pick** • The berries of the Oregon grape turn dark blue when they are ripe. Harvest them from the wild in the late summer and early fall, and wear gloves to avoid the prickly leaves.

**How to store** • Keep the berries unwashed and uncovered in the refrigerator in a shallow container on a paper towel to absorb moisture that can cause molding. They will keep for two to three days. Wash just before using.

To freeze, first rinse the berries (see page 69) and drain thoroughly, then transfer to a baking sheet lined with paper towels and pat dry. Discard immature and overripe berries. Put the lined baking sheet in the freezer until the berries are frozen. Pour the individually frozen berries into self-sealing plastic freezer bags and freeze for up to a year.

**Notes for the cook** • Berries of the Oregon grape are edible but tart; use them for jelly. In the spring, the tender leaves can be used in salads.

## BLACKBERRY

**Common names** • bramble, caneberry, mûre (France), mora (Italy), Brombeere (Germany), zarza (Spain), dewberry.

**Scientific classification** • Blackberries are in the same scientific family as roses (Rosaceae) and are closely related to strawberries. They are classified in the genus *Rubus* (from Latin *ruber*, meaning "red," which includes blackberries, dewberries, raspberries, and all their cultivars) and broken down even further into the subgenus *Eubatus*. There are so many recognized species, more than 250, that scientists have given the study of blackberries its own name—batology.

**Habitat and distribution** • These ancient fruit are native to most temperate regions of the world, which include most of Europe, parts of North and South America, Australia, and Asia.

Although blackberries have been classified in many different manners, one of the most straightforward is to classify them as trailing, erect, and evergreen. Trailing blackberries, also called *dewberries*, are a native North American wild blackberry, and they are named for the region where they grow—eastern, southeastern, and western dewberries. There are more than 90 species of wild trailing blackberries in North America, and they can be found in clearings and logged-over areas rich in decaying matter, growing on long sprawling vines with dime-size black fruit.

The western or Pacific dewberries are prized for their sweet and intensely flavored fruit. They are one of the parents, the other being raspberry, of most of the popular blackberry hybrids throughout the world today, such as boysenberries and loganberries.

Erect wild blackberries include the invasive Himalayan Giant (*R. procerus*), a native of Germany, introduced to the United States in 1885 by botanist Luther Burbank. This pesky plant grows in dense thickets and has become naturalized in Europe and the United States. The fruit produces juicy and moderately flavorful large berries that are seedy but make a good jelly. A number of other erect blackberries (e.g., *R. argutus, R. allegheniensis, R. pergratus*) are native to the eastern U.S., and these have served as the foundation material from which most of the blackberry cultivars grown for fresh eating have been developed.

The evergreen, or cut-leaf, blackberry, introduced to Oregon around 1850 by English explorers, is now naturalized throughout much of the northwestern United States and Canada, where its seeds have been spread by birds. These berries, which ripen in late summer, are firm and seedy with a mild flavor.

On the East Coast, dewberries are the common name for trailing blackberries. In the West, the native trailing blackberry, as well as the Himalayan Giant and cut-leaf evergreen, which have both gone native, are all called wild blackberries.

**History •** Blackberries have been written about as far back as the fourth century B.C. In the Old and New Worlds, these succulent berries were valued not only as a food source—they were eaten fresh and dried—but also as medicine. Blackberry juice was used to treat infections, and the bark and leaves were dried and ground as a remedy for dysentery. In Great Britain blackberries and honey were commonly used as a cure for sore throats and chest colds, and navy blue and indigo dyes were originally made from blackberry juice.

When the Europeans arrived in the New World, there were only a few distinct species of blackberries in this heavily forested country. As the settlers cleared the land, working their way west, the newly open spaces gave the blackberry plants room to grow, resulting in the widespread distribution and cross-pollination of wild blackberries.

The blackberry industry began in Europe in the seventeenth century, but not until the nineteenth century in North America, with cultivars brought from Europe. Within a few years America's wild blackberries were domesticated and hybridized, and commercial production eventually surpassed that in Europe.

**Where they are grown commercially** • Blackberries are cultivated in many areas in the world's temperate regions, including Europe, Russia, Asia, New Zealand, and North America. Oregon is the leading world producer of blackberries with more than 6,000 acres under production. Of the three types of blackberries commercially grown—the trailing, semierect, and erect—the most important economically are the trailing cultivars 'Marion', 'Boysen', and the 'Thornless Evergreen', accounting for 95 percent of all the blackberries grown in Oregon. Other trailing blackberries cultivated include the 'Kotata', 'Waldo', 'Siskiyou', and 'Logan'.

More than half of Oregon's commercial crop is the 'Marion' (developed in Marion County, Oregon, in 1956), prized for its complex and intense blackberry flavor, large fruit, and small seeds. The second most planted trailing blackberry is the productive 'Thornless Evergreen', which is slightly smaller and not quite as flavorful as the marionberry. It's processed and sold generically as "blackberries." Most of the crop is harvested mechanically.

About the same amount of 'Boysens' are grown as 'Thornless Evergreen', but boysenberries are highly valued for their large (almost twice as large as the 'Marion' and three times as large as the 'Thornless Evergreen'), fine-flavored maroon fruit.

The fresh blackberry market relies on a mix of erect ('Cherokee', 'Navaho'), semierect ('Chester Thornless', 'Triple Crown'), and trailing ('Olallie', 'Siskiyou', 'Kotata') cultivars, especially erect and semierect cultivars because they are better suited for shipping. However, the trailing cultivars have excellent flavor, ripen early in the season, and fill a market niche. Harvesting is done by hand in the cool mornings. The berries are taken to packing plants, where they are rapidly cooled and packaged for shipping. Berries that cannot be sold fresh are processed generically as blackberries for the retail market.

Blackberries for the fresh market are grown in Washington, British Columbia, Oregon, California, and the south central United States. Production has increased rapidly in the past 25 years, but so have imports, with the majority coming from Mexico, Chile, Guatemala, and Costa Rica.

**How to pick** • Harvest blackberries in the morning, before the hot summer sun softens their flesh, and when the berries are at the peak of ripeness. The fruit changes from white to red to black when they are ripe. When they first turn black, they are not immediately ripe, and they will not ripen off the bush, so pick only those berries that easily pull away from their receptacle with gentle pressure. Keep the berries cool and dry after picking.

### The Leading Commercial Blackberry Cultivars

**Boysen** • Commonly called *boysenberry.* Thought to be a cross between a red raspberry or a 'Logan' and a western dewberry. In the late 1920s, George Darrow of the USDA and southern Californian farmer Walter Knott found several berry vines in an abandoned garden plot on a farm previously owned by southern California botanist Rudolf Boysen. Mr. Knott planted the vines, and the resulting berries were called boysenberries, enormous deep maroon berries with large seeds and excellent flavor. By 1935 Mr. Knott started selling them at his farmstand along with jars of mouthwatering preserves made by his wife. These superb-tasting berries eventually made Knott's Berry Farm in Buena Park, California, famous.

**Brazos** • Blackberry cultivar developed from southern dewberries by Texas A&M University in the 1950s; widely grown in Texas and Mexico. Large, tart fruit with a soft texture.

**Chester Thornless** • Cross between 'Thornfree' and 'Darrow'. Developed by U.S. Department of Agriculture in Illinois but released in Maryland in 1985. It was the first thornless blackberry with hardiness; most winter hardy of all thornless blackberries. Medium, good-flavored firm fruit that will not soften or lose color during hot weather.

**Logan** • Commonly called *loganberry.* Cross between a red raspberry of European ancestry and a native western dewberry. Developed by Judge James Logan in his home garden at Logan Heights near Santa Cruz, California. Conical medium red berry with good flavor, although tart. While the shape and color of a raspberry, loganberry picks like a blackberry. To buy loganberry wine, contact Black Diamond Winery, 2976 Black Diamond Road, Port Angeles, WA 98363; 360-457-0748; www.wineryloop.com (loganberry wine, strawberry-rhubarb wine, and other fruit wine).

**Marion** • Cross between 'Chehalem' and 'Olallie'—commonly called *marionberry*. Introduced by George Waldo with the U.S. Department of Agriculture from his cooperative program with Oregon State University in 1956 and named after Marion County, where it was extensively garden tested. Medium-size dark red to black fruit with superior, complex blackberry flavor and medium seeds. Marionberries are the leading cultivated blackberry in the world. The majority of the crop is grown in Oregon's berry-basket-shaped Willamette Valley and then processed and sold worldwide.

**Navaho** • Thornless cultivar from a cross between two selections of blackberries developed from eastern U.S. native blackberries. Introduced by the University of Arkansas in 1988 and named after one of the Native American tribes. Medium-size, dark black, round, glossy, very firm fruit. This cultivar ships very well and is widely grown in the world for the fresh market. Grassy, green flavor typical of the eastern blackberry species.

**Thornless Evergreen** ('Everthornless') • The evergreen, or cut-leaf, blackberry (*Rubus laciniatus*) is a European native that has become naturalized in the western U.S. A thornless mutant was found that was called 'Thornless Evergreen'. The mutation for thornlessness is only in the outer cell layers of the plant, and so the plant often reverts to producing thorns if injured or pruned. Researchers, using cell cultures from the thornless layer of 'Thornless Evergreen', generated plants that are thornless in all cell layers and never revert to being thorny; 'Everthornless' was released from this effort. This late-season blackberry produces a medium-size berry, with sweet mild flavor and large seeds. It is a favorite of growers because it produces large yields and is disease resistant. In Oregon, it is the second most important commercial blackberry after the marionberry.

### Important Commercial Blackberry Hybrids (Europe)

**Tayberry** • Cross between an Aurora blackberry, from the USDA program in Oregon, and a European raspberry. Developed in 1979 by the Scottish Horticultural Research Institute. Elongated large berry with good flavor and acidity.

**Sunberry** • Cross between a western dewberry and a raspberry hybrid. Developed by Horticultural Research International in East Malling, England. Round, dark red fruit with good flavor.

**Tummelberry** • Cross between a 'Tayberry' and a sibling of 'Tayberry'.

**Veitchberry** • Cross between 'November Abundance' raspberry and English hedgerow blackberry (*R. ulmifolius*). Developed by Mr. Veitch of Bedford, England. Parent of the most commonly grown blackberry cultivar in England, the 'Bedford Giant'.

**How to buy** • Blackberries should be plump, without their stems, black, firm, and dry because moisture encourages mold. Avoid buying containers with signs of juice leakage, indicating overripe berries.

**How to store** • Keep the berries unwashed and uncovered in the refrigerator in a shallow container on a paper towel to absorb moisture that can cause molding. They will keep for two to three days. Wash just before using.

To freeze, first rinse the berries (see page 69) and drain thoroughly, then transfer to a baking sheet lined with paper towels and pat dry. Discard immature and overripe berries. Put the lined baking sheet in the freezer until the berries are frozen. Pour the individually frozen berries into self-sealing plastic freezer bags and freeze for up to two years. Fold frozen berries into batters just before baking except for pancakes. Defrost the berries first since the batter cooks so quickly the berries don't have time to thaw. For any recipe where the berries are to be used uncooked, thaw them on a paper towel for 20 minutes at room temperature and use them slightly frozen.

**Notes for the cook** • All the cultivars of blackberries and their hybrids have subtle flavor differences, and I like to mix them when I can. The slightly acidic 'Logan' (a blackberry-raspberry hybrid), for instance, is tart by itself, but when it is paired with marionberries in cobblers, the flavors of both fruits are enhanced. Like a lot of berries, blackberry cultivars vary widely in their sweetness, so adjust the sugar you add accordingly.

For wild blackberry pie, I use the prized Pacific dewberry (it's the berry we call the "real" wild blackberry) without any other berries as its flavor is unsurpassed. Serve blackberries at room temperature for their fullest flavor.

## BLUE HONEYSUCKLE BERRY

**Common names** • blue honeysuckle, Russian honeyberry, sweet honeysuckle, siniku-usama (Sweden), blåtry (Finland).

**Scientific classification** • *Lonicera caerula* belongs to the honeysuckle (Caprifoliaceae) family, the same as elderberries. Blue honeysuckle berries are named after Adam Lonitzer, a sixteenth-century botanist and author.

**Habitat and distribution** • These long-lived shrubs are native to Siberia, northern China, and Hokkaido (the northern island of Japan), where they thrive on acidic soils. They grow from four to six feet tall and produce large early-ripening (they are the earliest of all berries) dark blue fruit with a waxy coating similar to blueberries, in a variety of shapes from long and thin to plump ovals.

**History** • Blue honeysuckle berries have been a part of the diet of indigenous people in Siberia, northern China, and Hokkaido for thousands of years. The ancient people of Hokkaido, the Ainu, who lived in the northern part of the island 10,000 years ago, called the fruit *haskap,* which meant "many fruits on branches." These blueberrylike fruits ripen in the late spring and were especially welcome after the long, harsh winter.

**Where they are grown commercially** • This ancient fruit was not domesticated until the 1950s, when research began in the former Soviet Union. By 1998, 60 cultivars of blue honeysuckle had been released in Russia for home and commercial cultivation. Subsequent by-products have made it a minor commercial berry today. In Hokkaido, a minor industry processes this fruit into juices, sodas, wines, jams, jellies, ice cream, pastries, tea, and even chewing gum.

Blue honeysuckle trials are currently under way in the U.S. Dr. Maxine Thompson, a retired horticulture professor from Oregon State University, has a small test plot of blue honeysuckle plants in Corvallis, Oregon. These tasty fruits have the potential for a future industry as they are high in health-benefiting phytochemicals, and their anthocyanins are stable when processed, making the berries prime candidates for juice and other products.

Some nurseries sell the blue honeysuckle as an ornamental for home gardens.

**How to pick** • Pick the berries in the cool morning, when they are solid blue, plump, and fully ripe.

**How to buy** • Not available commercially.

**How to store** • Keep the berries in an uncovered container in the refrigerator for up to two to three days and wash just before using. Serve them at room temperature for their fullest flavor. Freeze in self-sealing plastic freezer bags for up to one year. These solid berries will not stick together when frozen.

**Notes for the cook** • This olive-shaped fruit has a pleasing sweet-sour flavor that is more intense than that of commercial blueberries. Eat blue honeysuckle berries fresh or cook them in pies and for preserves. Substitute these berries in any recipe that calls for blueberries.

## BLUEBERRY (*HIGHBUSH*)

**Common names** • rabbiteye, blueberry.

**Scientific classification** • Highbush blueberries (*Vaccinium corymbosum*) and rabbiteye blueberries (*V. ashei*) are members of the heath family (Ericaceae) and are related to lowbush blueberries and cranberries. More recently, some taxonomists have classified the rabbiteye blueberries with highbush blueberries. However, the rabbiteyes have traditionally been separated due to their southern range, their greater number of chromosomes, and the thicker skins and larger seeds of the fruit.

**Habitat and distribution** • Highbush wild blueberries grow in the East from Maine to Florida and west to Michigan, while the rabbiteyes are found from North Carolina to Florida and west to Texas. Both species typically grow in organic moist soils along lakes and streams; however, the rabbiteye blueberry is much more tolerant of mineral soils and hot summer temperatures. The domesticated version of these species is the common commercial blueberry.

**History** • The birth of the blueberry industry began in the early 1900s, when Dr. F. V. Colville, with the USDA in Beltsville, Maryland, began working with Ms. Elizabeth White, a commercial cranberry farmer in Whitesbog, New Jersey. Ms. White hired her workers to collect the finest wild highbush blueberry plants they could find from the surrounding New Jersey Pine Barrens. The best of these were planted on her property for Dr. Colville's breeding program. By the 1920s the industry was born when four cultivars, bred for flavor, size, light blue color, and hardiness, were released from crossbreeding and propagation of the wild plants. Dr. Colville spent 35 years crossbreeding blueberries from this wild selection. For more history, see Lowbush Blueberry, page 16.

**Where they are grown commercially** • North America is the world's leading producer of cultivated highbush blueberries. They are grown in more than 30 states and in the fertile Fraser Valley of British Columbia. The five top blueberry-producing states are Michigan, New Jersey, Oregon, North Carolina, and Washington. Half of the crop is sold fresh, and production is rapidly on the increase due to consumer demand both here and abroad. Chile, New Zealand, Australia, and many European countries are cultivating blueberries as well.

One of the more recent major successes in breeding has been the crossbreeding of native Florida species into the commercial blueberries to develop "low chill" or "southern highbush" blueberries that can be grown in areas with mild winters. This has allowed the expansion of the blueberry industry into Mexico, California, and southern Florida.

Now there are so many blueberry cultivars they can be divided into the time of the season they ripen—early, midseason, and late (early in Florida means March; in North Carolina, April; in Arkansas, May; etc.). In addition to the varying ripening times, blueberry cultivars differ in the size of the fruit, the color of their skin, their aroma, and flavor. Cultivars of the rabbiteye (*V. ashei*), which are tolerant to heat and drought, are grown mainly in the southeastern United States, where they are also indigenous. Georgia is the leading rabbiteye producer. Other notable production comes from North Carolina and a small amount from Florida. More recently, rabbiteyes have been planted in Oregon, where they grow well in the mild climate and the fruit ripens very late in the season.

**How to pick** • Highbush blueberries grow in clusters on thornless bushes within arm's reach, making them easy to harvest. Pick them in the morning when the berries are firm and cool. Refrigerate the berries as soon as possible after picking.

**How to buy** • Fresh blueberries should be firm and full with smooth skin with a silvery white bloom; there should be no traces of juice or mold on the berries or the container.

**How to store** • Cover berries or store in self-sealing plastic bags in the refrigerator for up to 10 days. Wash just before using and serve them at room temperature for their fullest flavor.

To freeze, first rinse the berries (see page 69) and drain thoroughly, then transfer to a baking sheet lined with paper towels and pat dry. Pick over and discard immature and overripe berries. Pour into self-sealing plastic freezer bags and freeze for up to one year. (These solid berries will not stick together when frozen.)

**Notes for the cook** • Blueberries can be used with sweet or savory, hot or cold, and spicy or delicate foods. Think of them as the chicken of the berry world. They are good mixed with other fruits and nuts, especially almonds. Blueberries can be used fresh or frozen with the exception of pancakes, when they should be thawed first. The thin batter cooks so quickly they might not have time to thaw. To keep the area surrounding the berries from turning blue, coat them with flour before adding them to dough or batter before baking. I take them on river float trips in a plastic container in an ice chest (not touching the ice) for cereal and snacking, and I'm always amazed at how well they hold up.

## BLUEBERRY (*LOWBUSH*)

**Common names** • wild blueberry; bosbes (Netherlands); myrtile, airelle, myrtillier (France); bolleber (Denmark); blea-berry (Scotland); mirtillo néro (Italy).

**Scientific classification** • Lowbush blueberries are members of the heath family (Ericaceae) along with 40 other varieties of wild berries, including huckleberries, bilberries, lingonberries, and cranberries. *Vaccinium angustifolium,* and to a lesser extent *V. myrtilloides,* are two species of wild blueberries harvested in Maine and eastern Canada for the wild blueberry industry. The bilberry (*V. myrtillus*), which is found in

Eurasia and the western United States, is roughly the European version of the lowbush blueberry. The wild lowbush blueberry may hybridize with the wild highbush blueberry (*V. corymbosum*) so that intermediate or half-high blueberries may be found in some fields. Half-high blueberry cultivars, such as 'Northblue', 'Northcountry', and 'Polaris', are grown for commercial production in very cold climates like Minnesota and are commonly grown as ornamental shrubs.

**Habitat and distribution •** Lowbush blueberries are deciduous shrubs that thrive in the acidic soils of northern Eurasia and North America. These diminutive plants are six to 18 inches tall and often grow in dense colonies with several species growing together. The most important commercial species in the United States, the low sweet blueberry (*V. angustifolium*), grows southward in the Alleghenies to West Virginia and from Minnesota to Maine, where it thrives in the open rocky uplands and sandy fields called *barrens.* Giant granite boulders are a striking contrast to the knee-high mounds of colorful blueberry bushes that grow in masses around them, like a perfectly landscaped garden.

The Canadian distribution of the lowbush wild blueberry is from eastern British Columbia to Labrador for *V. myrtilloides,* and eastern Manitoba to Newfoundland for *V. angustifolium.*

**History •** Wild blueberries became well established in North America after the last ice age. The berries flourished in the acidic soils left by the retreating glaciers, and early man quickly realized their value as a food source and a medicine. The berries were eaten fresh, dried, and smoked, often mixed with deer meat and fat to make pemmican, small high-protein cakes eaten during travel. The roots were brewed into a tea and used as a muscle relaxant during childbirth, and berry juice was given as a cough suppressant.

Wild blueberries were first canned in Cherryfield, Maine, during the Civil War for the Yankee troops. It was the birth of the industry, which continued to grow after the war with soldiers who had developed a taste for these berries returning home.

**Where they are grown commercially •** The lowbush blueberry industry in North America is concentrated in the northeastern corner of the continent, where the low sweet blueberry (*V. angustifolium*) and the sourtop blueberry (*V. myrtilloides*) are native and have grown naturally in the forest understory for thousands of years.

Farmers intensely manage these ancient barrens, where berries thrive in colonies or clones spreading out in a short, dense mat. Today the land is mowed or burned every other year to prune the plants, a technique colonists learned from the Indians hundreds of years ago. A blueberry field produces only every other year due to mowing/burning, but this practice makes harvest easier. It removes competing plants, pushes back the encroaching forest, and increases plant growth by returning nutrients to the soil.

Maine supplies half of the world's crop of wild blueberries and 99 percent of the production in the U.S on 60,000 acres. (New Hampshire has approximately 1,000 acres, and Massachusetts has another 500 acres.) Most of the berries are frozen with only 8 percent of them canned and 1 percent sold fresh. The majority of the crop is sold to the American baking industry; Europe and Japan buy the rest. Like cultivated blueberries, wild blueberry production has increased rapidly in the last few years because of improved production practices, and increase in demand has been fueled by the new findings on the health benefits of these antioxidant-packed berries.

Northeastern Canada produces the remaining half of the world's lowbush blueberry crop, selling 60 percent of the harvest to Europe and Asia and 20 percent to the U.S.

**How to pick** • When driving through Maine's blueberry country during harvest, you'll notice string dividing the barrens into 15-foot-wide vertical lanes. That's to help the pickers thoroughly work through one area and not miss any fruit. The berries are picked in the cool morning and evening hours from late July to mid-September with a hand rake that resembles a dustpan with a row of skinny metal teeth sticking out from the bottom. (It takes 6,000 to 8,000 rakers annually to pick the wild blueberries each summer!) The picker sweeps the rake through the berry bushes in a semicircular motion, forcing the teeth to pull off the berries, which roll into the bowl of the rake. After the rake is run through the blueberry plants two or three times, the berries are slowly poured into a bucket to winnow out unwanted debris. Many barrens offer U-pick, but you need a strong back before you try it. A tractor-mounted mechanical harvester now picks about 20 percent of the crop in Maine and 80 percent of the crop in Canada.

**How to buy** • The berries should be solid colored, well formed, and plump with smooth skin that has a silvery white bloom without any sign of mold. Blueberries won't ripen after harvest, so be sure the berries are fully ripe; avoid pale-colored or red berries in the container.

**How to store** • Pick the berries over and discard unripe fruit and debris. Cover or store in self-sealing plastic bags in the refrigerator for up to 10 days. Rinse just before using.

To freeze, first rinse the berries (see page 69) and drain thoroughly, then transfer to a baking sheet lined with paper towels and pat dry. Pour the berries into self-sealing plastic freezer bags and freeze for up to a year. Blueberries are solid and will not stick together when frozen.

**Notes for the cook** • Wild blueberries can be used fresh or frozen in everything from smoothies to the classic blueberry muffins or pies. Their unsurpassed flavor is enhanced greatly by cooking. To keep the area surrounding the berries from turning blue, coat them with flour before adding them to dough or batter. They are good mixed with other fruits and nuts, especially almonds.

## BUFFALO BERRY

**Common names** • Buffalo berry, rabbit berry, soapberry, soopoallie. Explorers, who learned from the Indians to eat buffalo berries with buffalo, named the berry.

**Scientific classification** • Buffalo berries (*Shepkerdia argentea*), members of the oleaster family (Elaeagnaceae), are named for Dr. John Shepherd, a Canadian botanist, and include the silver buffalo berry, russet buffalo berry, and roundleaf buffalo berry. They are closely related to sea buckthorn (*Hippophae rhamnoides*). The berries are named after their silvery leaf; *argentea* is Latin for "silvery."

**Habitat and distribution** • Buffalo berries grow throughout North America in small populations, but they are most common in the Great Plains, where they thrive in moist areas along streams or ponds, and are exceptionally tolerant of dry environments. They range in height from three to 20 feet and produce oval-shaped scarlet or golden berries that grow in clusters. While there are three species of buffalo berry, the berries commonly picked are from the thorny branched species (*S. argentea*); they are sour but have a good flavor.

**History** • Native Americans throughout North America used the buffalo berry plant in multiple ways. The tart berries were made into a sauce for buffalo, pressed into cakes and smoked, and used for stews and pemmican. A red dye was made from the berries, and medicine was concocted from the leaves and bark. When the pioneers arrived, they made the berries into jams and jellies.

**Where they are grown commercially** • Not grown commercially.

**How to pick** • The berries are harvested in late July or August by shaking the branches over a mat since their sharp thorns make them difficult to pick.

**How to buy** • Not available commercially, but buffalo berry jelly is sold in western Canada.

**How to store** • Keep the berries unwashed and uncovered in the refrigerator in a shallow container on a paper towel to absorb moisture that can cause molding. They will keep for two to three days. Wash just before using.

To freeze, first rinse the berries (see page 69) and drain thoroughly, then transfer to a baking sheet lined with paper towels and pat dry. Discard immature and overripe berries. Pour the berries into self-sealing plastic freezer bags and freeze for up to one year.

**Notes for the cook** • Buffalo berries make good preserves, such as jelly and syrup. Substitute them in any recipe calling for red currants.

## CHOKECHERRY

**Common names** • black cherry (a recent name change in Canada).

**Scientific classification** • Chokecherries (*Prunus virginiana*) are members of the rose family (Rosaceae) and are closely related to plums, peaches, and apricots. They are named after the Latin for "plum/cherry trees," *prunus* (from the Greek *prunos*), and the state, *Virginia*, where the tree was first discovered in North America.

**Habitat and distribution** • The most widely distributed tree in North America, chokecherries grow from the Arctic Circle to Mexico and in all but a few states in the Southeast. These New World natives grow to 25 feet and are widespread in open woods and along streams with berries that grow in dense clusters.

**History** • For the Plains Indians, the chokecherry was a dietary staple. The fruits were commonly dried and shaped into cakes that were used with buffalo or other game meat in making pemmican. A medicinal tea was made from the leaves.

**Where they are grown commercially** • Chokecherries are not cultivated commercially on a large scale for their fruit. A variety of chokecherry trees, with yellow, orange, or red berries, is sold at nurseries for ornamental gardens.

**How to pick** • Harvest wild chokecherries when they have turned from red to nearly black, usually during August.

**How to buy** • Not available commercially.

**How to store** • Keep the chokecherries unwashed and uncovered in the refrigerator in a shallow container on a paper towel to absorb moisture that can cause molding. They will keep for up to one week. Wash just before using.

To freeze, first rinse the berries (see page 69) and drain thoroughly, then transfer to a baking sheet lined with paper towels and pat dry. Discard immature and overripe berries. Put the chokecherries in self-sealing plastic freezer bags and freeze for up to one year. Chokecherries are solid and will not stick together when frozen.

**Notes for the cook** • Chokecherries are astringent (thus their name) but prized for their unique flavor. They have been used for centuries in the kitchen for preserves and wine. Make them into jelly, syrup, vinegar, jam, or liqueur. Like cranberry juice, their juice is too tart to drink straight; add one cup sugar for every three cups of chokecherry juice.

**Beware** • **Avoid chokecherry stones. They can make you sick.**

## CLOUDBERRY

**Common names** • salmonberry, yellowberry, baked apple berry, Moltebeere (Germany), lakka (Finland), molte (Norway), hjortron (Sweden), multebar (Denmark), braamsoort (Netherlands). The name *cloudberry* comes from the Old English word *clud*, meaning "rocky hill."

**Scientific classification** • *Rubus chamaemorus;* cloudberries are members of the rose family (Rosaceae) and are closely related to raspberries and blackberries.

**Habitat and distribution** • Cloudberries are circumpolar and grow in the subarctic regions of the Northern Hemisphere. In North America the berries grow as far south as British Columbia and New Hampshire. These perennial herbs are about three inches tall with a single berry. The plants spread by rhizomes and produce amber raspberry-like berries in moist tundra and bog habitats.

**History** • Cloudberries have been prized for centuries for their unique musky flavor and their exceptionally high level of vitamin C. The berries were (and still are) gathered by indigenous peoples and used both unripe and ripe for food. In North America the Inuit, Haida, and other local Indians traditionally stored cloudberries in cedar boxes or barrels. They are still a favorite for Indian ice cream, called *agutuq* (pronounced "a goo duck").

**WHERE THEY ARE GROWN COMMERCIALLY •** Studies, called the Northberry Project, are currently under way in a joint effort with Finland, Norway, Sweden, and Scotland on the development of new improved cultivars of cloudberries that could someday lead to their successful cultivation. Hundreds of seedlings are being grown in the test gardens for high flower production and large berry size. The goal is to domesticate wild cloudberry plants and selectively breed them for resistance to disease and improved yield. Not only would the berries be more readily available to the public, they would provide a secondary income for local farmers, increase tourism, and help to revegetate old peat bogs.

**HOW TO PICK •** Ripe berries turn from maroon to golden yellow, making them easy to spot in the sphagnum moss where they usually grow. Pick berries that are completely golden yellow without any traces of red.

**HOW TO BUY •** Not available commercially.

**HOW TO STORE •** This fruit is high in benzoic acid and consequently will keep covered in the refrigerator for up to two to three weeks. Freeze individually on a cookie sheet and then store airtight in self-sealing freezer bags for up to a year.

**NOTES FOR THE COOK •** Cloudberries are highly prized by cooks who are lucky enough to live in areas where they grow. They are traditionally eaten fresh, made into parfaits, stirred into ice creams, cooked into pies or preserves, or made into liqueur.

## CRANBERRY (*HIGHBUSH*)

**COMMON NAMES •** mooseberry, squashberry.

**SCIENTIFIC CLASSIFICATION •** Highbush cranberries (*Viburnum edule,* the North American native; *Viburnum opulus,* the European cranberry bush; and *Viburnum opulus var. americanum,* the American cranberry bush) are members of the honeysuckle family (Caprifoliaceae). *Viburnum* is Latin for "wayfaring tree," referring to the tree's bushy configuration, and *edule* acknowledges its edible berries.

**HABITAT AND DISTRIBUTION •** Highbush cranberries are distributed throughout the northern half of North America and in isolated populations in Colorado. They are straggly deciduous shrubs that range in height from two to 12 feet and produce bright reddish orange berries that grow in small clusters. Look for them at low to middle elevations near moist forests and on banks of rivers and creeks. These native berries have been domesticated and are popular as an ornamental plant in gardens. The fruit remains on the branch during winter, providing sustenance for local birds and animals.

**History** • Highbush cranberries were a favorite fruit of the Kwakiutl Indians of Vancouver Island. The unripe berries were harvested in late summer and fall and stored in cedar boxes with water and oil. These boxes of berries were greatly valued and given as prestigious gifts at special occasions. The bark of the highbush cranberry bush was used to treat a variety of medical illnesses, from colds to infections. For many tribes in this region, highbush berry patches were so important they were owned by families and passed down from generation to generation.

**Where they are grown commercially** • Not grown commercially.

**How to pick** • For jam, harvest the berries while they are still hard and underripe—their high pectin level will ensure superior preserves by producing a thick, luscious jam. The fruit will become sweeter and more full flavored as it reaches maturity after the first frost.

**How to buy** • Not sold commercially, but plants are available for home gardens from Raintree Nursery, 391 Butts Road, Morton, WA 98356-1700; 360-496-6400; www.raintreenursery.com.

**How to store** • Keep the unwashed fruit in an open container in the refrigerator. It will keep for up to a week. Rinse just before using. To freeze, first rinse the berries (see page 69) and drain thoroughly, then transfer to a baking sheet lined with paper towels and pat dry. Discard immature and overripe berries. Store in self-sealing plastic freezer bags in the freezer for up to one year.

**Notes for the cook** • These tart berries have a seed that needs to be removed by running the berries through a food mill. Use the pulp in any recipe that calls for cranberries.

## CRANBERRY (*LOWBUSH*)

**Common names** • cranberry, moss berry, bogberry, canneberge (France), tranbär (Sweden), Moosbeere (Germany), mortella di palude (Italy), arándano agrio (Spain). The Dutch named the cranberry, calling it *kraneberre* after the sandhill cranes that inhabited the coastal marshes during the birds' annual migration. Not only did the cranes eat the berries, but their heads resemble the unopened cranberry flower.

**Scientific classification** • Cranberries (*Vaccinium macrocarpon*) are members of the heath family (Ericaceae) and are directly related to huckleberries, blueberries, and lingonberries. Their species name, *macrocarpon,* is Latin, meaning "large" (*macro*) "fruit" (*carpon*).

**Habitat and distribution** • Cranberries are perennial plants native to North America, Europe, and Asia, where they thrive in bogs and marshes created from deposits left by the receding glaciers 10,000 years ago. As the ice melted, acid minerals were left in holes on a layer of clay that were eventually filled with water and organic matter, providing the ideal conditions for wild cranberries to flourish.

In the northern United States, the true native American cranberry or swamp cranberry (*Vaccinium macrocarpon*) has become the basis for the commercial cranberry industry worldwide. Several relatives, such as the small cranberry (*V. microcarpon*), southern mountain cranberry (*V. erythrocarpum*), and northern mountain cranberry (*V. vitis-idaea*), have somewhat similar fruit, and several unrelated plants with tart red fruit, such as European and American highbush cranberry (*Viburnum opulus* and *Viburnum opulus var. americanum*) and cranberry cotoneaster (*Cotoneaster apiculata*), have also been called *cranberry.*

**History** • Early man in both North America and Europe harvested the wild cranberry. The first record of cranberries being consumed comes from an analysis of a mug found in a Bronze Age tomb in Denmark that showed the remains of a fermented drink made from wild cranberries, grain, and bog myrtle.

In North America, the Native Americans in the Northeast used this plentiful indigenous fruit both in their diet and culturally. They made small pemmican cakes by mixing the mashed berries with dried venison, venison fat, and boiled cornmeal and drying them in the sun. Other favorites were cranberry succotash, made by cooking the berries with beans and corn, and a cranberry corn bread that was boiled and served with honey or maple syrup as a sauce. Cranberry juice was used as a dye for coloring blankets and clothing and as a medicine for wounds. Symbolically the cranberries represented peace and friendship among the tribes and were served at tribal gatherings.

The colonists learned how to harvest and cook cranberries from the Indians, and they found a new use for them—cleaning silverware! The silver items were boiled in their acidic juice, and consequently the berries were often called "goldsmith's berry."

During whaling expeditions and voyages to China, American ships carried barrels of the vitamin C–rich cranberries in spring water to protect sailors against scurvy.

Commercial cultivation started in the early nineteenth century on Cape Cod when a local farmer, Henry Hall, noticed that the wild cranberries in his bog that grew the best were the ones covered by a layer of sand blown in from the nearby sand dunes, a practice continued today. The sand helps protect the vines from weeds and insects, and the new roots that sprout from the stem in the sand layer invigorate the plant.

**Where they are grown commercially** • The world's commercial cranberry industry is based on the true American cranberry that is indigenous only to North America. Cranberries are grown commercially in Canada, Chile, and the northern United States, where the top producers are Wisconsin, Massachusetts, Oregon, New Jersey, and Washington.

Despite popular belief, cranberries do not grow in water. In production areas with cold winters, the bogs are flooded periodically to produce a protective ice layer over and around the plants. In the spring, the bogs are drained and the plants grow again. After the flowers finish blooming, the berries ripen in the warm summer sun until September or October, when they are harvested.

If a wet harvest system is used, the bog is flooded up to 1½ feet. A wheel churns the water, dislodging and floating the berries to the surface, creating a brilliant red bog that is a sight to behold. The berries are corralled onto conveyer belts by workers with long-handled rakes and taken to processing plants, where they are graded on color and size. Most of the berries from a wet harvest are made into juice and sauce.

While the majority of cranberries are wet-harvested for the juice market, some are dry-harvested with mechanical pickers manually pushed through the fields. They simultaneously prune the vines while picking the berries, which are then packed and sold for the fresh market.

**How to pick** • Wild cranberries grow in dense patches in marshy areas. Pick the berries in the late fall when they turn a deep burnished red, indicating ripeness.

**How to buy** • Fresh cranberries will vary in color from bright red to deep burgundy, depending on the cultivar. The berries should be plump and firm, without indentations or soft spots. Inspect the package for crushed or shriveled berries before buying.

**How to store** • Fresh cranberries will keep in the refrigerator for four to eight weeks. Wash the berries just before using them. Freeze them in the bags they come in and use the frozen berries directly from the freezer. They will be good for at least a year. Rinse the frozen berries just prior to using.

**Notes for the cook** • With the exception of dried cranberries, which are popular in salads and baked goods, cranberries are one of the most underutilized of all American berries. While most of us serve cranberry sauce during the holidays, few of us give this healthy fruit a second thought the rest of the year. Think of them as the lemons of the berry world. Their tartness acts as a flavor enhancer when they are mixed with other fruits or berries, bringing out the best in both. Some cultivars of fresh cranberries, such as the dark purple 'Stevens', are sweet enough to be eaten fresh. Cut the berries in half and sprinkle them in green salads to add a splash of color. Cranberries freeze exceptionally well, so stock up on them around the holidays.

## CURRANT (*BLACK*)

**Common names** • groseille noire, cassis noir (France); ribes (Italy, Sweden, Denmark); schwarze Johannisbeere (Germany); grosclla (Spain); zwartes-aalbes (Netherlands). *Currant* is derived from *corran*, a former British name given to the fruit because it resembled Corinths, the tiny Zante grapes imported from Corinth, Greece, and sold in English markets.

**Scientific classification** • Black currants (*Ribes nigrum*) belong to the currant family (Grossulariaceae) and are classified in the genus *Ribes* along with gooseberries. *Ribes* is derived from the Arabic name for these plants; *nigrum* is Latin for "black."

**Habitat and distribution** • Currants and their gooseberry cousins include 150 species that are native throughout northern Europe, Asia, North America, and in the mountainous areas of South America and northwestern Africa. These woody deciduous shrubs reach a height of three to six feet when mature and produce pea-size black, red, or white (an albino form of the red currant) berries in clusters. While currants and gooseberries have many similarities and differences, the distinguishing feature that separates one from the other is that currants have smooth wood and gooseberries have thorns.

The common black currant (*Ribes nigrum*), a native of eastern and central Europe, was first domesticated between 1500 and 1700 in western Europe.

Several black currant species are native to the United States, and the common European black currant is naturalized in the East.

**History** • Black currants were first mentioned in England during medieval times, when they were used to flavor wine. Imported from Holland, the plants were slow to catch on and not as popular as red currants. By the sixteenth century they were being grown in gardens for food in France, but they did not become popular until the eighteenth century, when they were accepted as a food and medicinal plant. In England the juice was boiled with sugar as a treatment for sore throats, and the berries were preserved in brandy. By the nineteenth century the commercial production of cassis began in Dijon, making the fruit even more popular. In Russia black currants were (and still are) greatly valued. They are fermented into wine with honey, made into preserves, and, in Siberia, brewed into a healthy medicinal tea with their leaves.

Currants were so highly regarded by the colonists that they brought plants with them when they came to the New World.

The Native Americans used wild currants as a medicine by boiling the bark and roots for tea, which they used for a variety of ailments and conditions, from sore eyes to childbirth, and as a food source.

**Where they are grown commercially** • The Russian Federation, Poland, Germany, Scandinavia, the United Kingdom, and more recently China are the leading world producers of black currants. Black currants have been popular for centuries in Europe and are widely grown for processing into juice, jams, jellies, liqueurs, desserts, meat sauces, and as flavorants and colorants. Black currant juice, particularly under the label Ribena, is consumed in even greater quantities in Europe than Concord grape juice is in the United States.

Production of black currants in the U.S. has been limited because some species of the European black currant are cohost to the white pine blister rust. To combat the spread of the rust in the white pine timber industry, in the early 1900s a ban was placed on planting currants in the U.S. Even though the federal ban on growing black currants was rescinded in 1966, and the decision was left up to the states, 17 states still prohibit their growth. The development of new genotypes resistant to this disease has allowed many states to lift their restrictions. Black currants are grown in the eastern United States mainly for fresh market sales. In the Pacific Northwest they are produced and shipped nationally for the fresh market and locally processed into coulis, juice, and jelly. Black currants have a short season, so buy them as they are available.

**How to pick** • Unlike most other fruits, currants can stay on the bush for up to two weeks after they are ripe without deteriorating. Strigs (the clusters of fruit) of currants are picked by hand and easily lift off the bush when ripe.

**How to buy** • Buy black currants that are plump and firm with solid-colored shiny skin without cracks or brown spots.

**How to store** • Store the strigs unwashed and uncovered in a single layer on paper towels in the refrigerator for three to four days. Before using, remove the currants from the stems with an upside-down fork or your fingers and rinse and drain.

Currants can be frozen either on or detached from the strigs. To freeze them on the strigs, first rinse the strigs (see page 69) and drain thoroughly, then transfer to a baking sheet lined with paper towels and pat dry. Discard immature and overripe berries. Put the strigs into self-sealing plastic freezer bags and freeze for up to one year. The currants detach from the strigs when they are frozen, and the strigs can easily be picked out by hand just prior to using. To freeze currants off the strig, follow the instructions above except remove the currants from the stems first.

**Notes for the cook** • Like lemons, currants have some degree of tartness that enhances the flavors of other foods they are cooked with. Black currants are more tart and intensely flavored than red currants and are generally cooked before being used. Their complex, dusky flavor is softened with a little sugar in juice, jams, and jellies, and their high pectin level means they set well. My favorite way to use black currants is in sauces for dark game birds and meat. They also make an excellent sorbet, or try a handful tossed in a peach or apple pie. Berries from different cultivars will vary in sweetness, so add sugar judiciously.

## CURRANT (*RED*)

**Common names** • groseille rouge (France); ribes (Italy, Sweden, Denmark); johannisbeere-aalbes (Netherlands); grosella (Spain). *Currant* is derived from *corran*, a former British name given to the fruit because it resembled Corinths, the tiny Zante grapes imported from Corinth, Greece, and sold in English markets.

**Scientific classification** • Red currants (*Ribes rubrum*) belong to the currant family (Grossulariaceae) and are classified in the genus *Ribes* along with gooseberries. *Ribes* is derived from the Arabic name for these plants; *rubrum* is Latin for "red."

**Habitat and distribution** • Red currants, native to the Northern Hemisphere, grow in northern Europe, Asia, Siberia, Manchuria, and the eastern United States as far south as Virginia. (Golden currants grow in most of the United States with the exception of Vermont and Maine.) The North American wild red currant (*R. triste*) is similar in taste and quality to European red currants, but it has not been developed for cultivation.

Like black currants, red currants are woody, fast growing, deciduous shrubs that reach a height of five feet when mature. The canes produce long flower clusters, called *strigs*, which bear about 12 pea-size red or white (an albino form of the red currant) berries.

**History** • There is little early written history about red currants. They first appear in literature as late as the fifteenth century with a description that refers to them as herbs with no mention of them as a food, but by the middle of the next century they had become common garden plants. In 1629 the apothecary to James I of England, John Parkinson, wrote that red currants were usually eaten fresh in hot weather or made into preserves, and the white currant, with a more pleasant "winey" taste, was popularly fermented into wine and distilled into brandy. As new improved cultivars were developed, the plants became more popular in cottage gardens for cooking, as well as for making wine, juice, and homemade vinegars. One nineteenth-century British horticulturist, John Phillips, noted how to store the berries so they would keep for years in corked bottles: "If they were gathered perfectly dry but not too ripe, and as long as they were stored away from air in a dry situation. If the bottle were packed, corks downwards, in a chest, and the space around them filled with sand, this would ensure their longest keeping."

In North America the Native Americans picked wild currants and ate them fresh and mixed and dried with other indigenous fruit. Their bark and roots were steeped for medicinal tea.

**Where they are grown commercially** • Germany, Poland, France, the Netherlands, Belgium, and Hungary are the main world producers of red currants. In the United States, 80 percent of the nation's crop is from Prosser, Washington, where there is plenty of rich, deep soil and an ample supply of irrigation water. These bush berries are shipped internationally, nationally, and locally for the fresh market and processed into juice and jelly. Luckily for cooks, they are gradually becoming more readily available at local farmers' markets.

**How to pick** • Modern red currant cultivars have been selected for their ability to ripen all the berries on a strig at once. The ripe berries, which contain three to 13 tiny seeds, are translucent. The fruit turns red before it is ripe, so let the currants hang on the bush for one to two weeks after developing their color to ripen completely. Unlike most other berries, currants can stay on the bush for up to two weeks after they are ripe without deteriorating. Strigs of currants are easily picked by hand and readily lift off the bush when ripe.

**How to buy** • Buy red currants that are plump and firm with solid red-colored shiny skin without cracks or brown spots.

**How to store** • Store the strigs unwashed and uncovered in a single layer on paper towels in the refrigerator for three to four days. Before using, remove the currants from the stems with an upside-down fork or your fingers and rinse and drain.

Currants can be frozen either on or detached from the strigs. To freeze them on the strigs, first rinse the berries (see page 69) and drain thoroughly, then transfer to a baking sheet lined with paper towels and pat dry. Discard immature and overripe fruit. Put the strigs into self-sealing plastic freezer bags and freeze for up to one year. The currants detach from the strigs when they are frozen, and the strigs can easily be picked out by hand just prior to using. To freeze currants off the strig, follow the instructions above except remove the currants from the stems first.

**Notes for the cook** • Red and white currants are milder and sweeter than black currants, which have a completely different flavor, and can be used either fresh or cooked. (White currants are slightly less acidic than red currants, but both can be used for the same recipes.) Fresh red and white currants can be tossed into fruit salads, turned into intensely flavorful sorbets, or baked into pies or cobblers. Their high acid and pectin levels also make them perfect for blue-ribbon preserves. (The famous French Bar-le-Duc jelly is made from white and red currants.) Raspberries and red currants are particularly good together. Red currant juice can also be used in salad dressings and barbecue sauces.

## ELDERBERRY

**Common names** • sureau (France); vlier amerikaanse, vlier zwartevlier (Netherlands); Holunder (Germany); sambuco (Italy). The name elderberry is likely derived from the Anglo-Saxon word *ellaern*, or *aeld*, meaning "fire," for the tree's hollow stems, which were used for blowing on a fire to get it started.

**Scientific classification** • Elderberries are members of the honeysuckle family (Caprifoliaceae). The scientific name for the black elderberry is *Sambucus nigra*, the American elderberry is *Sambucus cerulean*, and the red elderberry is *Sambucus racemosa*. *Sambucus* is derived from the Greek word *sambuké*, a type of harp, as well as a lute made from elder stems, which are hollow.

**Habitat and distribution** • There are at least 20 species of elderberry shrubs and small trees that are widely distributed in the temperate Northern Hemisphere and a few in the Southern Hemisphere. You can find them growing in the understory of forests as a small tree or shrub, depending on the species, with red, blue, black, or white berries. The red elderberries can cause stomach upset and should not be eaten.

**History** • The wild elderberry has been popular for centuries as both a curative and a culinary constituent. The leaves, flowers, bark, and berries have all been used for different purposes, which could fill an entire book. Hippocrates wrote about the healing properties of the elderberry in the fifth century B.C. Different cultures throughout history have used the elderberry and dried elderflowers to treat a variety of illnesses, from bronchitis to the flu.

During Roman times the berries were used as a hair dye and over the centuries have been used to color cheap wines. In Portugal, when shady winemakers began to regularly use black elderberries as a grape substitute in cheap ports, it became illegal to plant black elderberry trees.

These ancient trees played an important role in Old World folk history. In England and Russia they were planted near cottages to keep away witches, while Sicilians believed elderberry sticks would drive away robbers and serpents.

The Native Americans steamed elderberries in baskets on hot wet rocks and stored the fruit underground or in water for winter use. The leaves were used for infections and to reduce swelling, and the bark was steeped for tea for stomach problems and colds. The Quinault Indians removed the pith from the stem and used it as a whistle to bugle for elk, while colonists used it to tap sugar maples for collecting sap for syrup and sugar making.

**Where they are grown commercially** • The largest commercial producer of elderberries in the world is Austria. A thousand Austrian elderberry growers formed a co-op and built a large freezing facility in Thalhammerstrasse called Beerenfrost. The berries are sold throughout the world and used in juices, jams, fruit yogurts, wine, and extracts for nutraceuticals. Oregon has a few large plantings, and the fruit is primarily sold to companies, such as Smucker's, that make preserves and to out-of-state wineries. Germany and Denmark also grow elderberries, but on a much smaller scale.

Elderberries are raised commercially for nurseries and make lovely additions, especially the new, popular purpleleaf and cut-leaf forms, to ornamental gardens. Even if you don't use the berries in the kitchen, they are a favorite of many species of birds and will attract them to your yard.

In Kansas a new agricultural industry based on the elderberry has started. Semiretired wheat farmers and ranchers are growing elderberries for commercial products and are pleasantly surprised they can make as much money off a few acres of elderberries as a field of wheat. To order elderberry wine and other elderberry products, contact Wyldewood Cellars Winery, PO Box 205, Mulvane, KS 67110; 800-711-9748; www.wyldewoodcellars.com.

**How to pick** • Harvest blue or black elderberries when all the berries in their parasol-like blossom have turned color. Cut the entire bunch of berries off the tree and keep them cool until you get them under refrigeration. These firm berries travel well.

**How to buy** • Not for sale commercially.

**How to store** • To remove the berries, hold the entire cluster over a bowl and, with a table fork turned upside down, gently run the fork through the berries to dislodge them from their stems. Pick over the berries and rinse just before using. Store in the refrigerator for up to two to three days in a closed container. Freeze elderberries in self-sealing plastic freezer bags for up to one year.

**Notes for the cook** • Do not cook or eat red elderberries or their blossoms; they can cause stomach upset. Black and blue elderberries have been popular in Europe for centuries for making wines, jellies, and pies; in North America they were widely used by the Native Americans and pioneers. Elderberries are low in pectin and are best mixed with other high-pectin fruit like apples.

Blossoms from the black and blue elderberry trees have been as popular with cooks as the berries. Their spraylike flowers bloom in May and are traditionally made into elderberry wine or fried in a batter.

**Beware • The roots, leaves, and wood of elderberries are poisonous, so do not use them for tea.**

## GOOSEBERRY

**Common names** • worcesterberry; groseille épineux, groseille à maquereau (France); uva spina (Italy); Stachelbeere (Germany); grosellero espinoso, uva espina (Spain). No one is sure of the derivation of the name *gooseberry*, but it has been commonly used since the fifteenth century. Some suggest it comes from the old English custom of serving gooseberry preserves with a goose or from an adaptation of the French *groseille* (currant), or from the German *Jansbeere,* from "John's berry," named for the ripening period, which coincided with the Feast of St. John. The French name *groseille à maquereau* refers to the tradition that originated in England in the sixteenth century of serving gooseberries with mackerel.

**Scientific classification** • Gooseberries (*Ribes*) belong to the currant family (Grossulariaceae) and are classified in the genus *Ribes* along with currants. North American gooseberries are classified as *R. hirtellum* and European gooseberries as *R. uva-crispa.*

**Habitat and distribution** • Gooseberries are native to North Africa, Asia, northern Europe, North America, and the mountainous areas of South America. These low, fast-growing deciduous shrubs with spines prefer cool, humid weather with winter chilling. Their fruit is produced singly or in pairs from the stem of the plant and can be smooth or prickly.

Wild gooseberries grow in abundance in the United States, where at least 16 species grow in the north and west, although a few can be found as far south as Texas.

Worcesterberries are the fruit of the American coastal gooseberry (*R. divaricatum*), native to woodland stream banks in Oregon, Washington, and northern California. They are cultivated in home gardens in some regions of northern Europe.

**History** • Gooseberries were imported into England and northern France and became commercially important during the Middle Ages. By the 1800s more than 722 cultivars had been developed, attesting to their popularity. But during the next century, as England became more and more industrialized, gardens fell by the wayside as the manpower needed for cultivating specialty crops like gooseberries wasn't available. As a result, growers formed a network of gooseberry clubs—competing to grow the largest gooseberries; some of the oldest clubs still exist. A hundred years later apples replaced gooseberries as a source of pectin, and with the world wars of the twentieth century the gooseberry industry was greatly diminished.

In North America wild gooseberries were eaten by the Native Americans fresh, dried in cakes, and gathered green and kept for winter use. The roots were infused to make a tea for sore throats, while the bark was soaked and the juices used for eye ailments. The Nisqually used the thorns for tattooing with charcoal.

**Where they are grown commercially** • The Russian Federation, Germany, and Poland grow most of the world's gooseberries, which are derived from the European gooseberry. Small quantities are grown in North America, and their gene pool is from a combination of the European gooseberry (*Ribes uva-crispa*) and the American gooseberry (*Ribes hirtellum*).

Today there is a renewed interest in cultivating gooseberries, and several thousand cultivars exist in a multitude of colors from emerald green to ruby red and royal purple (only the green, white, and yellow fruit are used for processing). New cultivars not yet on the market include gooseberries that are teardrop and oval shaped that grow in a variety of colors.

**How to pick** • Gooseberries are woody perennial shrubs from three to six feet tall. These spiny plants produce berries borne singly along the stems that range from pea size to the size of a large cherry. For the best flavor, pick berries that are ripe with well-colored fruit in early to midsummer.

**How to store** • Unlike currants, gooseberries can be picked as they are beginning to ripen, just as the color starts to appear, and they will develop both flavor and color if kept in a self-sealing plastic bag with a damp paper towel in the refrigerator. They will keep for two to six weeks. Before using, tip and tail them with a paring knife or kitchen scissors. This step is not necessary if you are making a recipe that will be strained after the berries are cooked, such as a jelly or sauce. Rinse the berries just before using. Freeze whole gooseberries, rinsed, drained thoroughly, and patted dry, in self-sealing plastic freezer bags for up to one year. Tip and tail the frozen berries by rubbing the fruit between two damp kitchen towels. You do not need to thaw them before cooking.

**Notes for the cook** • This old-fashioned favorite can be divided into two groups. Culinary gooseberries, generally smaller with thick skins, are not suitable for fresh consumption. They are picked green, when their pectin levels are at their highest, making them ideal for jams, jellies, and preserves. If left on the bush, these berries will soften as the pectin level decreases, and they will get sweeter and can be eaten off the bush.

The larger and often thin-skinned dessert gooseberries can be eaten fresh without cooking when they are harvested ripe. They can also be picked unripe and used for pies and preserves, like their culinary cousins. Some gooseberry cultivars fall into both categories.

All gooseberries have a refreshing, distinctive flavor and astringency, similar to rhubarb, that is enhanced when the berries are cooked. Their tart kick particularly complements rich game meat, wild birds, such as goose and duck, and oily fish, so don't get trapped into thinking that gooseberries are used only for desserts.

To make a simple sauce with them, tip and tail the fruit with scissors and cook them with a little sugar and water over medium heat until the fruit collapses and thickens. Cook the mixture down further to make Gooseberry Cheese, page 173.

## GROUND-CHERRY, CAPE GOOSEBERRY, AND TOMATILLO

**Common names (ground-cherry)** • husk tomato, strawberry tomato.

**Common names (cape gooseberry)** • Peruvian ground-cherry, goldenberry, poha berry (Hawaii), coquerelle (France), jam fruit (India).

**Common names (tomatillo)** • Mexican ground-cherry; alkékenge du Mexique (France); mexikanische Blasenkirsche (Germany); tomate verde, miltomate (Spain).

**Scientific classification** • All ground-cherries (genus *Physalis*) are members of the potato family (Solanaceae) and distant relatives of the tomato, pepper, and eggplant. *Physalis* is Greek for "bladder," referring to the paperlike calyx that encases the fruit. There are more than 70 species of ground-cherries, and three of them have fruits that have been valued by cooks for centuries: husk tomatoes (*P. pruinosa*), Cape gooseberries (*P. peruviana*), and tomatillos (*P. ixocarpa*).

**Habitat and distribution** • While all ground-cherries are indigenous to North and South America, many have become naturalized throughout the world.

Tomatillos were domesticated in Mexico and were spread to Spain and the rest of the world with the Spanish explorers. While many varieties still grow wild, they are also a staple in home gardens, prized for the acidic bite they give to sauces and stews. Tomatillos are considered an essential ingredient in Mexican cooking.

Cape gooseberries are a native of South America and were also spread by Spanish explorers. The earliest mention of their growing in Europe was included in records from a German garden in 1614. During the next 200 years, these invasive plants spread throughout Europe, South Africa, Australia, and Hawaii. In temperate climates, Cape gooseberries are annuals, but they can live year-round in the topics, growing in a wide range of altitudes from 1,000 to 10,000 feet.

In the United States, husk tomatoes (*P. pruinosa*) are still grown by home gardeners, as well as growing wild in fields and pastures, where many consider them a weed.

**History** • These unusual plants are an ancient fruit native to North and South America. Of the three, only husk tomatoes (*P. pruinosa*) are native to North America, where they are widely distributed. Native Americans commonly ate them chopped in pemmican, and the colonists harvested these indigenous fruits until their cultivated crops, planted with seeds brought from Europe, began to produce. The Pennsylvania Dutch baked them in pies and made golden jelly with their tart fruit.

Tomatillos, native to Mesoamerica (from central Mexico to Central America), are an ancient fruit that has been found in archaeological excavations as far back as

900 B.C. In pre-Hispanic times, it was preferred over the tomato and even then was greatly valued by cooks.

The Incas knew another early fruit from the same family, Cape gooseberries. These golden berries grow wild in the Andes and were distributed around the world by the Spanish explorers.

**Where they are grown commercially** • Cape gooseberries are grown commercially in South America, China, California, Hawaii, New Zealand, Australia, India, Africa, and Great Britain. Although they are known most commonly as the *Cape gooseberry*, they are not related to the gooseberry family. Their name came from the Australians, who first imported them from the Cape of Good Hope at the turn of the nineteenth century. In Hawaii, where they have become naturalized, these marble-size fruits are known as *poha berries.*

Tomatillos are cultivated in Mexico and Guatemala, where their cultivation became industrialized about 10 years ago. Now 80 percent of the crop is shipped to the United States for the Hispanic community.

Husk tomatoes were domesticated in the seventeenth century but are not grown commercially for their fruit.

**How to pick** • Harvest tomatillos while they are still green and their husks have turned tan. If the fruit ripens too much, its flavor will become bland and tasteless. The husks on husk tomatoes and Cape gooseberries will turn straw colored and parchmentlike at maturity, and the fruit will have turned from green to golden yellow.

**How to buy** • Buy tomatillos and Cape gooseberries (from March to July) with a full and unblemished husk. Husk tomatoes are rarely available commercially.

**How to store** • Keep the fruit in its paper husk in a well-ventilated area. If kept dry, it will keep for up to two months. Rinse under cold water and discard the husk.

To freeze, scald for two minutes and drain. Put in self-sealing plastic freezer bags and freeze for up to one year.

**Notes for the cook** • Cape gooseberries are golden yellow and about the size of a cherry, with a pleasant tangy flavor. Cooks prize them for their high pectin, which ensures a thick, luscious jam when they are cooked. In India, in fact, these berries are called *jam berries.* They are also slightly acidic, making them perfect for sauces to serve with rich meat.

To use tomatillos, remove the husk and rinse the shiny green fruit in cold water. Some cooks like to cover them with cold water and gently simmer them for 15 minutes to remove some of the tart taste, but they can also be used fresh or chopped.

Use them as you would a mild lemon or tart green apple, to enhance the flavor of whatever you are cooking.

The husk tomato is much sweeter than the tomatillo and is most commonly used to make jam, pie, or dessert sauces.

## HARDY KIWI

**COMMON NAMES** • baby kiwi (Oregon), grape kiwi (British Columbia), tara, wild fig, wee-kee, bower vine, dessert kiwi, cocktail kiwi, yang-tao (China). The old name for the hardy kiwi was *Chinese gooseberry*. The name *kiwi* is a marketing term applied to the berry's larger cousin, the kiwifruit, by New Zealand exporters.

**SCIENTIFIC CLASSIFICATION** • Hardy kiwi (*Actinidia arguta*) is a member of the kiwi family (Actinidia), which includes more than 50 different species. This tiny kiwi is closely related to the kiwifruit (*A. deliciosa*). Hardy kiwi has male and female plants, so growers plant one male plant for every eight female plants to ensure pollination and fruit set.

**HABITAT AND DISTRIBUTION** • This smooth-skinned diminutive fruit, which looks like a grape, is native to northern China, Siberia, Korea, and probably Japan, where it grows in clusters on long vines that climb into trees up to 100 feet high. While kiwi is winter hardy to –10°F to –25°F and needs a long growing season, it is quick to break bud in the spring and often loses its crop to spring frosts.

**HISTORY** • Hardy kiwi has been a dietary staple for more than 2,500 years in Asia, where it's gathered in the countryside and sold in the cities' markets.

**WHERE THEY ARE GROWN COMMERCIALLY** • Small plantings are established in Canada, Germany, Italy, France, New Zealand, and the United States (about 62 acres in Oregon). Hardy kiwi have been cultivated as ornamentals since the early 1900s in the United States, but it is only recently that horticulturists have taken an interest in commercially growing these plants for their fruit. Because they need extensive trellis systems for commercial production, it is expensive to establish plantings.

**HOW TO PICK** • Harvest hardy kiwi (usually in the fall) when it easily comes off the vine. Usually it is picked at the mature stage and allowed to ripen off the vine, like kiwifruit.

**HOW TO BUY** • Buy fruit that is firm and plump without any traces of bruising. Many cultivars of hardy kiwi are available for the home garden at nurseries.

**How to store** • Store unwashed fruit in an open container in the refrigerator for seven to 14 days. Rinse just before using. Does not freeze well.

**Notes for the cook** • Hardy kiwi is aromatic and sweet with smooth, hairless skin and a pleasing, refreshing taste. It is sweeter than a kiwifruit and can be used in any recipe that calls for grapes. This tiny fruit has a range of ripeness and can be eaten when it is barely ripe and slightly tart; as it ages, the fruit will become softer, developing sweetness and a slight mint taste. I eat them raw as a snack food and sprinkled in salads. They can also be cooked into preserves, using a basic berry recipe.

## HUCKLEBERRY (*EASTERN*)

**Common names** • black huckleberry.

**Scientific classification** • True huckleberries are members of the heath family (Ericaceae) genus *Gaylussacia,* as are the blueberries and cranberries, and are native to the New World. There are 50 species, and each plant has pink flowers that eventually bear fruit with 10 large, bony seeds that make a crunch when you bite down on them. Eight species of huckleberries are grown in the eastern half of the United States and Canada. They are named for Joseph Gay-Lussac, a nineteenth-century French chemist and physicist. These perennial shrubs are not related to the garden huckleberry, which is a dark-fruited annual plant from the tomato and tomatillo family.

**Habitat and distribution** • Members of the genus *Gaylussacia* range from southeast Brazil to east of the Mississippi River. Huckleberries grow in a variety of sites from the coastal heathlands on Long Island to 4,000 feet in the southern Appalachian Mountains. These deciduous and evergreen shrubs require well-drained acidic soil that can range from moist woodlands and bogs to dry rocky slopes. They characteristically grow up to four feet and produce black berries with 10 seeds. The most common huckleberry is the black huckleberry (*Gaylussacia baccata*).

**History** • Huckleberries have played an important role in North American history, providing fresh berries in the late summer and fall and dried berries the rest of the year. The Lenape Indians of the Delaware Valley relied on the huckleberry as well as other wild berries to supplement their diet.

**Where they are grown commercially** • True huckleberries are cultivated only for ornamental garden plants.

**How to pick** • Not commonly picked for consumption.

# HUCKLEBERRY (*WESTERN*)

**Common names** • huckleberry, whortleberry, bilberry, black huckleberry, blue huckleberry, red huckleberry.

**Scientific classification** • Western huckleberries, members of the heath family (Ericaceae), are in the same genus (*Vaccinium*) as blueberries but are classified in different taxonomic categories. *Myrtillus* is the subcategory within *Vaccinium* that includes all western huckleberries. Their name is derived from the resemblance of the huckleberry leaves to myrtle leaves. Huckleberries are classified in a separate category because they produce single berries on new shoots, unlike highbush and lowbush blueberries, which grow clusters of berries on one-year-old wood. Huckleberries and blueberries have from 10 to about 30 small seeds per berry, depending on the species.

**Habitat and distribution** • Ten species of western huckleberries or bilberries are widely distributed west of the Mississippi and grow at a wide range of elevations from the coast to mountains. These small shrubs have berries that range in color from red to blue to purple to black and with and without a silvery bloom. You can occasionally find white-fruited plants.

The most common western huckleberry is *V. membranaceum*, found at elevations from 2,000 to 11,500 feet. It is known as the *black, thin-leaved,* or *globe huckleberry* and grows throughout Oregon, Washington, British Columbia, Idaho, and western Montana and Wyoming. Small pockets also grow in California, Utah, Arizona, and Michigan. This species is harvested from the wild by commercial fruit processors and made into an incredible array of food and cosmetic products.

Equally prized for flavor, the Cascade or blue huckleberry (*V.deliciosum*), which grows from 1,900 to 6,600 feet in the Cascade Mountains from northern California to British Columbia and in Washington's Olympic Peninsula. This diminutive shrub is two feet tall in subalpine forests and meadows and produces succulent blue berries. *V. ovatum*, the evergreen huckleberry, grows in forests along the Pacific Coast from California to Canada. It is often planted in home gardens.

Bilberries are widely distributed in the cool regions—the mountains, heaths, and moors—of both the Northern and Southern Hemispheres, thriving in the damp climate and acidic soils at elevations ranging from 1,200 to 7,500 feet. They are common in northern Europe and Asia and grow in two regions of the Cascade and Rocky mountains, from British Columbia to central Oregon, and in Colorado, New Mexico,

Utah, and Arizona. They are a small plant that grows from four to 24 inches tall with purplish black small berries.

**History** • Thousands of years ago natural wildfires created openings in forests, letting in light and giving huckleberries room to grow. Every few years after harvest the Native Americans burned the fields to keep the forest pushed back and to increase their huckleberry crop. (Many of these berry fields are still popular picking sites today.) Huckleberries provided fresh food in the late summer and fall and dried berries the rest of the year. Like salmon, this reliable food source allowed the prehistoric Columbia River people to remain in semipermanent villages throughout the year.

In late August entire villages would move to the high Cascade Mountains and set up camps for the women to gather berries while the men hunted and fished. The women dried the berries on tule mats placed in front of a fire built alongside a smoldering log. The berries were turned constantly with a long, oarlike paddle until they were dry, which took from six to eight hours. The fruit was packed into baskets and taken back to camp, where it was dried further in the sun. The dried huckleberries would keep for up to a year, providing valuable barter for fish and other goods at Indian trading gatherings along the Columbia River.

Today Native Americans still gather annually in the Cascades to camp and pick berries. Many still use their traditional Indian baskets. Huckleberries are one of three indigenous foods, the other two being salmon and roots, still honored annually by them in the Pacific Northwest. The annual Huckleberry Feast is held every fall to celebrate the arrival of the huckleberries and to give thanks to Mother Earth.

**Where they are grown commercially** • In the past horticulturists have not been successful domesticating huckleberries. Field trials are currently under way in growing huckleberries as well as managing areas of wild huckleberry stands, like the wild blueberry barrens of the East. Huckleberries are widely harvested from the wild for commercial use in the northwestern United States and western Canada.

**How to pick** • Pick full, well-formed berries without cracks or blemishes in the early morning, when the berries are cool and firm. If you are in bear country, make plenty of noise—many pickers wear a bell—and always be aware of your surroundings. You might even want to carry pepper spray. Remember, bears love huckleberries as much as you do, and they are bigger than you are.

**How to store** • Unlike blueberries, huckleberry skins tear when the berries are picked, and fresh berries do not store well. Use fresh berries within a few days of picking. To clean the berries, wrap a small, lightweight cutting board in a terry cloth towel with a high nap and rest it in the bottom of a colander. With the board tilted at a 45-degree angle, pour the berries down the board. The leaves and twigs will stick to the cloth. Briefly rinse the berries under cold running water and put in a colander to drain. Pour onto a baking sheet lined with a paper towel and pat dry. Store the berries in self-sealing plastic bags. Simply shake out the amount of berries you need and return the rest to the freezer. The berries retain excellent quality for several years when frozen.

**How to buy** • Buy berries that are firm and fresh looking, without mold or berry juice on the outside bottom of the container.

**Notes for the cook** • The intense and complex taste of huckleberries makes them prized by cooks. The berries are good eaten fresh or baked in pancakes, muffins, or desserts. Their flavor is enhanced even further when they are heated with a pinch of sugar and a few drops of lemon or orange juice. Huckleberries make excellent sauces for game meats and birds, pies, tarts, and other pastries, and jams, jellies, and preserves. Frozen berries can be used directly from the freezer.

## JOSTABERRY

**Common names** • Jostabeere (Germany), groseille jostabes (France), jostabes (Netherlands).

**Scientific classification** • Genus *Ribes*; same family (Grossulariaceae) as gooseberries and currants. These hybrids among *R. nigrum, R. uva-crispa,* and *R. divaricatum* are given the designation *Ribes × nidigrolaria.*

**Habitat and distribution** • Currently there are 18 hybrids between currants and gooseberries at the National Clonal Germplasm Repository in Corvallis, Oregon. 'Josta' is the most commonly known hybrid. In appearance, it looks like a cross between a gooseberry (*R. uva-crispa*) and a black currant (*R. nigrum*). Like its currant parent, it is a thornless, deciduous shrub with dark fruit, but the fruit is the size of a small gooseberry with a less intense flavor than black currant.

**History** • Pronounced "yustaberries" in English, jostaberries originated in Germany but were not made widely available until 1977.

**Where they are grown commercially** • Jostaberries are cultivated in very limited production but are available for the home garden.

**How to pick** • The berries hang in clusters of three to five, making them easy to harvest. Pick jostaberries when they are fully colored—reddish black to black—and soft.

**How to buy** • Buy berries that are plump with solid color without cracks or brown spots.

**How to store** • Store the berries unwashed in a plastic bag with a damp paper towel for up to four weeks. Wash just before using. To freeze, rinse the berries and drain thoroughly. Pour them onto a baking sheet lined with paper towels and pat dry. Freeze in self-sealing plastic freezer bags for up to one year.

**Notes for the cook** • Jostaberries have a pleasant tangy sweet flavor that is a culmination of the best traits from both their gooseberry and currant parents. Eat them fresh or use them as you would gooseberries or cranberries in sauces for meat or poultry or cooked in jams, jellies, and preserves. Their flavor is enhanced when mixed with other fruits.

## JUNEBERRY

**Common names** • serviceberry; saskatoon; Indian pear, petite poire (French Canada); amelanchier (France); shadbush; sarvis berry (Montana); honeyberry (Pennsylvania).

The colonists who lived in the frigid northern climate of North America gave these berries one of their common names, *serviceberry*. In the early years, when a resident died during the winter, his or her body was saved for burial in the spring, when the ground thawed. With the arrival of warmer weather, the snowy white blossoms of the Juneberry were the first to bloom, and they were always used to decorate the casket.

The French Canadians referred to the berries as *Indian pear* or *petite poire* since the berries of some of the species in this family resemble miniature pears.

*Shadbush* is the name given to these berries by the early explorers. It refers to the eastern variety that blooms as the shad are returning to their spawning grounds in the spring.

*Saskatoon* is either the anglicized version of the Cree name for this berry—mis-sask-qua-too-mina or mis-sask-a-too-mina (plural sask-a-too-mina)—or the name of the place where stems of the Saskatoon bushes were gathered for arrow shafts: Mane-me-sas-kwa-tan.

*Amélanchier* refers to the French Provençal name *amélanche* for the European species, *Amelanchier ovalis. Amélanche* is derived from the Celtic word *gauloise*, meaning "small apple." Most nurseries sell this shrub as Amelanchier.

**Scientific classification** • Juneberries (genus *Amelanchier*) are members of the rose family (Rosaceae), which includes apples, plums, cherries, and caneberries/brambles. There are at least 12 different species of this perennial fruit-bearing shrublike tree, although *Amelanchier alnifolia* is the most important for fruit production. Dr. Hatterman-Valenti, a researcher working on Juneberries at North Dakota State University, calls these fruits the "blueberries for alkaline soils." "They are actually a pome," she told me, "and more closely related to the apple than the blueberry. Their seeds resemble miniature apple seeds, giving them a chewier consistency when eaten fresh."

**Habitat and distribution** • The genus *Amelanchier* is native to North America, Eurasia, and northern Africa. Members of this genus range in size from a shrub to a tree, which can grow up to 40 feet tall in a range of habitats from the plains to hillsides and swamps.

**History** • Of all the species of *Amelanchier* in North America, historically the most famous is *A. alnifolia* and its subspecies, which grow from Mexico to close to the Arctic Circle and east to Ontario and south to Iowa. These berries played a significant cultural role for the Native Americans who lived in these regions. By holding the fruit up to the sun and burying it in the ground, they paid tribute to Mother Earth for her abundance of gifts. In the legends of the Klamath Indians of northern California, the first people were created from Juneberry bushes. For the Blackfoot Indians their blossom symbolized spring in the tobacco planting ceremony. The sun dance ceremony was always held in the moon when the Juneberries were ripe (July). When the four-day event was over, the chief would tell his people it was time to move to "Many-berries," distant sites where they traveled annually and set up summer berry-picking camps.

The berries were eaten in a variety of ways: fresh, dried like raisins, or mashed and drained. The pulp was formed into small cakes and dried in the sun. Pieces of the berry cakes were added to soups and stews or boiled with shredded berry shoots and dry leaves to make a tea. Pemmican, from the Cree word *pimikan*, meaning "manufactured fat," was also made with dried smoked buffalo or other game that was pounded and mixed with melted fat and dried Juneberries (or other dried berries or a mixture of dried berries). These high-protein cakes were not only sustenance for the Native Americans, but in later years the Indians sold them to the European explorers and buffalo hunters.

The straight-grained serviceberry wood was carved into arrows and used to construct basket frames and crosspieces for canoes, while the bark was used as a remedy for a variety of illnesses.

European settlers preferred *Amelanchier* wood for fishing poles and umbrella handles and the fruit for pies, jams, and jellies.

**WHERE THEY ARE GROWN COMMERCIALLY** • The Juneberry was first domesticated from the wild in 1878 in Illinois and in 1918 in Alberta, Canada. Today thousands of acres on the Canadian prairies are commercially producing serviceberries. The industry started slowly in the 1970s and has drastically increased in the last 10 years. There are approximately 300 saskatoon farms in Canada with a mixture of cultivars, and the supply does not begin to meet the demand. About half of the orchards are U-pick operations.

In the United States the industry is in its infancy, with growing areas centered primarily in North Dakota and Kansas. Dan Kelner of Velva, North Dakota, has three acres with 3,000 Juneberry trees (shrubs). With an annual crop of 3,000 pounds, he has found this native fruit a wise alternative crop to wheat. He sold more than 12,000 trees in 2003 to five different states, so expect to hear more about Juneberries in the future.

**HOW TO PICK** • Harvest the berries when they turn from pink to purple and blue-black. The berries ripen all at once, making the harvest a concentrated effort over a few days.

**HOW TO BUY** • Fresh Juneberries should be firm with full, smooth skin; there should be no traces of juice or mold on the berries or the container.

**HOW TO STORE** • Keep the berries unwashed and uncovered in the refrigerator in a shallow container on a paper towel to absorb moisture that can cause molding. They will keep for two to three days. Wash just before using.

To freeze, first rinse the berries (see page 69) and drain thoroughly, then transfer to a baking sheet lined with paper towels and pat dry. Discard immature and overripe berries. Put the lined baking sheet in the freezer until the berries are frozen. Pour the individually frozen berries into self-sealing plastic freezer bags and freeze for up to one year.

**NOTES FOR THE COOK** • Juneberries look like dark blueberries but have a muskier flavor. Substitute them in any blueberry or huckleberry recipe. Toss the berries with flour to keep the batter surrounding them from turning blue when baking. Use this fruit frozen directly from the freezer except when making pancakes. Thaw berries first for

20 minutes on a paper towel before adding them to the batter. (The thin batter cooks so quickly the berries do not have enough time to thaw completely.) When making jam, some frozen berries can be ground and cooked along with whole berries to give the jam a varied texture.

As with many berries, sprinkling them with acid, such as lemon juice, or cooking them with acidic fruits, like sour cherries or rhubarb, brings out their flavor. Almonds and almond extract enhance Juneberries' nutty taste.

## LINGONBERRY

**Common name** • cowberry (Britain); partridge berry (Newfoundland); rock cranberry, mountain cranberry, lowbush cranberry (Alaska and Canada); lingon (Sweden); tyttebaer (Norway, Demark, and Germany); puolukka (Finland); Preiselbeere (Germany); mirtillo rosso (Italy); airelle rouge (France).

**Scientific classification** • Lingonberries are members of the heath family (Ericaceae) and are closely related to blueberries and cranberries. Their species name, *Vaccinium vitis-idaea,* is derived from *vacca,* Latin for "cow"; *vitis,* Latin for "vine"; and *idaea,* referring to Mount Ida in Greece—literally translated as the vines of Mount Ida.

**Habitat and distribution** • Lingonberries are circumpolar in the Northern Hemisphere, growing in dense mats in the cold arctic, alpine, and temperate forests in northern Europe, Asia, and North America.

There are two subspecies/types of wild lingonberries. In the Old World, the subspecies *V. vitis-idaea* grows in northern China, Siberia, and a dozen northern European countries. In North America the smaller subspecies, *V. vitis-idaea minus,* grows from British Columbia to Greenland and throughout the northern United States.

These creeping, low-growing shrubs have adapted to a wide range of locations: as understory in forests, on the tundra, high on the moors and heath barrens, and in peat bogs and swamps. The plants bloom once a year, producing brilliant ruby-red berries similar in appearance to a red currant (about the size of a pea or smaller for the North American subspecies) but with far more flavor and undetectable seeds. During the winter any berries remaining on the vine are highly prized by children, who eat them as "frozen candy."

**History** • For centuries in the Old and New Worlds, indigenous people throughout the far north have valued lingonberries as an important part of their diet. The berries were eaten both fresh and preserved in oil to eat during the long, harsh winters. The leaves were made into medicine to treat a variety of disorders from gout to bladder problems.

**Where they are grown commercially** • The lingonberry was first cultivated in 1789, but even today most of the lingonberries sold on the world market come from the wild. Since 1978 plant breeders in southern Sweden have been working on the domestication of the wild lingonberry, and they have developed several cultivars. The initial seeds were gathered from Sweden, but since then plants and seeds have been added from Russia, Lithuania, and Latvia. Similar experiments are taking place in Finland and Russia and, after eight years, have shown that lingonberries can be cultivated successfully on berry farms. Today lingonberries are grown in limited areas in both Germany and Sweden.

In Sweden and Finland, lingonberries are considered "the red gold" of the forests and are the countries' most important berries. They are the world's leading exporters of lingonberries along with Russia and Canada—specifically Newfoundland and Labrador. The majority of these berries are picked from the wild.

In North America, lingonberries are grown commercially in six Canadian provinces and eight states, including Wisconsin, Alaska, Oregon, and Washington. It is interesting to note that while plants in the wild typically fruit once a year, when they are moved to a warmer climate with longer summers they will fruit twice. Most of the lingonberries imported to the United States come from Canada, and they are made into products for the American Scandinavian community.

**How to pick** • Lingonberries are harvested using hand rakes similar to those used for wild blueberries. Commercial growers are now planting lingonberries in rows like strawberries so they will be able to harvest them mechanically with strawberry-picking equipment.

**How to buy** • If you are fortunate enough to find fresh lingonberries, look for plump berries that are completely red without any signs of mold.

**How to store** • Lingonberries naturally contain a large amount of benzoic acid, a preservative, enabling them to be stored for long periods of time. Store in an open container in the refrigerator for up to six to eight weeks. Rinse the berries just before using. To freeze, first rinse the berries (see page 69) and drain thoroughly. Pour onto a baking sheet lined with paper towels and pat dry. Transfer to self-sealing plastic freezer bags and freeze up to a year.

**Notes for the cook** • Lingonberries, about the size of large pomegranate seeds, have a luscious, bright flavor. Substitute them in any recipe calling for cranberries.

## MANZANITA

**Common names** • Manzanita is a Spanish word meaning "little apple," given to these berries by the early Spanish Californians for their miniature apple appearance.

**Scientific classification** • Manzanitas (*Arctostaphylos manzanita*) are members of the heath family (Ericaceae) and closely related to the bearberry, blueberries, and cranberries. *Arctostaphylos* is derived from *Arctos*, Latin for the Great and Little Bear constellations, and *staphyle*, "bunch of grapes," referring to the bear's preference for the trees' berries, which grow in small clusters.

**Habitat and distribution** • Manzanitas are evergreen trees and shrubs native to North America, where they grow in the western United States. Of the 73 species, 60 can be found throughout California, from the coast to the Sierra Nevada. They grow in many shapes and sizes from dense shrubs to small trees.

**History** • Native Americans took full advantage of the multipurpose manzanita tree. In the winter the dried fruits were pounded into a pulp and used in drinks, while the seeds were ground into flour, pressed into a cake, and baked. The leaves were brewed into a medicinal tea and ground into a salve to treat poison oak, and manzanita wood was carved into pipes and utensils. When the Spanish settlers and homesteaders arrived in California, they learned how to use the berries from the Indians.

**Where they are grown commercially** • Commercially grown for nursery stock only.

**How to pick** • Harvest the berries in the fall, when they turn a deep reddish bronze.

**How to buy** • Not available commercially.

**How to store** • Keep the berries in an open container in the refrigerator for up to one week. Put the berries in self-sealing plastic freezer bags and store for up to one year. Rinse just before using.

**Notes for the cook** • Manzanita berries are edible fresh, but they are tart, mealy, and seedy. These pea-size berries produce a fine jelly.

## MAYHAW

**Common names** • apple hawthorn, mayhaw berry. Erroneously called a berry, this fruit is actually more closely related to an apple. It's named after the month the berries are ripe—May.

**Scientific classification** • Mayhaws (*Crataegus aestivalis*) are members of the rose family (Rosaceae) and related to apples and pears.

**Habitat and distribution** • Mayhaw trees are indigenous to North America, but only to a small geographical region. They grow in swamps and bogs in the temperate southern climate from east Texas to Florida and up through Virginia. The trees produce small fruit like crab apples that are commonly red but can also be orange or yellow. Locals traditionally make jelly with the fruit, a pantry item that has been prized in the South for centuries. The berries are also cooked into sauces for wild game and fermented for wine. May hawthorn trees are widely cultivated in the United States for hedges.

**History** • Native Americans used the unripe fruit medicinally to treat bladder ailments. The seeds were boiled or roasted and used to make a drink similar to coffee.

**How to pick** • The large thorns on the mayhaw tree make it challenging to pick the berries. The easiest way to get them is to lay a tarp on the ground around the tree and shake the trunk. If the trees are growing in swamps, the berries need to be shaken off the tree and gathered in a boat using nets.

**How to buy** • Fresh mayhaws are available locally at farmers' markets in the limited regions where they grow. Look for berries that are a solid color without cracks or brown spots. You can order mayhaw products from Hillside Orchard Farms, 18 Sorghum Mill Dr., Lakemont, GA 30552-1627; 706-782-4995; www.hillside@hillsideorchardfarms.com.

**How to store** • Keep the berries in an open container in the refrigerator for up to one week. Put into self-sealing plastic freezer bags and freeze for up to one year.

**Notes for the cook** • These small berries are tart and seedy with a good flavor. Crush them first, either by pulsing two or three times in the food processor or with a potato masher, then simmer in a small amount of water. Strain through several thicknesses of cheesecloth and use the juice to make jelly (page 170).

## MOUNTAIN ASH

**Common names** • mountain ash berry; rowanberry; Ebereschenbeere, Vogelbeere (Germany); bacca del sorbo (Italy); sorbier (France).

**Scientific classification** • Rowan trees are members of the rose family (Rosaceae), native to both the Old and New Worlds. The European mountain ash (*Sorbus aucuparia*), historically called the *rowan tree* in Europe, has become naturalized in some regions of the United States. The two main species in the U.S. are *Sorbus decora* and *Sorbus Americana. Sorbus* is the Latin name Pliny used for the fruit of this tree in his writings.

**Habitat and distribution** • Rowan trees are widespread throughout the world, growing in Europe, Africa, the Middle East, and North America. They have become naturalized in eastern North America from Nova Scotia, along the Appalachian Mountains, to North Carolina. They grow up to 50 feet tall and prefer moist habitats in clearings from swamps to hillsides.

In the United States, mountain ash trees are much smaller than their European cousins, growing to a height of 10 to 20 feet, but they do prefer a similar habitat.

All of the *Sorbus* species produce a large number of tart yellow to red edible berries in late summer and early fall.

**History** • Rowan trees, named from the Nordic word *rune*, which means "magic," have a fascinating history going back to Celtic times, when they were planted next to stone circles and ancient villages. The trees were thought to have magical properties that provided protection against evil and were a source of spiritual strength. Small crossed branches were placed over the door and in stables, and necklaces of rowanberries were worn to ward off evil spirits.

In North America, the berries were not generally eaten except by the Haida Indians in British Columbia.

**Where they are grown commercially** • The trees are sold only at nurseries for ornamental gardens. One nursery in Molalla, Oregon, sells these as fruit trees. You can order them from One Green World Nursery, 28696 South Cramer Road, Molalla, OR 97038–8576; www.onegreenworld.com.

**How to pick** • Pick the berries late in the fall after the first freeze. A good indication that they are ripe is when the birds start eating them.

**How to store** • Run a fork turned upside down through the clusters to remove the berries. Rinse them in a strainer under cold water, drain well, and transfer the berries to a plate lined with paper towels to remove all the moisture. Pour them into a self-sealing plastic bag and store in the refrigerator for up two weeks. Freeze airtight in self-sealing plastic freezer bags for up to one year.

**Notes for the cook** • These berries are tart and must be cooked before using. If you wait to pick them until after the first freeze, they will be less astringent. These berries are high in pectin and exceptionally tart, making them prized for jelly that in Europe is traditionally served with rich meats, especially wild game. You can buy wild rowan jelly from ChefShop.com, PO Box 3488, Seattle, WA 98114–3488; 800-596-0885; www.chefshop.com (rowan jelly and berry jams).

## MULBERRY

**Common names** • black mulberry, mûrier noir (France), gèlso nèro (Italy), schwarzer Maulbeere (Germany), white mulberry, mûrier blanc (France), gèlso comune (Italy), weisser Maulbeere (Germany).

**Scientific classification** • Mulberry trees belong to the mulberry family (Moraceae). Botanically the fruits from mulberry trees are not berries but collective fruits that look like large loganberries. The generic name for these trees, *Morus*, is thought to be derived from the Latin word *mora*, meaning "delay," referring to the late expansion of their buds compared to other trees.

**Habitat and distribution** • Amazingly, there are more than 1,200 different species of mulberry trees. The three major species that are grown for fruit are the black mulberry (*Morus nigra*), the white mulberry (*Morus alba*)—both native to the Old World—and the red mulberry (*Morus rubra*), which is indigenous to North America.

The white mulberry, originally from China, has been cultivated for centuries for its leaves, which are the main food of the silkworm. This noble tree is named for its white blossoms, not its exceptionally sweet fruit, which can be white, lavender, or black. The white mulberry has become naturalized in both Europe and the eastern and southern United States.

The red or American mulberry, *Morus rubra*, grows in moist bottomlands from Canada to southern Texas. It produces a deep red, almost black fruit with a good flavor.

The black mulberry, *Morus nigra*, is native to western Asia and has been grown in Europe for its fruit since Roman times. It produces large, flavorful berries ranging in color from purple to black that often drop off the tree before ripening.

**History** • The black mulberry was introduced from Persia to southern Europe, where it was already widespread 2,000 years ago. These ancient trees were highly esteemed by early man and commonly referred to in writings of the Greeks and Romans. Mulberry leaves were found in a mosaic in Pompeii, and it is known that the Romans served mulberries at their feasts.

**Where they are grown commercially** • The only mulberry tree grown commercially is the black mulberry in Europe and Turkey.

**How to pick** • For the best flavor, pick fruit when it is perfectly ripe. White and red mulberry fruits ripen in the late spring, while the black mulberry fruits are later, toward the end of summer. The fruit of the latter is especially soft and collapses when picked. Always transport the berries in a bucket with a lid as these juicy berries are delicate and stain whatever they come in contact with. (The carpet in the trunk of my car can prove it.)

**How to buy** • Not available commercially except at the occasional farmers' market.

**How to store** • Because the berries are soft and juicy, they are extremely perishable. They can be stored unwashed in an open container in the refrigerator for several days. Rinse just before using. To freeze, rinse and drain the berries, then transfer to a baking sheet lined with paper towels and pat dry. To freeze, store in self-sealing plastic freezer bags for up to one year.

**Notes for the cook** • Use mulberries as you would raspberries or blackberries, for sauces, pies, tarts, jellies, syrups, and wines.

## OHELO BERRY

**Common names** • ohelo.

**Scientific classification** • Ohelo (*Vaccinium reticulatum*) is a member of the heath family (Ericaceae) closely related to huckleberry and cranberry. The genus name is derived from the Latin *vacca*, for cow (associated with pastures) and *reticulatum*, referring to their reticulate leaves.

**Habitat and distribution** • Berries from the ohelo are one of the few native fruits of Hawaii. They are low-growing, sprawling shrubs and are common within and around Kilauea Caldera on the Big Island of Hawaii and throughout Haleakala Crater on Maui, where they thrive on volcanic ash deposits. Ohelo is considered rare on Kauai, Oahu, and Molokai.

**History** • According to ancient Hawaiian tradition, ohelo berries are sacred to Pele, the fire goddess of the Hawaiian volcanoes. According to an ancient custom, before eating the berries, you should make an offering to Pele by throwing a few into the volcano.

**Where they are grown commercially** • Not grown commercially but harvested outside national parks on Maui and Hawaii for commercial production of preserves. You can order preserves from the Made in Hawaii Store, PO Box 96, Aiea, HI 96701-0096; 800-870-1055; www.madeinhawaiistore.com. Hawaii Volcanoes and Haleakala National Parks permit taking a quart of berries per day, for home consumption only.

**How to pick** • Pick the berries from late summer and fall.

**How to buy** • Berries are not sold commercially except in preserves.

**How to store** • Keep the berries chilled after picking and store unwashed in the refrigerator for two to three days in an open container lined with paper towels. To freeze, rinse (page 69) and drain thoroughly, then pour onto a baking sheet lined with paper towels and pat dry. Put into self-sealing plastic freezer bags and freeze for up to one year.

**Notes for the cook** • The round red, orange, and yellow ohelo berries vary in size from one-quarter to one-half inch in diameter. They are juicy and slightly sweet and can be eaten fresh or made into pies or preserves.

**Beware** • Do not mistake them for poisonous akia berries (*Wikstroemia uva-ursi*), which look similar to the ohelo berries and can grow next to them. The akia berry has one large seed, while the ohelo berry has many small seeds.

## PYRACANTHA

**Common names** • pyracantha, firethorn, and burning bush, named after its bright coral-red fruits. While the red-fruited pyracantha is the most popular, there are also plants with orange, yellow, and white fruits.

**Scientific classification** • Pyracanthas (*Pyracantha coccinea*) are members of the rose family (Rosaceae) and cousins to the crab apple and apple. Their fruits, while often called berries, are actually more like tiny apples. *Pyracantha coccinea* is derived from the Greek *pyr* ("fire"), *akantha* ("thorn"), and *kakkos* ("berry").

**Habitat and distribution** • These plants are native to parts of Asia and southeastern Europe. They have become naturalized in many regions of the world, including southern Africa and the United States, especially the South.

**History** • In 1629, pyracanthas were introduced to Great Britain from China as a wall shrub and have been popular for centuries.

**Where they are grown commercially** • Pyracanthas are not grown commercially for their fruits, but they are a popular ornamental garden plant throughout much of the world.

**How to pick** • Harvest the fruit when it is fully ripe, in the fall. A good indicator is to watch the birds in your garden—when they start eating them, hurry up and get out there.

**How to buy** • Not available commercially.

**How to store** • Store the unwashed berries in an open container on a paper towel in the refrigerator. Rinse just prior to using. To freeze, rinse the berries (see page 69) and drain thoroughly, then transfer to a baking sheet lined with paper towels and pat dry. Put the berries in self-sealing plastic freezer bags and freeze for up to one year.

**Notes for the cook** • Both the red and orange fruit produce a lovely, brilliant-colored jelly that tastes similar to apple jelly.

**Beware** • Ingesting too many raw pyracantha berries can cause nausea.

## RASPBERRY (*BLACK*)

**Common names** • blackcap, wild black raspberry, framboise de Virginie (France), schwarze Himbeere (Germany), frambueso negro (Spain). *Raspberry* comes from the old English name for this berry, *raspis berry*. No one is quite sure of its derivation, but it could be from the Anglo-Saxon word *resp*, meaning "a shoot or sucker," or from the Middle English word *raspis*—"a kind of wine"—or from the word *rasp*, meaning "to scrape," referring to the berries' thorny cane.

**Scientific classification** • Black raspberries (*Rubus occidentalis*), in the raspberry subgenus *Idaeobatus*, are members of the rose family (Rosaceae) and are closely related to red raspberries (*R. idaeus*) along with the blackberries. While yellow raspberries look and taste just like red raspberries, black raspberries have a look and flavor that is quite distinct from those of red raspberries.

**History** • Like many berries, the black raspberry was a utilitarian fruit for Native Americans. They ate them fresh and dried and often mixed them with other berries, meat, and fish. During the summer the berries were dried either in the sun or over a fire and then stored in wood boxes for winter use. In the springtime the young shoots were peeled and eaten raw. Black raspberries were also mashed with other berries and used as a dye while the roots were infused for a tea to treat the flu.

**Habitat and distribution** • Wild black raspberries, commonly called *blackcaps*, are native to North America and grow throughout the continent. There are two species—one ranging in the western half of North America and the other in the eastern half—

and both are indigenous to the New World. Blackcaps turn from red to black when they are ripe and, in hot climates, can be dry and seedy.

**Where they are grown commercially** • The black raspberry was not domesticated until 1850, and it took another 30 years before serious cultivation got under way. It wasn't until the early 1880s, when the European raspberry was crossed with the wild black raspberry to produce a purple raspberry, that interest was taken in domesticating wild black raspberries for hybridization and commercial crops. The late 1800s and early 1900s saw a flourish of selecting superior genotypes from the wild and breeding efforts to develop cultivars. By 1925 there were 193 cultivars bred from various programs in the eastern United States and Canada. Since the early 1900s, fewer than a dozen new black raspberry cultivars have been developed.

The industry was centered in western New York, western Michigan, and central Maryland. Today the industry has shifted to Oregon's Willamette Valley, where 1,200 acres are cultivated for processing. Until recently the USDA used black raspberry juice as the organic dye to stamp graded meat.

Black raspberries are also grown in small numbers on the East Coast, specifically Ohio and Pennsylvania, where they are sold to the fresh market.

**How to pick** • Raspberries differ from blackberries in that they detach from the receptacle when they are harvested, leaving a soft, hollow fruit that is exceptionally fragile. Always pick black raspberries in the morning, before the hot summer sun softens them even more and when the berries are at the peak of ripeness. Perfectly ripe fruit will be full colored with its characteristic fruity flavor and aroma, and it will come off the receptacle with the slightest pull.

**How to buy** • Ripe black raspberries should be dry and well formed without soft spots, discoloration, or any signs of mold. There should be no signs of juice leakage on the container.

**How to store** • Because raspberries are fragile, they have a short shelf life of only two to three days. Store unwashed and uncovered in the refrigerator in a shallow container on a paper towel. Wash just before using.

To freeze, first rinse the berries (see page 69) and drain thoroughly, then transfer to a baking sheet lined with paper towels and pat dry. Discard immature and overripe berries. Put the lined baking sheet in the freezer until the berries are frozen. Pour the individually frozen berries into self-sealing plastic freezer bags and freeze for up to one year.

**Notes for the cook** • Raspberries are delicate berries and should be added to dishes at the last minute. Black raspberries have one of the highest antioxidant levels of all foods, making them one of the most health-benefiting of all berries; eat them frequently. Snack on a bowlful, toss them into smoothies, sprinkle them over ice cream, or make them into a pie and serve slices covered with a big scoop of vanilla ice cream—use low-fat if you have to. If they are particularly dry and seedy, toss them with ½ cup blueberries. Because of their seediness, it is often best to strain out half or all of the seeds when making a sauce. You can buy black raspberries from Sturm's Berry Farm Inc., 1037 Evans Road, Corbett, OR 97019-9621; 866-402-9058; www.sturmsberryfarm.com (black raspberries, other berries, and preserves).

## RASPBERRY (*RED*)

**Common names** • framboise (France), Himbeere (Germany), lampóire (Italy), fram-bueso (Spain). *Raspberry* comes from the old English name for this berry, *raspis berry*. No one is quite sure of its derivation, but it could be from the Anglo-Saxon word *resp*, meaning "a shoot or sucker," or from the Middle English word *raspis*—"a kind of wine"— or from the word *rasp*, meaning "to scrape," referring to the berries' thorny cane.

**Scientific classification** • Raspberries (*Rubus idaeus*—from the Latin *ruber*, meaning "red," and *idaeus*, referring to Mount Ida near Troy, where the first-century Roman scholar Pliny visited and later wrote about the region's raspberries) are members of the rose family (Rosaceae) and are related to blackberries. The raspberry subgenus, *Idaeobatus*, is further divided into the red (and their yellow forms) raspberry (*R. idaeus*), black raspberry (*R. occidentalis*), and purple raspberry, which is a hybrid between red and black raspberry.

**Habitat and distribution** • Red raspberries are native to Europe, North America, and Asia and grow in a wide range of climates from the tropics to the Arctic. However, *R. idaeus* is native to the northern temperate zone of the Northern Hemisphere, where the same species grows in both Europe and North America. In the U.S., wild red raspberries grow almost everywhere except the Deep South. They thrive in Alaska, the northern U.S., Canada, and east of the Cascade Mountains in the Pacific Northwest. Wild red raspberries are less common in the other western states. These perennial shrubs grow in thickets, clearings, and open woods with sweet and intensely aromatic fruit.

**History** • Besides eating the fruit, the ancient Greeks made an eye ointment out of raspberry blossoms and used the leaves to treat stomach problems. By the fourth century, raspberries were already being grown in Italian gardens, as documented in the agricultural records of Palladius. In medieval Europe, raspberries were a source of dye for paintings and manuscripts, as well as being used medicinally. During the next

200 years, the cultivation of raspberries gradually spread from the nobility to the masses, and they became common garden plants. By the end of the 1800s, there were more than 400 cultivars; unfortunately, fewer than half of them still exist.

Native Americans gathered and ate wild red raspberries and dried them in cakes to use during the winter. The leaves and roots were used as a medicinal herb for various ailments.

The earliest record of raspberry cultivation in the U.S. was in 1771 in a list of plants sold by William Price in Virginia. At the time, all the red raspberries grown in North America were of European stock. As the wild American red raspberries were eventually domesticated, they were crossed with the European stock, which is the ancestry of most of America's cultivated raspberries today.

**Where they are grown commercially •** Of the more than 200 species of raspberries in the world, only the red and black raspberry of Europe, North America, and Asia, and their hybrids are widely cultivated. The raspberry industry is concentrated in the Northern Hemisphere. In North America, red raspberry production is centered on the West Coast, where mild winters, warm summer sun with long days of uninterrupted growth, and little rain produce superior berry crops.

The industry was slow to start, but by the mid-1940s more than 60,000 acres were being cultivated for red raspberry production in New York, Pennsylvania, Ohio, Michigan, and Oregon, with a high percentage of the berries being sold fresh. After World War II, a combination of a severe labor shortage, a devastating plant disease, and loss of land to housing rapidly decreased red raspberry production in the eastern and midwestern United States.

With the introduction of aphid-resistant cultivars and new propagation techniques, the industry survived, but the center of large-scale commercial production shifted entirely to the West Coast, where farmland was still readily available. Today approximately 20,000 acres of raspberries are under production in British Columbia, Washington, Oregon, and California. Washington, the leading producer, has 122 growers and harvests 40 million to 70 million pounds a year. Unlike British Columbia, Washington, and Oregon, California's raspberries are sold primarily to the fresh market.

When seeds of red raspberries are grown, about one out of every 1,000 produces yellow or apricot-colored fruit rather than red. Other than color, these raspberries are the same as typical red raspberries. The most widely grown cultivar is 'Fall Gold'.

**How to pick •** Always pick raspberries in the morning, before the hot summer sun softens them further, and when the berries are at the peak of ripeness. Raspberries differ from blackberries in that they detach from their receptacle when they are harvested, leaving a soft, hollow fruit that is exceptionally fragile. Perfectly ripe fruit will be a deep color with its characteristic fruity flavor and aroma, and each berry easily comes off the receptacle with the slightest touch.

**How to buy** • Fresh raspberries should be dry and well formed without soft spots, discoloration, or any signs of mold. There should be no signs of juice leakage on the container. Be aware that a 6-ounce container of raspberries (called a clamshell) contains 1¾ cups berries, not 2 cups.

### The Raspberry Family

**Arctic raspberry** • A circumpolar dwarf raspberry.

**Black raspberry** • Cultivars are descendants of the wild black raspberry indigenous only to North America. It wasn't until the early 1800s, when the European red raspberry was crossed with the wild black raspberry to produce a purple raspberry, that interest was taken in domesticating wild black raspberries for hybridization and commercial crops.

**Purple raspberry** • A cross between a black and red raspberry; the fruits are large and have a dull purple color that has never caught on with consumers, who prefer red or black raspberries. 'Brandywine' and 'Royalty' are the most widely grown cultivars. They make outstanding processed products, like jams and jellies.

Yellow-fruited red, purple, and black raspberries are commonly found mutations. The fruits, other than color, are nearly identical to the species they came from.

**Mora (*Rubus glaucus*)** • Thought to be a hybrid between a blackberry and raspberry species, this raspberry grows from 6,000 to 12,000 feet in Mexico, Ecuador, Colombia, and Costa Rica. It is cultivated on a small scale and sold in large cities.

**Wineberry (*Rubus phoenicolasius*)** • Of Japanese origin, but it has become naturalized in parts of the U.S.

**How to store** • Because raspberries have a hollow center and are easily crushed, they are especially delicate and have a short shelf life of two to three days. Store unwashed and uncovered in the refrigerator in a shallow container on a paper towel. Rinse just before using.

To freeze, first rinse the berries (see page 69) and drain thoroughly, then transfer to a baking sheet lined with paper towels and pat dry. Discard immature and overripe berries. Put the lined baking sheet in the freezer until the berries are frozen. Pour the individually frozen berries into self-sealing plastic freezer bags and freeze for up to one year. I freeze them in ½-pint (2-cup) self-sealing plastic freezer bags so I have the exact amount for making Melba Sauce (page 230).

**Notes for the cook** • Raspberries are delicate and should be added to dishes at the last minute. Always serve them at room temperature for their fullest flavor. For desserts, I often sprinkle them whole or pureed for a sauce with framboise liqueur to enhance their flavor. If I'm serving a dessert with whipped cream, I add a splash of framboise instead of vanilla while whipping.

Use red raspberries in batters directly from the freezer, and they'll hold their shape perfectly. Raspberries are good mixers with other red berries, such as red currants or cranberries in sauces, and rhubarb, and they have an affinity for the exotic scent of rose geranium.

You can order tea made from wild raspberry leaves from the Algonquin Tea Company, RR # 1, Goldenlake, ON, Canada K0J1 X0; 800-292-6671; www.algonquintea.com/bulk.shtml (bulk herbs and organic teas, including berry teas).

## SALAL

**Common name** • Salal is the Northwest Indian name for this plant.

**Scientific classification** • Salal (*Gaultheria shallon*) is a member of the heath family (Ericaceae) and is related to blueberries and cranberries. It is named after Dr. Jean-François Gaulthier, a famous French Canadian botanist and physician.

**Habitat and distribution** • Salal is an evergreen shrub indigenous to North America. It grows profusely from the Pacific Coast inland up to 2,500 feet in the Cascade Mountains and from southeastern Alaska and central British Columbia to southern California. It thrives in the damp understory of coastal Douglas fir and redwood forests and in the sunnier and drier forests inland, where it grows in dense, low thickets.

**History** • Salal berries were a staple of all the Pacific Northwest Indians and one of their most important berries. In British Columbia, the Indian women mashed the berries, formed them into cakes, and left them to dry in the sun. The cakes were soaked in water and dipped in seal or whale oil before being eaten. For winter storage, the fruit were crushed and then dried in rectangular cedar frames set on skunk cabbage leaves over a smoldering alderwood fire. The dried cakes were then folded and stored in cedar boxes.

The Chinook Indians who lived along the lower Columbia River dried the berries into loaves that weighed from 10 to 15 pounds. The early settlers made jelly with salal berries, often mixing them with Oregon grape.

**Where they are grown commercially** • Not sold commercially. Plants are available for ornamental gardens.

**How to pick** • Harvest in the morning when it's cool. The berries grow in clusters and turn from red to blue-black when they are ripe, usually around the first part of August.

**How to buy** • Not sold commercially, but the plants are sold in nurseries for ornamental gardens. Stems with their dark, glossy leaves are often sold with florist bouquets.

**How to store** • Pick the berries over and discard unripe or over ripe fruit and debris. Store unwashed in the refrigerator in an open container on a paper towel for up to three days. Rinse the berries just before using. To freeze, first rinse the berries (see page 69) and drain thoroughly, then transfer to a baking sheet lined with paper towels and pat dry. Put the lined baking sheet in the freezer until the berries are frozen. Pour the individually frozen berries into self-sealing plastic freezer bags and freeze for up to one year.

**Notes for the cook** • Salal berries are dark and juicy (especially along the moist coastal areas) and make a good jelly when mixed with Oregon grape or blueberries.

## SALMONBERRY

**Common names** • The name *salmonberry* is derived from the berries' use by the Native Americans, who ate fresh salmonberry bush shoots in the spring with dried salmon and later in the season with the fresh fish. The berries range in color from yellow to salmon colored to crimson and ripen in late spring, when local salmon are returning to the rivers of their birth.

**Scientific classification** • Salmonberries (*Rubus spectabilis*) are members of the rose family (Rosaceae) and closely related to raspberries. Their scientific name is derived from Latin: *Rubus,* meaning, "red," and *spectabilis,* meaning "spectacular," referring to their lovely blossoms. The salmonberry naturally hybridizes with the nagoonberry (*R. arcticus*) to produce the Alaska bramble (*R.* × *alaskensis*).

**Habitat and distribution** • Salmonberries grow from the Aleutian Islands to northern California and east to Idaho. They were first introduced to Great Britain in 1827 as garden plants but have since become naturalized and invasive, growing in regions with mild and wet winters, especially along the northern coast.

These deciduous bushes grow from three to 12 feet tall with erect or arching stems and raspberrylike berries. They are a part of the shady understory in a wide range of coniferous forests that includes most firs, western hemlock, red cedar, redwood, Sitka spruce, and hardwoods, like alder and black cottonwood. These brightly colored berries add a bit of color to the banks of creeks, where they thrive in dense thickets. Other varieties of wild berries—wild black raspberries, thimbleberries, and trailing blackberries—often grow nearby, but salmonberries are the first to ripen.

**History** • Salmonberries were eaten only fresh by the Native Americans in the Pacific Northwest, as they are too soft and juicy to dry. In the spring the young shoots of the salmonberry bush were peeled and eaten fresh and steamed as a vegetable with smoked salmon. The astringent bark and leaves were used as medicine for burns and toothaches and brewed into a tea for labor pains. Branches with the pith removed were made into pipe stems.

**Where they are grown commercially** • Not available commercially.

**How to pick** • Pick these fragile berries when they have turned from yellow to orange or crimson and easily come off the receptacle. They are soft and delicate, even more fragile than a raspberry, and great care must be taken not to crush them. Salmonberries grow sparingly on bushes, usually just enough to satisfy passing hikers. They are best eaten fresh right off the bush, and I particularly like the berries that have turned crimson, as their flavor seems more intense.

**How to buy** • Not available commercially.

**How to store** • Not recommended.

**Notes for the cook** • Salmonberries have an exceptionally delicate flavor. Some would say they are flavorless, but as anyone who hikes knows, everything always tastes twice as good outdoors as it does inside, and their flavor would be lost if they were cooked. Besides, the berries are so fragile they would completely disintegrate by the time you got them home.

## SEA BUCKTHORN BERRY

**Common names** • buckthorn, Sandorn (Germany), oblepikha (Russia), argousier (France), finbar (Sweden). The name *sea buckthorn* is derived from its habit of growing near the sea with its thorny spines.

**Scientific classification** • Sea buckthorns (*Hippophae rhamnoides*) are a member of the oleaster family (Elaeagnaceae) and related to the Russian olive and the oleaster. Their name is derived from the Greek language: *hippo,* meaning "horse," *phoas,* meaning "light," and *rhamnoides,* from their resemblance to the genus *Rhamnus*—the buckthorns. The ancient Greeks fed this plant to their horses to improve their health and to make their coat shiny. The Russian name for this plant, *oblepikha,* means "to cling to," referring to the berries, which are firmly attached to the branches.

**Habitat and distribution** • Sea buckthorns are deciduous shrubs with round, orange berries (they can be red or yellow, too, but not as commonly) that are native to the northern regions of Eurasia. They are particularly widespread in northern Europe and on the seacoasts of Romania, Mongolia, and China and are divided into eight subspecies by geographic location. They grow from sea level, preferring the slopes of riverbanks and the seashore, to 10,000 feet in the Himalayas.

In Russia families grow sea buckthorns in the gardens at their dachas. The berries are harvested at the end of summer and canned or made into jams or taken to the cities and sold at farmers' markets.

North American gardeners grow sea buckthorns as ornamentals for their colorful bright orange berries that remain on the bush all winter long.

**History** • Legend has it that sea buckthorns were the food of Pegasus, the flying horse of Greek mythology. The medicinal qualities of these historic fruits are recorded in ancient Greek and Tibetan texts from as early as the seventh century, when sea buckthorn was considered a universal healing agent. It was used to treat rheumatism, scurvy, tumors, skin diseases, and intestinal disorders.

**Where they are grown commercially** • Sea buckthorns were domesticated in Siberia in the 1930s and are often called *Siberian pineapple* after their similar flavor. In Eurasia this shrub is one of the most widely grown northern fruits.

Russia, Mongolia, and China are the largest producers of sea buckthorn products in the world. The berries are harvested commercially and processed for jellies, juices, liqueurs, candy, vitamin C tablets, tea, ice cream, cosmetics, and medicines.

Currently, many countries, including Canada, Russia, China, and Scandinavia, have breeding programs for this berry. With recent scientific studies showing their high antioxidant levels, which give them protective and anti-inflammatory properties, production is likely to increase in North America if a sea buckthorn can be developed that can separate easily from the plant so it can be harvested mechanically.

Sea buckthorn plants are available for home gardens. To order, see One Green World's Web site, www.onegreenworld.com.

**How to pick** • The sea buckthorn has sharp thorns, so wear a long-sleeved shirt when picking berries. The fruits can be round or oval and are shiny orange, yellowish red, or yellowish gold when ripe.

**How to buy** • Not available commercially.

**How to store** • Keep the unwashed berries in an uncovered container in the refrigerator for up to two weeks. Wash just before using. To freeze, first rinse the berries (see page 69) and drain thoroughly, then transfer to a baking sheet lined with paper towels and pat dry. Discard immature and overripe berries. Pour the berries into self-sealing plastic freezer bags and freeze for up to one year.

**Notes for the cook** • The fruits of the sea buckthorn are enjoyably sweet and sour with a pineapple–passion fruit flavor. In Belarus, the juice is known as *Russian pineapple juice.* They are too acidic to be eaten fresh but make excellent thick jellies, sauces, juices, and syrups. Use them as you would gooseberries.

## STRAWBERRY

**Common names** • strawberry; fraise, fraise des bois (France); Erdbeere (Germany); fràgola (Italy); aardbei (Netherlands); fresa (Spain); frutilla (Spain/Chile). No one is certain how the strawberry was named. It could have come from the medieval European practice of street vendors selling strawberries strung on pieces of hay or from the fact that the fruit ripened at the same time as hay (the Anglo-Saxon word for *hay* is *streaw*) or, more likely, from the runners around the strawberry plant, which resemble *streaw* (hay).

**Scientific classification** • Strawberries (*Fragaria* sp.) are members of the rose family (Rosaceae), like raspberries and blackberries. Their genus name is derived from the Latin *fragrans*, after the fruits' exquisite fragrance.

**Habitat and distribution** • Of all cultivated fruit, strawberries are found in the greatest number of places. They grow at sea level on the sandy dunes, in meadows and subalpine forests, and high up on the slopes of many of the world's highest mountains, including the Himalayas, the Alps, and the Andes.

While a number of wild species of strawberries found worldwide are well known regionally, the four most important are alpine (wood) strawberry/fraise des bois (*F. resca*), found throughout the northern hemisphere; scarlet or Virginia strawberry (*F. virginiana*), found throughout North America; beach strawberry (*F. chiloensis*), found along the Pacific Coast of North and South America; and musk strawberry (*F. moschata*), found in Europe.

The hybrid between the North American *F. virginiana* and South American *F. chiloensis* produced the cultivated strawberry (*F. ananassa*), which has become naturalized in parts of North America, Europe, Russia, Hawaii, Japan, and China.

**History** • Although wild strawberries grew in Europe before the first century, there are few written references to them. One of the first was in the Roman poet Ovid's *Metamorphoses*, written in the first century, about a spurned lover trying to win his sweetheart back: "With thine own hands thou shalt thyself gather the soft strawberries growing beneath the woodland shade." Pliny listed the wild strawberry as *fraga*, one of the natural fruits of Italy. In the thirteenth century, a Greek doctor wrote about using the strawberry to treat depression. These picture-perfect fruits were also popular in Italian, Flemish, and German art, and in English miniatures they were the symbol of modesty and humility.

By the fourteenth and early fifteenth century, strawberries were being cultivated in European apothecary gardens. All parts of the plants were used in medicinal teas and ointments intended to treat a long list of illnesses from throat infections to broken bones. But by 1530, the succulent fruit of the alpine strawberry (*fraise des bois*) took on a new role as a delicacy for the table. By the end of the century, the European species—the alpine strawberry and the musk strawberry—were domesticated, and botanists had begun breeding experiments in earnest. The alpine strawberry was still the favored species, but events were taking place in the New World that would forever change cultivated strawberries.

In South America, the Huilliche people of Chile were already cultivating the wild South American strawberry (*F. chiloensis*). By the time of the Spanish Conquest in the 1550s, strawberry cultivation was commonplace throughout all of central Chile. As the Spaniards traveled north, they spread the strawberry, which they called *frutilla,* meaning "little fruit," into different countries of South America, including Peru and Ecuador.

In 1711 a 30-year-old French spy, Lieutenant Colonel Frézier, was sent by King Louis XIV of France to get information on the Spanish West Indies. While posing as a captain on a merchant ship, he was secretly documenting ports and making detailed drawings of Spanish fortresses. At the same time, he was taken with the cultivation of the enormous strawberries growing in Concepción. "They plant whole Fields, with a Sort of Strawberry Rushes, differing from ours, in that the Leaves are rounder, thicker and more downy. The fruit is generally as big as a Walnut, and sometimes as a Hen's Egg....The berries are brought back in such abundance to the city of Concepción and the vicinity that people sell them at the market like other fruits. For half a real, which is the lowest money, one gets one or two dozen, wrapped in a cabbage leaf."

Frézier began his return voyage to France in 1714 with his clandestine military notes and five Chilean strawberry plants. Upon his arrival, he gave two plants to the officer in charge of the ship's precious fresh water for keeping his plants alive on the long journey home; one went to Paris for the king's garden, one was given to his superior, the minister of fortifications, who lived in Brest, and he kept one for himself.

Unfortunately, all five strawberry plants were female (likely collected for their large fruit—it was not known then that there are male and female strawberry plants and the males, essential for fruit set, do not produce fruit), and botanists had difficulty getting them to bear fruit. Plants propagated from the fruitless plant were sent to Holland and from Holland to England. But the Chilean strawberry grew best in Brest, where it was accidentally crossed with *F. virginiana*—brought to Europe from the New World in the late 1500s—which was growing in a field next to *F. chiloensis.* The resulting hermaphroditic (no longer male and female plants, but both sexes on one plant) hybrid was subsequently given the name *F. ananassa,* which is the commercial strawberry commonly grown throughout the world today.

In North America, the tiny wild strawberry was mostly eaten fresh by Native Americans as it was too small and fragile to transport. These berries were so abundant that no one bothered to cultivate them until centuries later.

**Where they are grown commercially** • Leading states growing strawberries are California, Florida, and Oregon. The U.S. industry began around 1800 with the domestication of *F. virginiana,* and subsequently *F. ananassa* replaced it in cultivated fields. Today California is the world's leading producer and grows 85 percent of North America's crop.

The semitropical climate of Southern California allows growers to start picking berries for shipping in January, and picking continues north as the berries ripen with the arrival of warmer weather. Even in November the state's northern berry fields are still producing fruit, giving California an almost year-round strawberry season. The majority of the berries are sold to the fresh market, with only 25 percent of them being processed.

Florida grows 12 percent of the nation's crop, producing 192 million pounds of strawberries a year. The industry, located in central Florida, 18 miles east of Tampa, began in the 1880s when Henry Plant built a railroad to Tampa, which provided transportation so farmers could ship their strawberries north during the winter. Today the town is known as the winter strawberry capital of the United States—it grows all the fresh strawberries sold in the South and Northeast during the winter months. (Fresh winter strawberries in the Midwest and West are supplied by Mexico and California.)

The 120-year-old Oregon strawberry industry began in 1846 when Henderson Luelling traveled the Oregon Trail, bringing two wagons filled to the brim with fruit and nut trees and berry plants. The plants thrived in the fertile Willamette Valley, and by the late 1870s Oregon strawberries were being processed and shipped across the country by Southern Pacific Railroad. In the 1920s, the first freezing plants for fruits and vegetables were developed in Oregon. Berries were frozen in barrels and shipped to factories in the East for processing. Of the 3,100 acres of strawberries grown in Oregon today, 90 percent of them are processed.

Just mentioning the names of two famous Oregon cultivars, 'Hood' and 'Marshall', will bring tears to the eyes of old-timers, who consider them to be the standard for all cultivated strawberries. Oregonians pride themselves on their local strawberries, which have excellent flavor, are sweet, juicy, and red throughout. Their juiciness, intense flavor, and color mean they are perfect for processing and eating but too soft to be shipped. They are sold fresh only locally, so plan to visit Oregon around the first or second week of June, when the first berries arrive in the markets.

Other strawberry-growing centers are in North Carolina, Washington, New York, and Michigan.

**How to pick** • Harvest strawberries in the cool morning or evening hours, before the summer heat makes the berries soft and easily perishable. Strawberries need to be perfectly ripe before you pick them. They should be plump and completely red and just starting to soften.

**How to buy** • Look for berries that are fully formed, bright red, without bruising or soft spots, and with fresh-looking green caps. Beware of buying out-of-season strawberries. Some growers pick their strawberries when they are only 40 percent ripe. The berries turn red during shipping but will never develop sweetness, and they will be hard and pithy as if they've been crossed with an apple.

**How to store** • Unwashed strawberries should be stored uncovered on a paper towel in the refrigerator for two to three days. Hull and rinse just before using. To freeze, first hull and rinse the berries (see page 69). Drain thoroughly, then transfer to a baking sheet lined with paper towels and pat dry. Discard immature and overripe berries. Put the lined baking sheet in the freezer until the berries are frozen. Pour the individually frozen berries into self-sealing plastic freezer bags and freeze for up to one year.

**Notes for the cook** • When strawberries are at the peak of their season, I make simple dishes that allow the fruit to speak for itself, like strawberry shortcake or homemade lemon sherbet topped with fresh strawberries. I also buy flats of local strawberries and freeze them to use throughout the winter.

The rest of the year is different. Strawberries are in the market year-round now, but you never know what you are going to get. If you buy a basket of particularly good berries, ask the produce manager for their cultivar name and keep requesting those berries. Until consumers start demanding higher-quality berries, stores will keep selling inferior fruit. And be aware that the name on the container, such as Driscoll's, is the name of the company selling the berries, not the name of the cultivar.

I have included some recipes in this book just for when you get stuck with a basket of those marginal strawberries and guests are due in an hour. Try the Sautéed Strawberries with Balsamic Vinegar (page 248) or the Shortbread with Warm Berry Port Sauce (page 222).

And don't forget that the age of a strawberry plant affects the flavor of the fruit—the older the plant, the less flavor and pectin it has (a good tip to know when making preserves late in the season).

## SUMAC

**Common names** • sumac (England, France); Sumach, Essigbaum (Germany); sommacco (Italy); zumaque (Spain); sumak (Turkey). The German name *Essigbaum* means "vinegar tree," after its sour berries, while the Dutch name, *zuukkruid*, translates as "sour condiment."

**Scientific classification** • Sumac trees belong to the cashew family (Anacardiaceae), along with cashews and pistachios and mangoes. The most common North American species is the staghorn sumac (*Rhus typhina*); in addition to being widely naturalized, it is also commonly planted in landscapes as an ornamental. Sumac's name is derived from the Arabic *summaq*, meaning "dark red"—referring to the trees' red berries.

**History** • Ground sumac berries are one of the oldest spices used by man. Their mildly bitter and fruity/woody flavor reminiscent of tamarind has been used for centuries to season dishes. The Romans stewed these small berries and added the fruity pulp to meat and vegetable dishes. In North America, the Native Americans of central Arizona and southern California used the berries of the sugar sumac as a sweetener. Other tribes steeped the dried berries of the smooth, lemonade, and fragrant sumac in water as a refreshing drink.

**Habitat and distribution** • The large *Rhus* genus contains 250 varieties of trees and shrubs that grow in a range of climates from tropical to subtropical and temperate. They are widely distributed in the Mediterranean area, eastern Asia, the tropics, and North and South America. While the majority of the varieties grow in the warmer climates, 20 different sumac species grow in the United States, and 13 of them are native.

These sun-loving plants are characteristically small shrubs that thrive in soil that has been heavily disturbed, such as along roads and railroads. They usually grow in clumps and produce brilliant-colored fall leaves with bright dry red berries.

**Where they are grown commercially** • Sumac trees are grown in North America as an ornamental garden plant.

**How to pick** • Pick the berries in the fall, when they turn bright red.

**How to buy** • Whole sumac berries are not for sale commercially, but ground sumac berries are available at specialty food stores.

**How to store** • Sumac berries are dry and can be stored in a cool place in a closed paper bag for several months.

**Notes for the cook** • Sumac berries are an ancient spice still used in Middle Eastern cooking. The berries are dried and ground with a little salt, then mixed with thyme and sesame seeds in a blend called *zatar*, used as a table condiment over rice or grilled meats. Brush pieces of pita bread with olive oil, season with a sprinkling of zatar, and bake in a 350°F oven for 5 minutes.

Plain dried sumac berries and salt are also available commercially—think of this spice as lemon salt with a pleasant fruity/woody taste. Use it sprinkled over Middle Eastern dishes like hummus. Ground sumac berries and zatar are both available at specialty food stores that carry products from the Middle East. You can order them from Penzeys Spices, 19300 West Janacek Court, Brookfield, WI 53008-0924; 800-741-7787; www.penzeys.com.

Dried sumac berries from the staghorn, lemonade, and smooth sumac can be used to make a refreshing drink.

**Beware** • *Toxicodendron diversilobum* and *T. radicans,* commonly known as *poison oak* and *poison ivy,* have often been called *poison sumac* because their resin can cause irritation to the skin. They were once in the *Rhus* genus but were reclassified to separate them from the other sumacs. The fruits of poison oak and poison ivy are usually fleshy and white or greenish. While it would be difficult to confuse them with the dry red berries of staghorn sumac (*R. typhina*), you should be careful.

## THIMBLEBERRY

**Common names** • thimbleberry, western thimble raspberry, white flowering raspberry. Thimbleberry is an appropriate name for these domelike berries.

**Scientific classification** • Thimbleberries (*Rubus parviflorus*) are members of the rose family (Rosaceae) and closely related to raspberries. Their scientific name is derived from the Latin *ruber,* meaning "red"—referring to its red berry—and *parviflorus,* Latin for "small flowered."

**Habitat and distribution** • Thimbleberries grow from Alaska to northern Mexico and east to the Great Lakes, where they thrive as forest understory, along stream banks, and in open, moist sites. These shrubs can grow to be eight feet tall in dense thickets with soft, maplelike green leaves and deep pink or pinkish red berries.

**History** • Native Americans ate thimbleberries if they grew nearby. The Nuu-chah-nulth of British Columbia dried the berries with smoked clams and ate the young shoots raw as a vegetable. The Nuxalk, also from British Columbia, felt the berries were inferior and mixed them with wild raspberries and wild black raspberries before drying them into cakes. In Oregon, the Lower Umpquas ate the thimbleberries only fresh.

**Where they are grown** • Not grown commercially except as plants for ornamental gardens.

**How to pick** • Thimbleberries tend to be dry and seedy. Leave them for trail food for hikers or for the birds and animals.

**How to buy** • Not sold commercially.

**How to store** • Not recommended.

# BERRY BASICS

### *Simple Syrup*

At the beginning of berry season, make this simple syrup and keep it in a covered glass jar in the refrigerator so you can whip up berry drinks and some desserts in no time. In a saucepan, heat 2 cups sugar with 2 cups water. Cover and simmer for 2 minutes, until the sugar dissolves, and then remove from the heat. When the syrup is cool, pour it into a glass jar with a lid. Simple syrup keeps in the refrigerator for up to 6 months.

### *Washing Berries*

Berries need to be rinsed before being used. I pour the berries into my over-the-sink expandable colander and spray them with cold water, gently shaking the basket a couple of times. Another easy method is to put the berries in the basket of a salad spinner. Fill the salad spinner with cold water and give the berries a good dunking—just a few seconds in the water will do. Let the berries drain before using them. Raspberries, with their hollow cores, are particularly fragile, so rinse them only a pint at a time.

### *Fresh vs. Frozen Berries*

Some berries, like strawberries, raspberries, and lately blueberries, are available fresh almost year-round, but they can often be of inferior quality. If you plan ahead, you can freeze your own local berries in the summer, when they are at the peak of the season.

Rinse the berries and pour them onto a baking sheet lined with a paper towel and pat dry with another paper towel. Put the baking sheet in the freezer until the berries are completely frozen. Transfer to self-sealing plastic freezer bags and freeze. The only exceptions to this are the firmer solid berries—wild blueberries, blueberries, huckleberries, cranberries, and currants, for example. Once they are washed and completely dry, they can be put directly into freezer bags and frozen. Their solid shape keeps them from sticking together so they do not need to be frozen individually like caneberries (known as *brambles* in the East). It important to freeze berries in exact amounts, such as pints or quarts, since frozen berries become compressed when thawed, making it impossible to measure them accurately.

If you don't have your own frozen stash, buy high-quality frozen berries rather than using mediocre fresh fruit. Frozen fruit is individually quick frozen (IQF) at the height of the season, just hours after being picked. Some brands are better than others, so always read the label and buy fruit grown in known berry-growing regions. (Processed blackberries and raspberries from the Northwest are bred to have intense color and flavor—vital characteristics for frozen berries.) IQF berries are washed before they are frozen, so there is no need to wash them again.

Most berries should be frozen for only up to a year. After that ice crystals will begin breaking down the berries' flesh, and eventually they will lose their flavor. Every May I make jam or syrup with all the berries left in my freezer to make space for the forthcoming summer crop. (It is interesting to note that several studies have shown that freezing caneberries does not diminish their nutraceutical health benefits.)

Thaw frozen berries (except strawberries, which will become mushy) for 20 minutes at room temperature on a plate lined with a paper towel, or quick thaw in the microwave. Set the power to "Defrost" and place berries in a single layer on a paper towel-lined plate. Microwave 2 minutes for blackberries, blueberries, gooseberries, cranberries, black currants, and huckleberries, and 1 minute 20 seconds for red or white currants and all raspberries. They should still be slightly frozen and hold their shape. If they are still too frozen, continue to microwave on the defrost cycle for 10 more seconds at a time.

Frozen berries (except strawberries) can be baked in batters, cobblers, and pies by simply adding another 5 or 6 minutes to your baking time, or use them for making homemade berry vinegars, liqueurs, or purees. For jams, jellies, and soups—any recipe that is going to be cooked—berries can also be used directly from the freezer.

### *Berry Purees*

Berry purees, known as *coulis* in France, a term I use interchangeably in this book, are easy to make. Rinse and thoroughly drain the fruit or use frozen berries, unthawed. Process the berries in a food processor. If the berries have large seeds, as do raspberries and boysenberries, push half or all of the puree through a strainer with the back of a spoon. Add a little sugar and a few drops of berry liqueur, such as cassis or framboise, and the puree is instantly transformed into a sauce rivaled by none. Berry purees will keep covered in the refrigerator for three to four days, or they can be frozen for up to a month. You can buy unsweetened berry purees at Perfect Puree, 2700 Napa Valley Corporate Drive, Suite L, Napa, CA 94558; 800-556-3707; www.perfectpuree.com. Commercial purees are expensive—it takes 20 pounds of blueberries to make one 32-ounce bottle of concentrate, but the concentrate will go a long way, and it can be frozen for up to a year.

### *A Pureeing Guide*

Use these measurements as a general rule. The size of berry cultivars varies widely throughout the country.

**1 cup whole blackberries = ½ cup pureed and strained**
**1 cup whole loganberries = ½ cup pureed and strained**
**1 cup whole raspberries = ⅓ cup pureed and strained**
**1 cup whole boysenberries = ⅓ cup pureed and strained**
**1 cup whole lingonberries = ⅓ cup pureed and strained**
**1 cup whole wild blueberries = ½ cup pureed and strained**
**1 cup whole huckleberries = ½ cup pureed and strained**
**1 cup whole blueberries = ½ cup pureed and strained**
**1 cup whole red currants = ¼ cup pureed and strained**
**1 cup whole black currants = ⅓ cup pureed and strained**
**1 cup whole large (California) strawberries = heaping ⅔ cup pureed and strained**
**1 cup whole small (Pacific Northwest) strawberries = ½ cup pureed and strained**

### *Other Helpful Berry Measurements*

**One 3-pound package frozen marionberries = 10 cups**
**One 12-ounce package frozen blackberries = 1¾ cups**
**One 10-ounce package frozen raspberries = 1 cup**
**One 16-ounce package frozen strawberries = 3 cups**
**One 16-ounce package frozen blueberries = 3 cups**
**One 16-ounce package cranberries = 4 cups**
**One 12-ounce package cranberries = 3 cups**
**One 6-ounce raspberry clamshell = 1¾ cups**

### *Dried Berries: The Next Generation of Dried Fruit*

High-quality dried berries have only recently become available, and they are so good they seem more like guilty pleasures than the perfect nutraceutical snack food. Thanks to new technology, the fruit is picked during the peak of the season and flash-frozen within hours. This ensures the berries' quality when they are processed later throughout the fall and winter months. These nonsulfured and wholesome dried fruit are exceptionally soft textured, with a rich color and an unmatched fresh flavor. Eat them as they are or use the berries to add a bright, bold taste to salads, yogurts, baked goods, trail mixes, cereals, stuffings, sauces, candies, or desserts. This new generation of dried fruits is naturally rich in antioxidants, and any way you eat them will be beneficial to your health. Their long shelf life of 12 months makes them especially convenient to have on hand, too. Trader Joe's has a good selection of high-quality dried berries under its own label.

To dry your own, place rinsed and thoroughly drained berries in a single layer on a baking sheet in a warm (160°F to 200°F) oven for four to five hours, until the berries are thoroughly dry.

### *A Sneaky Way to Remove Berry Stains*

To remove a berry stain, heat the teakettle to boiling. Stretch the fabric over a small bowl and hold the kettle at least two feet above the dish. Slowly and carefully pour the boiling water on the fabric. You might have to do this a couple of times.

### *Cream*

Berries and cream are inseparable. Buy heavy cream without any additives, because berries deserve the best. Pure cream is naturally rich and sweet with a delicate flavor.

All cream sold in supermarkets today is either pasteurized (heated to 145°F or 161°F, depending on the process, with a shelf life of 20 days) or ultrapasteurized (heated to 280°F or higher, with a shelf life of 60 days). While the heat kills harmful bacteria and extends the shelf life, it also destroys the delicate flavor of the cream and decreases its ability to whip and hold peaks, making it necessary to add emulsifiers and stabilizers. When possible, therefore, buy pasteurized heavy cream without additives, as it has been subjected to lower heat.

**Whipped cream** made from pasteurized heavy cream is magnificently thick textured with a sweet, buttery flavor that holds its peaks for a day or longer. Whipped cream made from ultrapasteurized heavy cream is thick textured but does not have the delicate flavor of whipped pasteurized heavy cream. Whipped cream made from pasteurized whipping cream produces a thin-textured whipped cream that lacks flavor and becomes watery after a few hours. Ultrapasteurized whipping cream produces a thin-textured whipping cream that lacks flavor and will become watery after a few hours.

**Crème fraîche** is made in France from unpasteurized cream that thickens naturally from its own bacteria. Until recently it was almost impossible to buy crème fraîche in the United States since all our cream is pasteurized. Now, however, it is becoming more readily available, but it's made by a slightly different technique from the French method. Fresh pasteurized cream is inoculated with a bacterial culture that produces acidity and a wonderful thick and rich crème fraîche with a tangy flavor all its own. To mail-order, contact Vermont Butter and Cheese Creamery, Websterville, VT 05678; 800-884-6287; www.vermontcreamery.com.

If you want to make your own crème fraîche, mix 1 cup heavy cream with 1 tablespoon buttermilk. Cover and let sit in a warm place for six to eight hours, until the cream is thick. Keep it stored in the refrigerator for up to three weeks.

**Clotted cream** is produced in southwestern England from Jersey cows and other breeds that produce high-fat milk. The cream is separated from the milk and heated slowly, evaporating the water in the milk and concentrating the fat solids. The result is a thick, heavy cream the consistency of softened butter. It is traditionally used on scones with strawberry jam and served with tea during the summer months. Look for it at specialty markets and grocery stores.

**Double Devon cream** is a thick, high-fat (48–50 percent) pasteurized cream developed during World War II because it didn't need refrigeration and had a long shelf life. It is named after Torrington, Devon, the town in southwestern England where the cream is produced. Made by heating the cream in a vacuum, it is known for its unique flavor. Like clotted cream, it is served with scones and jam.

## *Roasting Nuts*

The intense flavors of nuts and berries have a natural affinity for each other. The acid in the berries counterbalances the richness of the nuts. Toasting nuts before adding them to a recipe not only makes them crisper but intensifies the rich flavor of their natural oils as well. Most nuts can be toasted spread in a single layer on a baking sheet for eight minutes at 400°F. The denser nuts, such as hazelnuts, need to be toasted slowly so that the nutmeat cooks evenly throughout. Toast in a 275°F oven for 20 minutes, until their skins crack. Take the pan out of the oven and, while the nuts are still warm, remove as much of the skin as possible by rubbing them between your hands or a rough dish towel.

### *Substitutions*

Caneberries grow on long canes instead of bushes or ground plants and include all blackberries and red and black raspberries. They can all be substituted for one another in recipes, with the exception of black raspberries, which can often be seedy. Red, yellow, and purple raspberries can be used interchangeably. And wild blueberries, Juneberries, blueberries, and huckleberries can be substituted for one another. Red and black currants have completely different properties and are not interchangeable.

### *Strainers*

To make a berry puree, you will need some type of strainer, and there are many choices available. For small amounts, use a 5-inch fine-mesh strainer and a spatula to push the pulp through; for larger amounts, you can use a food mill fitted with a sieving dish with the smallest holes, a chinois (a French cone-shaped sieve) with a pestle, or an electric mixer, such as KitchenAid with its fruit/vegetable strainer.

### *Baking Utensils*

**Pie pan with juice saver rim**—A 9-inch-wide rimmed pie pan with an indentation that catches drips instead of having them bubble over onto the bottom of your oven.

**Pie crust shield**—A metal ring, about 10¼ inches wide, that covers the raised rim of the pie, protecting it from getting too brown.

**Pyrex pie plates**—They come in various sizes and allow you to keep an eye on your crust as it bakes. Pyrex conducts heat faster than metal, so remember to decrease the cooking time by 10 minutes or lower the temperature by 25°F.

**Mary Ann pan**—A 7-inch heavy-gauge tinned steel pan raised in the center. When the cake is unmolded, the depression in the center of the cake is filled with fresh fruit—perfect for berries. (Serves about 6.)

**Fluted German Obsttortenform pan**—A 9½-inch pan, same as a Mary Ann pan, with small fluted edges. (Serves about 8.)

**Bundt fluted Obsttortenform pan**—A 10¼-inch Mary Ann pan with wide fluted edges. Can be purchased with helpful Teflon lining. (Serves about 8.)

**Loose-bottomed tart pan**—These are available in various sizes, from 9 to 11¼ inches. These pans are all fluted and made of tinned steel. Some of the larger tart pans are available in black steel. The advantage of the black is that the dark finish will give an even color to your crust. (Serves 8 to 10.)

**Tartlet pan**—Small fluted and unfluted tart pans made of tinned steel, ranging in size from 1 to 4 inches wide and in shapes from round to oval to square. (Serves 1 to 2.) Some of the 4-inch tartlet pans have loose bottoms.

**Coeur à la crème mold**—This heart-shaped mold can be made of wicker or porcelain and comes in two diameters, 3¼ inches (serves 1) and 6 inches. (Serves about 6.)

**Ice cream maker**—There are a variety of ice cream makers on the market that do a good job at a moderate price. Many of the newer ones are electric and simple to use. Put the quick-freezing, double-insulated cylinder in the freezer overnight, and the next day simply add the ingredients and turn the machine on. Thirty minutes later you have homemade ice cream. All of them come with recipe booklets, too. Most make 1 or 2 quarts.

**Carbon dioxide whipped cream dispenser**—These handy dispensers make whipped cream in seconds. The canisters will hold a pint of heavy cream. Simply add sugar and a flavoring, then attach the lid and the carbon dioxide cartridge. Put on one of the decorative tips that come with it. Turn the canister upside down and gently shake it; that's all you have to do. The cream will keep in the canister in the refrigerator for 2 to 4 weeks.

**Over-the-sink expandable colander**—These handy colanders are perfect for working with large quantities of berries, and I wouldn't be without one. They are stainless steel and fit over the sink with expandable arms. Berries can easily be rinsed under cold running tap water and left to dry. I use a large slotted spoon to scoop the berries up.

All of the equipment listed is available at Sur La Table. To mail-order, contact Sur La Table, PO Box 34707, Seattle, WA 98124; 800-243-0852; www.SurLaTable.com.

# COOLERS, COCKTAILS, SMOOTHIES, AND OTHER DRINKS

The lovely color and intense flavor of berries provide the perfect media for a tempting roster of beverages. Here is a wide variety of drinks from old-fashioned berry sodas to upscale mixed drinks, such as the luscious Blackberry Martini.

For many of the drinks, if you have berry puree (page 70) and simple syrup (page 69) on hand, you'll be able to make them on a moment's notice. The sugar syrup will keep for up to six months in a covered jar in the refrigerator. If you are a Cosmopolitan fan, prepare the Sweet-and-Sour Mix ahead, too—it's a sugar syrup with fresh lemon and lime juice, and it's what sets this Cosmopolitan apart from all others.

Berry purees will keep in the refrigerator for only three days, and then they lose their freshness. If you are having a party, make them in advance and store them in a covered jar in the refrigerator. A few berry purees have recently become available at grocery stores. With the recent scientific studies confirming the health benefits of eating berries, expect to see an increase in the availability of purees and other berry products in the future.

For making berry liquors and liqueurs, I buy large (7½-cup) Italian canning jars at Cost Plus World Market. They are a lovely bell shape with a wide, flat bottom that allows all the fruit to be in contact with the spirits, and they have convenient attached glass lids that clamp down with a metal clasp. If you can't find them, use a gallon or ½-gallon jar, depending on the recipe, and put a piece of wax paper over the top before attaching the lid to keep the metal from corroding.

There are two methods for making smoothies, one using frozen fruit and another using fresh fruit with ice cubes. Both work beautifully. Just be sure to use a blender if you're using ice cubes, which would dull the blade of your food processor. Berry smoothies are an easy way to load up on antioxidants—be sure to try the Marionberry Antioxidant Elixir.

I've also included two different methods for making berry liqueurs. You can either make them from scratch or make a berry-flavored liquor and sweeten it with sugar syrup when you want to serve an after-dinner liqueur. The advantage of the latter method is you have two different drinks from one recipe.

Serve all cold berry drinks in chilled glasses by placing the glasses in the refrigerator for an hour before serving.

## *Agua Fresca*

Agua fresca, which literally means "fresh water," is a favorite thirst-quenching drink in Mexico. It is simply water flavored with a puree of fruit and enhanced with a splash of lime and a little sugar.

**MAKES 3 TO 4 SERVINGS**

**2 tablespoons sugar**
**1 pint basket (about 2 cups) fresh raspberries, rinsed and drained, or frozen raspberries, thawed with juice, pureed, and seeded (see page 70), to make about ⅔ cup puree**
**Juice of ½ lime, plus 3 to 4 lime slices for garnish**
**1 sliced star fruit**
**1 fresh mint sprig**

In a 1-quart pitcher, dissolve the sugar in 2 tablespoons hot water. Add the raspberry puree and lime juice and stir to blend. Add the star fruit, 2 cups ice, and 2 cups cold water. Stir again. Float the sprig of mint on top and serve immediately in chilled glasses.

## *Berry Spritzer*

A refreshing nonalcoholic summer drink with a bright taste—and pretty to look at, too.

**MAKES 4 SERVINGS**

**½ pint (1 cup) fresh raspberries, rinsed and drained, or frozen raspberries, thawed with juice, pureed (see page 70), to make about ⅓ cup puree**
**¼ cup Simple Syrup (page 69)**
**2 cups soda or sparkling water**
**4 lime wedges**
**4 fresh mint sprigs**

Fill four 9-ounce glasses with ice cubes. Put 2 tablespoons of raspberry puree and 1 tablespoon of sugar syrup in each glass and fill with soda. Stir and garnish each drink with a lime wedge and a mint sprig.

### Berries on the Road

Shirley Collins, who founded Sur La Table cookware store in Seattle, and her husband flew to Texas one July to visit her mother at the height of the Pacific Northwest's berry season. While they were waiting for their luggage to come by on the conveyor belt, her mother said, "Oh, look, there's a baby coffin. How sad." Shirley replied, "No, Mom, that's mine, and it's a salmon box from Pike Place Market, packed to the brim with fresh berries!"

## *Staghorn Sumac Lemonade*

Sumac berries from the staghorn sumac have been used for centuries to make a refreshing drink that was known to the pioneers as *Indian lemonade.* You will have to gather these berries from the wild, so be sure you can positively identify them before picking.

**MAKES 2 QUARTS**

**2 cups ripe red sumac berries, rinsed and drained**
**Sugar**

Remove the berries by holding them over a bowl and, with a fork turned upside down, gently run the fork through the berries to dislodge them from their stems. Put the berries in a bowl with 2 quarts cold water. Cover and let sit overnight in the refrigerator. Strain, sweeten to taste, and serve over ice. Drink sumac lemonade within 1 to 2 days, or it will lose its flavor.

## *Homemade Strawberry Lemonade*

Homemade berry lemonades add a festive touch to a summer table, and they taste as good as they look. Frozen berries do not need to be thawed. This lemonade can be made up to two days in advance.

**MAKES 1 QUART**

- **1 cup sugar**
- **1 cup fresh lemon juice (from 5 large lemons), plus the zest from the lemons, coarsely grated**
- **1 pint (2 cups) fresh strawberries, raspberries, marionberries, or other blackberries, rinsed and drained, or frozen berries**
- **Fresh mint sprigs**

Dissolve the sugar in 2 cups simmering water. Add the lemon juice, zest, and 2 more cups of water and let cool.

Puree the berries and stir into the lemonade. Strain and chill. To serve, pour into tall, ice-filled glasses. Garnish each with a sprig of fresh mint.

*Note:* For a quick version of this recipe, substitute 1 quart good-quality prepared lemonade, such as Odwalla, and stir in the pureed berries.

### The American Fraise des Bois

The famous fraise des bois (*F. vesca*), also known as the *wood* or *alpine strawberry,* has four subspecies throughout the world. While this is the most widely distributed and common of all strawberry species, the alpine strawberry is generally associated with Europe, where it grows wild in the woods and is prized for its aromatic petite oval fruit. If you are lucky enough to be in Italy when the fraises des bois are in season, you can buy them from street vendors who sell them in little paper cones. Surprisingly, the same species exists in North America (and Asia, too). One subspecies grows in the woods from eastern North America to British Columbia, another in the woods of western North America, and a third in the forests of California's Sierra Nevada range, as well as in the state's coastal woods and headland scrubs.

### Two Plus Two Equals Prize-Winning Elderberry Wine

Although Dr. John Brewer has a Ph.D. in physics, he quit building high-tech companies in 1995 and embarked on a new career, this time in the agricultural world. He converted the 37-acre family wheat farm he inherited in Kansas into an award-winning winery. "I spent six years doing research on how to make this family farm more profitable. I knew I wanted a high-tech agricultural product, which was wine. We decided what was really great was Grandma's elderberry wine, and she's not around anymore, so we put two and two together, and that's how it came about." Dr. Brewer has won over 130 international awards for his wine in just six years, and he is the only professional wine judge in Kansas. He is also the largest producer of elderberry wines in the United States. "I'm still trying to figure out what I'm going to do when I grow up," he says. You can buy his elderberry wine along with elderberry concentrate, fudge, and preserves at Wyldewood Cellars Winery, PO Box 205, Mulvane, KS 67110; 800-711-9748; www.wyldewoodcellars.com.

## *Citrus-Elderberry Summer Cooler*

Chad Finn, small-fruit breeder at Oregon State University and berry expert extraordinaire, enjoyed this elderberry cordial while on a research trip to England. "Last summer in England at a friend's house we had a wonderful alcohol-free elderberry flower cordial. The kids loved it, and we plan to make it this spring with blossoms from our elderberry tree." If you don't have a blue or black elderberry in your yard, you'll have to gather the blossoms from the wild. My friend Marlene Parrish, who lives in Pittsburgh, says, "I keep a tablet in the glove compartment in the spring and note where I see elder flowers. Then, in late August, I cruise early and try to beat the birds." For this recipe, do the reverse. In August, jot down where there are elderberry trees with blue or black berries so you can go back in the spring for the elderberry blossoms. *Never pick red elderberries or their blossoms—they can cause stomach upset.*

**MAKES 1½ TO 2 QUARTS CONCENTRATE, UP TO FORTY 8-OUNCE SERVINGS**

**Juice of 4 large oranges**
**Juice of 1 large lemon**
**2 ounces tartaric acid (available at beer- or wine-making supply shops)**
**6 cups sugar**
**25 elderberry blossoms from a blue or black elderberry, rinsed**

Blend the orange and lemon juices with the tartaric acid in a large bowl until the tartaric acid is completely dissolved. Add 6 cups cold water, the sugar, and the blossoms, poking them down into the liquid. Cover and macerate for 24 hours in the refrigerator. Strain through cheesecloth or a fine strainer and discard the blossoms. Pour the citrus-elderberry cordial into bottles and serve diluted, 4 parts water to 1 part concentrate, over ice. It will keep for one month in the refrigerator or frozen for up to 2 months.

## *Blackberry Atole*

When we were in central Mexico, I was surprised to see luscious, giant blackberries in the markets. As I quickly found out, wild blackberries grow in the mountains, and when they are in season they are used in atoles, an ancient drink made from dried corn that dates back to pre-Columbian days. When I asked Diana Kennedy about the blackberries where she lives, she said, "Curiously enough here in Michoacan, the little wild ones, with lots of seeds, are picked in the mountains just before the rainy season in May and brought down to market by the Indians who live there. They are at their sweetest then. Later, as the rains come, they begin to spoil and are sour. Still they have that wonderful, penetrating flavor and are just perfect to mix with the dried corn gruel called *atole.*"

These thin, porridgelike drinks can be drunk warm or at room temperature.

This is Diana's recipe from her book *The Essential Cuisines of Mexico.*

**MAKES 2 QUARTS**

**1½ pints (3 cups) fresh blackberries, rinsed and drained, or 3 cups frozen blackberries**
**1 cup masa**
**Raw dark brown sugar or piloncillo (Mexican name for raw brown sugar), to taste**

Put the blackberries into a saucepan with 2 cups water and bring to a boil. Lower the heat and simmer for 5 minutes. Strain the blackberries into a bowl, pressing out as much of the juice from the flesh as possible. Discard the seeds. Set the blackberry puree aside. You should have about 3 cups.

Dilute the masa with 1½ cups water. Put another 5 cups water in a heavy saucepan and bring to a boil. Add the diluted masa through a strainer, pressing out any lumps with a wooden spoon. Cook over medium heat, stirring from time to time to prevent sticking, until the mixture is just beginning to thicken, about 5 minutes.

Stir in the strained blackberry puree with sugar to taste and continue cooking over medium heat, stirring and scraping the bottom of the pan to prevent sticking, until the mixture thickens—it should make a thin coating over the back of a wooden spoon—about 15 minutes.

Serve either warm or at room temperature.

## *Summer Water*

Linda Wisner, past president of the Portland Culinary Alliance, hosts many events at her lovely old Portland home. For her summer garden parties, she often hangs a 5-gallon industrial cooler from Sanderson Industrial Supply in Portland, filled with Summer Water, from her fencepost for her guests to help themselves. She makes this refreshing drink with herbs and edible flowers from her rambling garden. For more formal parties, she uses a punch bowl with a tisane ice ring and edible flowers and/or lemon slices. Here is how to make Summer Water in Linda's own words.

**MAKES 1½ GALLONS, SERVING 16**

"I start by making a tisane [infusion] from a combination of equal portions of fresh mint, lemon verbena, and lemon balm, using 2 big colanders full for a gallon of water. I bring the water to a steady simmer in a large pot while I strip off the woody stems of the herbs and rinse the herbs. With the heat off, I immerse all the leaves in the hot water and let them steep for no more than 3 minutes, occasionally muddling them to release their flavor. (A longer steeping makes it taste too vegetative.) Then I strain the tisane and refrigerate it for several hours or overnight. Before serving, I combine with ice, 1 quart cranberry juice (or other berry juice), 1 quart of ginger ale or lemon-lime soda, and lots of sliced fresh lemons in a punch bowl, pitcher, or large industrial beverage cooler. I do not add sugar. For a punch bowl or pitcher, it's pretty to float verbena and mint leaves and/or edible flowers such as pansies, borage, fuchsia, or tuberous begonias. The pansies have a slight licorice flavor, the borage has a cucumberlike flavor, and the fuchsia and begonias don't have much flavor at all."

### *Basic Berry Smoothie*

Berry smoothies are an easy way to get your daily dose of antioxidants, fiber, and vitamins. These flavorsome drinks are simple to make, too, once you know the essential ingredients. They are nothing more than fruit, dairy, juice, sugar, lemon juice, which is optional, and ice.

**MAKES 2 SERVINGS**

**1 pint (2 cups) fresh berries, rinsed and drained, or frozen berries**
**½ cup juice, such as orange or cranberry**
**½ cup whole or skim milk, soy milk, or yogurt**
**1 to 2 teaspoons sugar or honey, to taste (optional)**

Puree the berries, juice, and milk together in a blender, with ½ cup ice cubes if using fresh berries, until smooth. Sweeten with sugar or honey if desired.

#### Dried Berries in a Jar

It's impossible to buy good fresh berries year-round, but recently high-quality freeze-dried berries have become available online. The fresh berries are pureed, then immediately freeze-dried, creating an intensely berry-flavored powder loaded with antioxidants and other health benefiting phytochemicals; 1 tablespoon is the equivalent of eating ½ cup of fresh berries. Stir into yogurt, add it to smoothies, or sprinkle it over a dish of ice cream. To order online, contact: Nutri-Fruit, 7510 SE Altman Road, Gresham, OR 97080; 866-343-7848; www.nutrifruit.com (freeze-dried red raspberry, black raspberry, marionberry, boysenberry, blueberry, and strawberry and frozen berries).

### *Marionberry Blastoff*

"You can serve this with or without the seeds," says my friend Jan-Marie Schroeder. "I don't bother taking out the seeds, because that is where a lot of nutrients are, but most people would prefer seedless."

**MAKES 2 SERVINGS**

**½ pint (1 cup) fresh marionberries, crushed and pushed through a strainer with the back of a spoon to remove the seeds if desired, or other blackberries, rinsed, or frozen marionberries**
**1 cup vanilla nonfat frozen yogurt**
**½ cup milk or soy milk**
**Sugar to taste if necessary**

Blend until smooth. Serve immediately.

### *Raspberry-Nectarine Smoothie*

The penetrating flavor of raspberries is especially refreshing in a smoothie. To make other berry smoothies, substitute another berry for the raspberries and add a heaping ½ cup fruit such as peaches for the nectarine.

**MAKES 2 SERVINGS**

**½ cup fresh raspberries, rinsed and drained, or frozen raspberries**
**½ nectarine, pitted and cut into quarters**
**1 banana, peeled**
**¼ cup low-fat milk or soy milk**
**¼ cup fresh orange juice**
**2 to 3 teaspoons honey, to taste (optional)**

Put all the ingredients in a blender, adding ½ cup ice if using fresh berries, and process until smooth.

### *Strawberry Energizer*

This nutritious drink, sponsored by the California Strawberry Commission, was on the 2002 Olympic menu for the athletes and coaches of the U.S. ski and snowboard team. Strawberries are an excellent source of vitamin C, folate, potassium, and fiber. For more information on strawberries contact: California Strawberry Commission, PO Box 269, Watsonville, CA 95077; 831-724-1301; www.calstrawberry.com.

**MAKES 2 SERVINGS** **2 cups plain nonfat yogurt**
**1 cup ice**
**½ pint (1 cup) fresh strawberries or other berries, rinsed and drained, or 1 cup frozen strawberries**
**1 cup granola**
**2 tablespoons wildflower honey**

Put all the ingredients in a blender and process until smooth.

## *Loganberry-Cantaloupe Smoothie*

Loganberries are tart and bring out the cantaloupe's flavor in this smoothie recipe.

**MAKES 2 SERVINGS** **2 cups cantaloupe or honeydew melon**
**½ pint (1 cup) fresh marionberries or other blackberries, rinsed and drained, or frozen marionberries**
**½ cup plain nonfat yogurt**
**½ cup fresh orange juice**
**½ cup milk or soy milk**
**2 to 3 tablespoons honey, to taste**

Put all the ingredients in a blender, with 1 cup ice if using fresh berries. Process until smooth.

## *Papaya-Strawberry-Banana Smoothie*

This tropical smoothie is a family favorite. I've added canned coconut milk—made by extracting all the liquid from freshly grated coconut—to give it an exotic flavor.

**MAKES 2 SERVINGS** **½ cup fresh strawberries, rinsed and drained, or frozen strawberries**
**½ medium banana, peeled**
**½ cup sliced and peeled papaya**
**¼ cup reduced-fat canned coconut milk**
**¼ cup pineapple-orange-guava juice or other slightly acidic juice, such as orange juice**
**Seeds from ½ purple passion fruit**
**1 to 2 tablespoons honey, to taste (optional)**

Put all the ingredients together in a blender, with ½ cup ice if using fresh berries. Process until smooth.

### *Marionberry Antioxidant Elixir*

Jan-Marie Schroeder is the executive director of Berry Works, an organization that provides a variety of services to members of the berry industry. She is also the mother of seven-year-old twins. One night, as they were watching the Miss America pageant, one of the daughters asked her what she would do for the talent contest if she were participating in Atlantic City. The other daughter said, "I know—Mommy could make smoothies!"

Making prize-winning smoothies is one of Jan's many talents. "This is our everyday smoothie at my house—we have it at least once a week. As an alternative, I have tried blueberry juice. In a taste test with blueberry and black raspberry, 100 percent of my tasters (guess who they are) chose the black raspberry. It really is better, but the blueberry is fine, just less complex," she says.

Bananas can be frozen in the skin and used as needed directly from the freezer. Simply peel and add them to the blender with the berries. Fresh bananas can also be used.

**MAKES 2 SERVINGS**

**½ pint (1 cup) fresh marionberries or other blackberries, rinsed and drained, or frozen marionberries**

**1 cup black raspberry juice (best) or Blackberry Crush (both from Trader Joe's)**

**½ frozen or fresh banana, peeled**

Blend until smooth. Serve immediately.

#### Blackberry Canes

She put down her hammer and seemed to relax. Her trousers, he could plainly see, were a pair of old work pants cut off with scissors. What a thing to do. "You know what I really admire, this time of the year?" she asked him.

"I wouldn't dare to guess, Miss Rawley."

"Blackberry canes," she said. "Now you go ahead and laugh at me, because everybody else does; I know they're an awful nuisance. But they're amazing, too."

"I expect they're the fastest-growing plant this side of China," he said.

"Yes, sir! They shoot up out of the ground and by mid-June they're eight feet tall. Then the top starts to bend back down to the ground, and by August they've made an arch of a size to walk under, if you wanted to. Did you ever notice how they do that?"

"I've noticed, and noticed," he said. "I've gone through about eight bush hogs in my lifetime, noticing how blackberries grow."

"I know. I'm not defending them. They'd eat up my whole orchard if I didn't keep them cut back to the fence. But sometimes in winter I just have to stand back and stare at those arches going down the road, up and down, like a giant quilter's needle sewing its way across Zebulon County, one big arched loop per year. You can love them or hate them, either one, but there's no stopping them." She looked at him sideways, like a mother scolding. "And you have to admit, the berries make the best pie there is."

—From *Prodigal Summer* by Barbara Kingsolver

## *The Devil-Made-Me-Drink-It Dessert Smoothie*

Barbara Durbin, food writer for the *Oregonian*, created this dessert smoothie recipe for an article she wrote for the paper's food section, FOODday. It's elegant and tastes as good as it looks. "These are creamy, like milkshakes, a beautiful deep pink if you use red raspberries, or purplish pink if you use black raspberries or blackberries. Serve for dessert, following a light dinner, such as grilled chicken salad."

**MAKES 2 SERVINGS**

- **½ pint (1 cup) fresh black or red raspberries, marionberries, or other blackberries, rinsed and drained (a few reserved for garnish), or frozen berries**
- **1 cup raspberry or blackberry nonfat yogurt**
- **¼ cup plain nonfat yogurt or half-and-half**
- **½ cup boysenberry or raspberry sorbet, slightly softened**
- **½ cup vanilla-raspberry-swirl frozen yogurt or ice cream**

Put the fruit, yogurt, and half-and-half in a blender or food processor and puree. Add the sorbet and process until just blended. Pour into tall, stemmed goblets, being careful not to splash up the sides. Gently place a scoop (about ¼ cup) of frozen yogurt or ice cream on top of each. Garnish with a few berries. Serve immediately.

## *Berry Ice Cream Sodas*

The first ice cream sodas were sold in the United States in 1874, and while they aren't nearly as popular as they used to be, they are way too good to be forgotten. These refreshing drinks please young and old alike and are especially satisfying when made with berries. Prepare the berry puree by crushing the fruit in a food processor or blender and pushing it through a strainer to remove the seeds (if you don't mind the seeds, you can eliminate this step), then make a simple sugar syrup and chill the glasses. And don't forget to buy some straws—sodas just aren't the same without them. They let you get to the bottom of the glass, where all the flavors are concentrated—even the passion fruit seeds sink, but they are small enough to pass through the straw and give a delightfully fresh burst of flavor. Each of these recipes makes 1 soda for a 9-ounce glass.

### *Strawberry Ice Cream Soda*

**1 tablespoon Simple Syrup (page 69)**
**2 scoops reduced-fat vanilla ice cream**
**3 tablespoons strawberry, red or black raspberry, boysenberry, loganberry, or blackberry puree (see page 70), a few reserved for garnish**
**¾ cup soda or sparkling water**
**Dollop of whipped cream**

Pour the Simple Syrup into the bottom of a chilled 9-ounce glass and add 1 scoop of ice cream and the berry puree. Stir to blend. Keep stirring and fill the glass ¾ full with soda or sparkling water. Add the remaining scoop of ice cream and a dollop of whipped cream. Garnish with the reserved whole berries, put in a straw and a dessert spoon, and serve immediately.

### *Marionberry-Coconut Ice Cream Soda with Passion Fruit*

**1 tablespoon Simple Syrup (page 69)**
**3 tablespoons canned, reduced-fat coconut milk**

**¼ cup marionberry or other blackberry, strawberry, red or black raspberry puree (see page 70), a few whole berries reserved for garnish**

**¾ cup soda or sparkling water**

**1 scoop reduced-fat vanilla ice cream**

**Dollop of whipped cream**

**1 teaspoon passion fruit seeds (see Note)**

Pour the Simple Syrup into the bottom of a chilled 9-ounce glass and stir in the coconut milk and marionberry puree. Keep stirring and fill the glass ¾ full with soda or sparkling water. Add the ice cream and a dollop of whipped cream. Garnish with the reserved whole berries and passion fruit seeds, put in a straw and a dessert spoon, and serve immediately.

*Note:* Passion fruit can be found at Asian markets and larger grocery stores from early spring to summer. Cut the fruit in half and scoop out the seeds with a spoon. There is about 1 tablespoon of seeds and pulp per passion fruit.

## *Chocolate-Espresso Soda with Raspberries*

**1 tablespoon Simple Syrup (page 69)**

**2 scoops chocolate espresso ice cream**

**3 tablespoons brewed espresso**

**¾ cup soda or sparkling water**

**Dollop of whipped cream**

**5 fresh or frozen raspberries**

Pour the Simple Syrup into the bottom of a chilled 9-ounce glass and add 1 scoop of ice cream and the espresso. Stir to blend. Keep stirring and fill the glass ¾ full with soda or sparkling water. Add the remaining scoop of ice cream and a dollop of whipped cream. Garnish with the raspberries, put in a straw and a dessert spoon, and serve immediately.

## *Bella, a Blackberry Martini*

Lucy Brennan, of Mint, in Portland, Oregon, makes the best blackberry martinis. She named this cocktail after her faithful dog, Bella, whom she misses dearly because she spends most of her days at the restaurant. The secret to these remarkable martinis, Lucy says, "is to use superfine sugar to make a wide, 1-inch coating around the rim of the glasses, then chill them. Use plenty of ice and shake the drink quickly before it has a chance to melt. Sip these slowly. They go down easily, but they are powerful, and the alcohol can catch up with you in a hurry."

**MAKES 1 MARTINI**

**1 lemon quarter, cut in the middle of the flesh down to but not through the rind**
**Superfine sugar**
**¼ cup vodka**
**¼ ounce Triple Sec**
**¼ ounce fresh lemon juice**
**¼ ounce Simple Syrup (page 69)**
**¼ ounce blackberry, raspberry, or strawberry puree, seeded (see page 70)**

**MAKES 4 MARTINIS**

**4 lemon quarters**
**Superfine sugar**
**1 cup vodka**
**1 ounce Triple Sec**
**1 ounce fresh lemon juice**
**1 ounce Simple Syrup (page 69)**
**1 ounce berry puree (page 70)**

Prepare 1 (or 4) 9-ounce martini glasses. Rub the cut lemon around the rims, moistening a 1-inch-wide band. Sprinkle the sugar on a small plate and coat the rims. Chill the glasses until serving time. Fill a martini shaker with ice and add the vodka, Triple Sec, lemon juice, Simple Syrup, and blackberry puree. Shake robustly for 10 seconds and strain into the glasses. Serve immediately, but sip very slowly and enjoy.

Superfine sugar, called castor sugar in Great Britain, is finely granulated and makes a smooth coating on glassware for drinks. While you can buy it at some specialty food stores, it's easy to make your own by processing granulated sugar in a blender or food processor with the steel blade for 1 minute.

## *Cosmopolitan Lucere*

Lucere, one of Portland, Oregon's few restaurants overlooking the beautiful Willamette River, serves the best Cosmopolitans. Michael Paul, the head bartender, says the secret is the sweet-and-sour mix, a combination of sweetened fresh lime and lemon juice, and a good-quality unsweetened cranberry juice, such as Northland.

**MAKES 1 COSMOPOLITAN**

**1¼ ounces vodka**
**¾ ounce Triple Sec**
**2 ounces Sweet-and-Sour Mix (recipe follows)**
**¼ cup cranberry juice**
**1 lime wedge**
**3 fresh cranberries (if available—for looks only)**

**MAKES 4 COSMOPOLITANS**

**5 ounces vodka**
**3 ounces Triple Sec**
**1 cup Sweet-and-Sour Mix (recipe follows)**
**1 cup cranberry juice**
**4 lime wedges**
**12 fresh cranberries**

Have ready 1 (or 4) chilled 9-ounce martini glasses. Put the vodka, Triple Sec, Sweet-and-Sour Mix, and cranberry juice in a martini shaker. Shake the mixture vigorously for 10 to 15 seconds. (Note: Michael Paul says, "Robust shaking is vital to properly dilute the mixes.") Strain into martini glasses and serve immediately, garnished with lime wedges and a few fresh cranberries if available.

## *Sweet-and-Sour Mix*

This recipe makes more Sweet-and-Sour Mix than you'll need for 1 Cosmopolitan. Keep it in a covered glass jar in the refrigerator for up to 1 month. Double for 4.

**MAKES ½ CUP**

**2 tablespoons fresh lime juice (from 1 lime)**
**1 tablespoon fresh lemon juice (from about ½ lemon)**
**2 tablespoons superfine sugar**

Combine the lime juice, lemon juice, and sugar in a ½-cup measuring cup and stir with a spoon to dissolve the sugar. Fill the measuring cup to the top with water. Stir to blend. Store covered in the refrigerator.

## *Homemade Berry Liqueur*

The following recipe from the *Oregonian*'s FOODday section can be used for any berry. Strawberries, blackberries, raspberries, and black currants make particularly good liqueurs. You can buy berry liqueurs from Internet Wines & Spirits, 10800

Lincoln Trail, Fairview Heights, IL 62208; 618-394-9800; www.internetwines.com (berry liqueurs, many imported, made from real fruit).

**MAKES ABOUT 3 QUARTS**
**2 to 2½ pounds (3 to 3½ pints) fresh whole berries, extremely ripe but not bruised, rinsed and drained, or 2 to 2½ pounds frozen berries**
**Zest of 1 lemon, cut into strips**
**1½ to 2 cups sugar (see Note)**
**About 6 cups vodka**

Put the berries and lemon peel in a clean glass gallon jar. Set aside.

Put a small saucepan over medium heat and dissolve the sugar in 1 cup water. Let cool and pour over the fruit in the jar. Add the vodka and enough water to fill the jar—about 1 to 2 cups. Place wax paper under the lid and close. Put the jar in a cool, dark location, shaking gently every day for at least 1 month, preferably 3 months.

Remove the lid and taste for sweetness. If it's not sweet enough, make and add a small amount of Simple Syrup (page 69). Replace the wax paper and lid; place in a cool, dark place for another 3 months; don't shake during this time.

Strain through a cheesecloth or decant the liqueur by siphoning liquid off the top. The liqueur may be a little cloudy. Pour into small containers and store either at room temperature or in the refrigerator. It will keep for up to 3 years.

*Note*: Adjust the amount of sugar depending on the sweetness of the berries. For instance, use 1½ cups sugar for raspberries and strawberries, but 2 cups for blackberries and black currants. The sweeter the berry, the less sugar you will need.

## *Homemade Berry-Flavored Liquor*

Many berry-flavored liquors are available commercially—Absolut Kurant from Denmark, Stoli Razberi from Russia, cranberry vodka from Finland, to name a few—but it's easy to make your own. Fresh or frozen berries are simply added to neutral spirits, such as vodka or grain alcohol (diluted with water), with or without herbs and spices, and left to macerate for 3 days to 2 weeks or longer—it's up to you how intensely flavored you want it. As the fruits' tissues break down, the berries' lush flavors are released into the alcohol. The pulp is strained out, and the flavored liquor can be used in a variety of festive drinks, from berry-flavored martinis to after-dinner drinks. Or, give as a gift in a decorative bottle.

So, start with high-quality fruit. As with anything else, the finished product is only as good as the ingredients that go into it.

I use Italian canning jars that come with convenient lids attached by wire clasps. Their wide, bell-shaped bottom allows all the fruit to macerate in the alcohol.

**MAKES ABOUT 1 FIFTH**

**1 quart (4 cups) perfectly ripe but not bruised fresh raspberries, rinsed and drained, or frozen raspberries**
**1 fifth 80-proof vodka**

Rinse the fruit in a strainer and let it drip-dry. Transfer to a nonporous bowl (such as glass) or an Italian bell-bottom canning jar and add the vodka. Cover tightly with plastic wrap or the lid and let steep in a cool, dark place for 3 days to 2 weeks. Strain and pour into decorative bottles and attach the lids. Age the liquor for at least 2 months before using. It will keep for up to 3 years.

*Variations*: In place of the raspberries, use any of the following:

**1 quart (4 cups) fresh or frozen raspberries and the crushed seeds from 4 cardamom pods**
**1 quart (4 cups) fresh or frozen strawberries and 5 torn rose geranium leaves**
**1 quart (4 cups) fresh or frozen boysenberries and 5 slices fresh ginger**

*Note*: It's easy to make a berry liqueur from berry liquor by simply sweetening the homemade liquor with Simple Syrup (page 69). Or you can make individual glasses of liqueur by adding enough Simple Syrup to a small glass of liquor to make it sweet enough to your liking. Berry liqueurs are good served on the rocks with a splash of soda.

### Eighty Pounds of Raspberries in a Bottle

Have you ever wondered why framboise is so expensive? It takes 80 pounds of raspberries to make one 375 ml bottle! You can buy American-made framboise at Clear Creek Distillery, Box: 2389 Northwest Wilson Street, Portland, OR 97210; 503-248-9470; www.clearcreekdistillery.com (pure fruit spirits, including framboise).

### *Kaspar's Cranberry-Apple Holiday Cheer*

Chef Kaspar Donier, who owns Kaspar's Restaurant and Wine Bar in Seattle, sent this recipe for hot spiced cranberry-apple cider one year in a Christmas card, and I've been making it ever since. In addition to the luscious red color, the cranberries add a tangy, bold taste. For a nonalcoholic version, omit the applejack. A good source for cranberry information can be found at Cape Cod Cranberry Growers' Association, 3203 Cranberry Highway, East Wareham, MA 02538-4703; 508-295-4895; www.cranberries.org.

**MAKES 4 SERVINGS**

- **1 cup fresh cranberries, rinsed and drained, or frozen cranberries, mostly thawed**
- **1 quart natural apple cider**
- **1 2- to 3-inch cinnamon stick**
- **3 cloves**
- **Zest of ½ lemon, cut into strips**
- **Zest of ¼ orange, cut into strips**
- **¼ cup applejack (optional)**
- **4 fresh mint leaves or dried apple rings**

Warm 4 glasses, such as brandy snifters, by filling them with hot water and letting them sit for a few minutes.

Put the cranberries into a saucepan and mash with a potato masher. Pour the apple cider into the pan and add the cinnamon, cloves, lemon zest, and orange zest. Bring to a simmer.

Discard the water in the glasses. Pour 1 ounce of applejack into each of the glasses. Strain the cider into the glasses and garnish with mint leaves or apple rings.

#### Coquille Indians and Gathering Berries

The Coquille Indians on the Oregon coast used wild berries as most Indians did. Some berries, such as black huckleberries, blackberries, and salal, were picked and dried for storage. Salmonberries, red huckleberries, strawberries, black raspberries, red and blue elderberries, blueberries, thimbleberries, currants, and gooseberries were eaten fresh during the season. Young shoots of the salmonberry and thimbleberry were eaten in the spring.

## *Madame Rose Blanc's Crème de Cassis*

Anne Messelink is a delightful Dutch woman who lives in Provence. We rented a vacation home from her last year, and she generously gave me her prized recipe for black currant liqueur, better known as *crème de cassis.* "I used to make this with my landlady, Madame Rose Blanc, who had a lovely, old-fashioned vegetable garden along with succulent rows of raspberries and bushes loaded with black currants," she said. "This recipe has far more perfume than any cassis you can buy."

I prefer drinks on the dry side, so I use only ¾ cup sugar to 1 pint berries, even though the original recipe called for 1½ cups sugar. Start with the lesser amount of sugar and adjust the sweetness to your liking.

A splash of crème de cassis in a glass of chilled dry white wine is a kir, the French aperitif. In a kir royale, champagne is substituted for the wine. I drink this homemade liqueur straight as I would a small glass of dry port or sherry.

**MAKES ABOUT THREE 8-OUNCE BOTTLES**

**1 pint (2 cups) fresh black currants, rinsed and drained, or frozen black currants, thawed with juice**
**1 bottle (750 ml) Côtes-du-Rhône or other dry red wine**
**¾ to 1½ cups sugar, to taste**

Combine the currants and the wine in a nonporous bowl, such as glass, and cover tightly with plastic wrap. Allow the fruit to steep for 2 days at room temperature in a cool, dark place.

Strain the mixture into a nonreactive pan through a fine strainer or several layers of cheesecloth. You should have about 1½ cups juice. Discard the fruit. Add the sugar to the juice and heat slowly to boiling, stirring constantly. Boil for 5 minutes, then remove from the heat. Let cool completely. Pour into three 8-ounce bottles and seal with a cap or cork. Store in the refrigerator for up to 1 year.

*Variation:* Make this with commercial black currant juice. It won't be quite as good, but it is still tasty. Blend 2 cups black currant juice with ¼ cup sugar in a nonreactive pan and heat gently until the sugar dissolves. Pour in the red wine. Let cool, pour into three 8-ounce bottles, and seal with a cap or cork.

## *Sangría Blanco*

Portland food writer Kathryn Kurtz and her husband, Gary, lived in Spain for several years, where she perfected this white sangría. "If you like your sangrías more on the dry side, don't add the sugar. You can use any flavor schnapps, but I find the peach especially mellow and nice. The amount of berries is variable, depending on how much you want to splurge. One cup actually works fine, but 2 gives the sangría more berry flavor," she says.

**MAKES 6 SERVINGS**

**2 oranges, thinly sliced and halved**
**2 lemons, thinly sliced and halved**
**¼ cup sugar**
**1 bottle (750 ml) white wine, sweet or semisweet but not dry, such as Riesling**
**1 to 2 cups mixed fresh berries, rinsed and drained**
**¼ to ½ cup peach schnapps**

Put the orange and lemon slices in a glass pitcher. Add the sugar and mash with a spoon to release the juice and dissolve the sugar. Pour the wine over the fruit and add the berries. Cover and chill for 2 hours. Chill six 9-ounce martini glasses or 11-ounce white wine glasses in the refrigerator for 1 hour.

Just before serving, stir in the peach schnapps and add a tray of ice cubes.

### Sambuca-Elderberry Liqueur

Sambuca is an Italian liqueur made from the distillation of the oil and white blossoms of the black elderberry tree with anise seeds and various other ingredients. This popular liqueur is named after the scientific classification for this tree, *Sambuca nigra*, which grows throughout much of the temperate world.

## *Sicilian Strawberry Liqueur*

Anna Tasca Lanza is a cooking teacher and author of *The Heart of Sicily: Recipes and Reminiscences of Regaleali, a Country Estate.* When the prized fraises des bois, the tiny wild strawberries, are in season, she makes this strawberry liqueur to serve after dinner with coffee. Use cultivated strawberries in place of wild.

**MAKES ABOUT 2 QUARTS**

**2 heaping pints (about 4 to 5 cups) fresh strawberries, rinsed and drained, or frozen strawberries, thawed with juice**
**1 fifth 180- to 190-proof grain alcohol (available at liquor stores)**
**2 cups sugar**

Put the strawberries in a nonporous bowl (such as glass), add the alcohol, and cover tightly with plastic wrap. Let the fruit steep for 2 days at room temperature in a cool, dark place.

Heat 1 quart water and pour in the sugar. Stir until the sugar dissolves. While the sugar syrup is still warm, blend with the berry mixture. Strain through a fine strainer or several layers of cheesecloth and let cool. Discard the fruit. Pour the liqueur into bottles and seal with a cap or cork. Store in either the refrigerator or at room temperature for up to 3 years.

## *Spicy Blackberry Brandy*

The Oregon Raspberry and Blackberry Commission recommends making this spicy brandy in the summer to give as a gift during the holidays.

**MAKES ABOUT 1½ QUARTS**

**2 pints (4 cups) fresh marionberries, other blackberries, or raspberries, rinsed and drained, or frozen marionberries, thawed with juice**
**¾ cup sugar**
**¾ teaspoon ground allspice**
**One 2-inch cinnamon stick**
**10 whole cloves**
**2 cups brandy**

Combine all the ingredients in a ½-gallon glass jar. Cover the jar with a piece of wax paper, then screw on the lid. Shake the jar daily for 7 days to dissolve the sugar. Store for about 2 months in a cool, dark place. Strain through a fine strainer or several layers of cheesecloth and let cool. Discard the fruit. Pour the liqueur into bottles and seal with a cap or cork. Let age for 1 month before serving. Store in either the refrigerator or at room temperature for up to 3 years.

*Strawberry Mojito*

A mojito is a lime- and rum-based drink that originated in Cuba in the early 1900s. When the weather gets hot, it is almost as refreshing as a splash in the lake. These drinks are made right in the glass, so you'll need 10- to 12-ounce chilled glasses and the back of a wooden spoon to muddle the mint and berries.

**MAKES 1 DRINK**

**1½ ounces Simple Syrup (page 69)**
**4 fresh strawberries or a handful of raspberries or blackberries, rinsed and drained, or 4 frozen strawberries or blackberries, thawed with juice**
**5 fresh mint sprigs, plus 1 for garnish**
**Soda or sparkling water**
**½ lime**
**2 ounces light rum or Bacardi Limón**

In a tall (10- to 12-ounce) chilled glass, muddle the Simple Syrup, 3 of the strawberries, 5 mint leaves, and a splash of sparkling water together with the back of a spoon until you smell the mint.

Squeeze the juice from the lime half into the glass, add the rum, and stir. Fill the glass with ice and top off the drink with soda water. Garnish with the remaining strawberry and mint sprig.

# BREADS

When you are baking with berries, keep the following tips in mind to get the best results:

- Huckleberries, Juneberries, and all blueberries can be baked in batters and breads either fresh or frozen. Their solid spherical shape keeps the berries intact and makes them prime candidates for any batter or dough recipe.
- The larger berries, such as blackberries and raspberries, hold their shape better if they are added straight from the freezer. Fresh raspberries, especially, with their hollow core, are fragile when thawed and will easily fall apart if folded into a batter, but adding them frozen works like magic.
- For stiff doughs and batters, dried berries hold up better, and they don't become gummy like fresh or frozen berries. Trader Joe's carries dried red and black raspberries, marionberries, black currants, and blueberries of exceptional quality. The berries are all grown in Oregon and marketed under the Trader Joe's brand name. The stores carry them in the West but will sell them anywhere if people start requesting them. They are handy to have on hand for baking and for snacking, too.

Berries are especially good in baked foods because their intensity is perfect for partnering with the exotic flavors of spices. Included in this chapter are recipes for Blackberry-Blueberry Cardamom Muffins, Ginger Scones with Lemon-Blueberry Filling, and French Toast with Oatmeal Crust. And, although almonds are not a spice, their richness is a nice counterpoint to the fresh, pure berry taste, as in the Raspberry–Marcona Almond Coffee Cake.

Baked goods with berries benefit from the fruits' moisture, making the breads last longer before drying out. Tightly wrap them in plastic wrap and then foil or store in self-sealing plastic bags. More often than not, you won't have to worry about having too much left over.

### *Blackberry-Blueberry Cardamom Muffins*

These mixed berry muffins not only taste good, they are a sight to behold: once baked, the batter becomes a rich golden color and the sugared blackberries invitingly poke out of the top. Red raspberries are good substitutes for the blackberries.

**MAKES SIX 4-INCH JUMBO MUFFINS OR SIXTEEN 3-INCH MUFFINS**

**¼ pound (1 stick) unsalted butter, softened**
**¾ cup plus 3 tablespoons sugar**
**2 large eggs**
**1 cup buttermilk**
**2 cups all-purpose flour**
**½ teaspoon coarse salt**
**¾ teaspoon baking soda**
**1 teaspoon ground cardamom**
**½ pint (1 cup) frozen or dried blueberries**
**½ pint (1 cup) frozen or dried marionberries or other blackberries**

Preheat the oven to 375°F. Grease or line muffin tins.

Cream the butter with ¾ cup of the sugar in a mixing bowl. Break in the eggs and beat well. Pour the buttermilk over all and beat until smooth. Add the flour, salt, baking soda, and cardamom and mix until blended. Gently fold in the blueberries. Divide the mixture equally among the muffin cups.

Roll the blackberries in the remaining 3 tablespoons sugar. Put 3 berries on the top of each muffin, pressing them down slightly into the batter.

Bake for 30 to 35 minutes for jumbo muffins, 15 to 20 minutes for smaller muffins, until a cake tester or toothpick stuck in the center comes out clean. Serve warm.

### *Brioche French Toast with Sautéed Berries*

Brioche French toast makes a festive breakfast, especially during the holidays, when fresh strawberries are often available. Frozen strawberries can be substituted, but they won't hold their shape quite as well, and they will be a little juicier. Try serving this dish with crispy slices of applewood-smoked bacon and glasses of freshly squeezed tangerine juice.

### Japan Loves Blueberries

The Pacific Northwest is one of the largest producers of blueberries in the nation. Production has increased dramatically in the last few years to supply Japan's growing love affair with these popular berries.

"We have a tradition to eat food as it is—so fruits are eaten as they are. In some areas where they are grown the berries are made into jam or a fruit sauce. During World War II there was a concentration of Americans in the middle of the main island in an area called Karuizawa. It's in the country, surrounded by woods and mountains, where a lot of wealthy people have summer homes. During the war the Americans planted blueberries, and they still grow in that area today."

—Keiko Hayashi, cookbook author, Tokyo, Japan

**MAKES 4 SERVINGS**

**3 large eggs**
**2 tablespoons milk**
**2 tablespoons unsalted butter**
**1 pint (2 cups) fresh strawberries, rinsed and drained, or frozen strawberries with juice, sliced**
**1 pint (2 cups) fresh blueberries, rinsed and drained, or frozen blueberries with juice**
**1 pint (2 cups) fresh raspberries, rinsed and drained, or frozen raspberries with juice**
**2 tablespoons vegetable oil**
**Eight ½-inch-thick slices brioche, crusts removed**
**Pure maple syrup**
**Sour cream**
**Confectioners' sugar**

Warm 4 plates.

In a shallow bowl, wide enough for a slice of brioche, beat the eggs with the milk and set aside.

Melt the butter in a sauté pan and add the berries. Warm gently over medium heat until they are hot but not boiling.

Pour the oil into a large skillet and put it over medium-high heat. When the oil is hot, quickly dip both sides of the brioche in the egg mixture and fry in the hot oil. In 2 to 3 minutes, when the bread is golden brown, turn it over and cook on the other side. Put 2 pieces of toast on each plate.

Drizzle the berries lightly with maple syrup and divide the mixture equally over the French toast. Put a dollop of sour cream on top of the berries and add a sprinkling of confectioners' sugar. Serve immediately, accompanied by more syrup and a bowl of confectioners' sugar.

## *French Toast with Oatmeal Crust*

This is an adaptation of a recipe from the lovely cookbook *The Flavours of Canada*, by Anita Stewart. At the Normaway Inn in Cape Breton, Nova Scotia, owner-innkeeper David Macdonald serves oatmeal-crusted French toast with local maple syrup. Here I topped it with a mixture of summer berries instead. Because the crust already has brown sugar in it, you shouldn't need to add sugar to the berries.

**MAKES 3 TO 4 SERVINGS**

**3 large eggs**
**¼ cup milk**
**1 cup old-fashioned or quick-cooking rolled oats**
**2 tablespoons dark brown sugar**
**½ teaspoon ground cinnamon**
**2 tablespoons canola oil**
**1 tablespoon unsalted butter, plus butter for serving**
**8 slices sourdough or other interesting bread**
**1 pint (2 cups) mixed fresh berries, such as raspberries, blackberries, and blueberries, rinsed and drained, or frozen berries, partially thawed**
**1 cup sour cream or crème fraîche (optional; see page 73)**

Warm 4 plates.

Beat the eggs and milk together in a dish wide enough for the bread. Stir together the oats, sugar, and cinnamon in another wide dish.

Heat the oil and butter together on a griddle or in a skillet over medium heat until the butter melts—don't let it burn. Dip each piece of bread in the egg mixture, then coat in the seasoned oats. Fry on both sides until golden brown. (They burn easily, so keep an eye on them.)

Serve slathered in butter with a healthy sprinkling of berries on top and a dollop of sour cream or crème fraîche if you wish.

*Variation:* Omit the fruit and serve with cranberry butter.

## *Cranberry Butter*

During the holidays, when edible flowers are often available commercially, I make fresh cranberry butter rolled in a layer of colorful flower petals to add a splash of color to my table.

**MAKES 1 SCANT CUP**

**1 cup fresh or partially thawed frozen cranberries**
**¼ pound (1 stick) unsalted butter, softened**
**1 to 2 tablespoons honey, to taste**
**Edible flowers (optional)**

Put the cranberries, butter, and honey in a food processor and process until the butter turns a soft pink color with tiny flecks of chopped cranberry. Put the cranberry butter in a small bowl and refrigerate until it is just firm enough to handle. Turn it out onto a sheet of wax paper and shape into a log. (This can be made up to 1 week ahead. Store tightly wrapped in wax paper in the refrigerator.)

One hour before serving, coarsely chop the flowers and lay them on another sheet of wax paper. Roll the cranberry butter log in the chopped flowers and leave it wrapped up in the wax paper in the refrigerator until you need it. Use within 1 to 2 hours.

## *Dutch Pancakes (Poffertjes)*

In the Netherlands, streetside vendors sell these silver-dollar-size yeast pancakes smothered in butter and confectioners' sugar. I've been making them for more years than I care to remember from a recipe that I clipped out of *Sunset* magazine when my children were little. Dutch pancakes are a family favorite at our cabin. We serve them topped with sour cream, heaps of freshly picked berries, and plenty of confectioners' sugar. Since you make them with yeast, they need to rise for 45 minutes before being cooked.

**MAKES 4 TO 6 SERVINGS**

**One ¼-ounce envelope active dry yeast**
**2 tablespoons sugar**
**½ teaspoon coarse salt**
**1 cup milk**
**1 large egg**
**½ teaspoon ground cardamom**
**1¾ cups all-purpose flour**
**Vegetable oil or unsalted butter**
**1 pint (2 cups) fresh berries, rinsed and drained**
**1 cup sour cream**
**Confectioners' sugar for sprinkling**

Warm 4 plates.

Put ¼ cup warm water (about 110°F) in a mixing bowl. Sprinkle with the yeast and stir until dissolved. Stir in the sugar, salt, milk, egg, cardamom, and flour until smooth. Cover and let rise in a warm place until doubled, about 45 minutes.

Heat about a tablespoon of oil or butter in a skillet over medium heat. Drop tablespoons of the batter onto the hot skillet, being careful not to let their sides touch or they will run together. Cook for about 2 minutes, until they are golden brown on the bottom and you see bubbles rising to the surface of the batter, then flip them over and cook for another 2 minutes. Don't undercook them or they will be soggy in the center. Add more oil or butter to the pan as needed.

Serve with fresh berries, a dollop of sour cream, and a sprinkling of confectioners' sugar.

## *Farina-Almond Muffins with Wild Blueberries*

Uncooked farina, a wheat cereal enriched with iron and folic acid, is a healthy addition to berry muffins. I have modified the original recipe, which came from a booklet of farina recipes developed by noted food writer Nancy Verde Barr, by replacing half of the farina with all-purpose flour. These flavorsome muffins are still moist and tender after the second and third day.

**MAKES TWELVE 3-INCH MUFFINS**

TOPPING
**¼ cup sugar**
**2 teaspoons ground cinnamon**
**¼ cup chopped almonds**

**Batter**

**1 cup farina**
**¾ cup all-purpose flour**
**½ cup packed light brown sugar**
**1 teaspoon baking powder**
**1 teaspoon baking soda**
**1 teaspoon coarse salt**
**1 cup buttermilk, plain yogurt, or sour cream**
**1 large egg**
**1 teaspoon pure almond extract**
**¼ pound (1 stick) unsalted butter, melted**
**½ pint (1 cup) frozen or dried wild blueberries, huckleberries, or blueberries**

Preheat the oven to 400°F. Grease or line a muffin tin. Combine all the ingredients for the topping and set aside.

Blend the farina, flour, sugar, baking powder, baking soda, and salt together in a medium bowl. In a separate bowl, whisk together the buttermilk, egg, almond extract, and melted butter. Combine with the dry ingredients. Fill each muffin cup two-thirds full and sprinkle with the topping.

Bake for 12 to 15 minutes, until the muffins are golden brown and a cake tester or toothpick inserted in the center comes out clean. Serve warm.

### Forty-Seven American Berries Beat Out Nuts

"The types of berries used by the Indians surpass even the nuts. Nearly every part of North America had several varieties of berry bushes that the local Indians nurtured. Forty-seven types of American berries have been identified. Some of these types, such as the blueberry, had up to twenty variations, and the gooseberry came in at least a dozen different varieties."

—From *Indian Givers* by Jack Weatherford

## *Ginger Scones with Lemon-Blueberry Filling*

Imagine biting into a scone that is moist with a rich lemon curd filling, studded with fresh blueberries, that is as good on the third day as the day it was baked. These tasty double-deckers have enough room in the middle to poke in a few fresh berries. If you like, substitute ½ teaspoon berry jam for the berries.

**MAKES TEN 3-INCH SCONES**

**3¼ cups all-purpose flour, plus flour for rolling the dough**
**½ cup sugar, plus sugar for sprinkling**
**2½ teaspoons baking powder**
**½ teaspoon baking soda**
**½ teaspoon coarse salt**
**12 tablespoons (1½ sticks) unsalted butter, cut into pieces**
**½ cup diced crystallized ginger**
**1 teaspoon grated lemon zest**
**1 cup buttermilk**
**Scant ¼ cup store-bought lemon curd or homemade, page 232 (see Note)**
**½ cup fresh wild blueberries, huckleberries, or cultivated blue berries, rinsed and drained, or 5 teaspoons berry jam**

Preheat the oven to 400°F. Lightly grease a large baking sheet. Sprinkle a little flour on a pastry cloth or a work surface.

Combine the flour, sugar, baking powder, baking soda, and salt in a large bowl. Cut in the butter with 2 knives or a pastry cutter until coarse crumbs form. Stir in the ginger, lemon zest, and buttermilk until the mixture is evenly moistened, then knead the dough in the bowl until it holds together.

Turn the dough out onto the floured surface and roll out to ¼-inch thickness. Cut out 20 scones with a 3-inch biscuit cutter. Put 1 teaspoon lemon curd in the center of 10 of the scones and spread it around, not quite to the edge, with the back of the spoon. Push 5 or 6 fresh blueberries or ½ teaspoon jam into the lemon curd–covered dough and then top with another pastry. Pinch the edges together to seal. Sprinkle the tops of the scones with sugar and bake for 20 minutes or until a cake tester or toothpick poked in the center of the top half (not all the way to the lemon curd filling) comes out clean. Serve hot or transfer to a rack to cool. Store the scones in the refrigerator in a self-sealing plastic bag for up to 3 days.

*Variation without the filling:* Roll out the dough into a 9-inch circle, about ½-inch thick, and cut out 5 scones. This will make 5 extra-large scones.

*Note:* Store remaining lemon curd in a covered jar in the refrigerator for up to 1 week.

### Huckleberry Hound

"I have trained my Australian Shepherd to pick her own huckleberries. She learned at an early puppy age what a huckleberry was and the following year started to sniff them out even before the flowers bloomed. There must have been a subtle scent only a dog could pick up. She smelled their progress carefully after that. She can scrape the ripe berries off with her teeth, like artichoke meat from a leaf, another talent of hers. However, she doesn't contribute any berries to the communal basket, and I sometimes have to fight her for an especially luscious cluster."

—From "Huckleberries and Hounds" by Jude Lutge,
executive editor of *Steppin' Out,* and an avid forager

## *Lemon Tea Bread*

The historic Packard House in Bath, Maine, makes this tea bread for guests. It's dense and moist and perfect to serve with a mound of fresh berries and a dollop of crème fraîche. Or serve it for dessert with fresh strawberries and a scoop of Blood Orange Vodka Berry Sorbet (page 188). To avoid wasting any glaze, I keep the bread in the baking pans until after they are glazed.

**MAKES THREE 5½ × 3½-INCH LOAVES**

**BREAD**

**4 tablespoons (½ stick) unsalted butter, softened**
**¼ cup vegetable shortening**
**1 cup sugar**
**2 large eggs, beaten**
**Grated zest of 1 lemon**
**1¼ cups all-purpose flour**
**1 teaspoon baking powder**
**½ teaspoon coarse salt**
**½ cup milk**

**GLAZE**

**5 tablespoons fresh lemon juice (from about 2 lemons)**
**¼ cup sugar**

Preheat the oven to 350°F and grease and flour 3 mini-loaf pans.

Using an electric mixer, cream the butter and shortening with the sugar and beat in the eggs and lemon zest.

Sift together the flour, baking powder, and salt. Alternately add the dry ingredients and milk to the creamed mixture. Pour the batter into the prepared pans and bake for 35 minutes or until a cake tester or toothpick poked in the center of a loaf comes out clean. Let the bread cool on a rack in the pans for 5 minutes.

For the glaze, stir together the lemon juice and sugar until the sugar dissolves. Pierce the loaves with a cake tester or toothpick and brush with the glaze until it is completely absorbed.

When the loaves are cool, run a knife around the edge of the pan to release the bread. Wrap them airtight in plastic wrap and store at room temperature for 4 days. Or wrap in foil over the plastic wrap and then put them in self-sealing freezer bags and freeze for up to 1 month.

## *Marionberry Biscuits*

This recipe comes from the Sisters Bakery in central Oregon. The berries make these biscuits special, and their thin confectioners' sugar glaze adds a pleasingly sweet taste.

**MAKES 16 BISCUITS, SERVING 8 GENEROUSLY**

**BISCUITS**
**2 cups bread flour**
**2 cups cake flour**
**½ cup granulated sugar, plus extra for the berries**
**⅛ teaspoon coarse salt**
**2 tablespoons baking powder**
**4 tablespoons (½ stick) cold unsalted butter**
**2 large eggs**
**1 cup buttermilk**
**1½ pints (3 cups) fresh marionberries, other blackberries, or red raspberries, rinsed and drained**

**GLAZE**
**1 cup sifted confectioners' sugar**
**½ teaspoon vanilla extract**
**2 tablespoons buttermilk**

Preheat the oven to 350°F. Grease a 9 × 13-inch pan.

Combine the bread and cake flours, sugar, salt, and baking powder in a medium bowl. Cut in the butter until crumbly.

Whisk together the eggs, ¼ cup water, and the buttermilk. Add to the flour mixture and stir until just combined.

Turn out onto a lightly floured board and divide in half. Pat each half out into a 6 × 8-inch rectangle, then cut each rectangle into 8 biscuits. Place half of the biscuits in the prepared baking pan and top each with about ⅓ cup marionberries. Sprinkle with granulated sugar if desired. Place the remaining 8 biscuits on top of the marionberries. Bake for 30 to 35 minutes or until golden brown.

Stir together the confectioners' sugar, vanilla, and buttermilk until smooth. When the biscuits have cooled slightly, drizzle glaze over each biscuit. Serve warm. These biscuits are best eaten the day they are made.

## *Morning Glory Muffins with Blackberries*

This muffin recipe, made famous by the Morning Glory Restaurant in Nantucket, is one of my favorites. The muffins are flavorful and stay moist for days. I've added fresh blackberries, but other berries, like huckleberries or blueberries, would be equally tasty. The batter makes 15 muffins, so you need to bake them in 2 batches. Fill empty muffin tins half full with water.

**MAKES 15 MUFFINS**

**2 cups all-purpose flour**
**1¼ cups sugar**
**2 teaspoons baking soda**
**2 teaspoons ground cinnamon**
**½ teaspoon coarse salt**
**2 cups coarsely grated carrot**
**½ cup sweetened shredded coconut**
**1 tart apple, peeled, cored, and grated**
**3 large eggs**
**1 cup canola oil**
**1 teaspoon vanilla extract**
**⅔ cup frozen marionberries or other blackberries**

Preheat the oven to 350°F. Grease or line a muffin tin.

Measure the flour, sugar, baking soda, cinnamon, and salt into a large bowl. Stir in the carrots, coconut, and apple. In another bowl, whisk together the eggs, oil, and vanilla and pour into the flour mixture, mixing well. Gently stir in the berries. Fill the muffin cups to the top and bake for about 25 minutes or until a cake tester inserted in the center comes out clean. Let the muffins cool for 5 minutes and then turn out onto a rack.

*Variation*: Substitute ¾ cup applesauce (Boysenberry Applesauce, page 154, is especially good) and use only ½ cup canola oil for a lower-fat muffin. Add the applesauce when you add the oil.

## *Mrs. Rogers's Bucket Dumpling*

I was amazed when I first tried this charming-sounding recipe, contributed by Mrs. W. Davis Rogers (Julia Dill) to *Charleston Receipts* (1950). I improvised by making it in a charlotte mold instead of a lard can, and baking it in the oven instead of steaming it on top of the stove. When it had baked for 2 hours, curiosity got the best of me. (The original recipe called for steaming it for 3 hours.) I removed it from the water bath and let it sit on the counter for 5 minutes before running a knife around its perimeter. Then I turned it upside down in a large shallow bowl. It unmolded beautifully, standing tall and perfectly shaped to rival any charlotte. The biscuit outer layer was a delicate golden color with traces of purple that hinted of the blackberry treasure inside, and a lovely puddle of blackberry juice began to collect around the bottom. Best of all, it sliced into perfect pieces, which I served with a spoonful or two of crème fraîche for dessert that night.

**MAKES 6 TO 8 SERVINGS**

**1 mounded tablespoon unsalted butter, softened**
**1 mounded tablespoon vegetable shortening, softened**
**2 cups all-purpose flour**
**2 teaspoons baking powder**
**2 large eggs, lightly beaten**
**¾ cup milk**
**1 quart (4 cups) fresh marionberries or other blackberries, rinsed and drained**
**¾ cup sugar**
**Crème fraîche**

Preheat the oven to 350°F. Lightly grease a 6-cup charlotte mold. Prepare a water bath by putting a baking pan large enough to hold the mold in the oven and partially filling the pan with water.

Stir together the butter, shortening, flour, and baking powder in a medium bowl. Add the eggs and milk and thoroughly blend.

Smear the dough around the sides of the mold. Combine the berries and sugar and carefully pour them into the center. Cover the mold tightly with foil and place it in the water bath in the oven. (The water should come up halfway on the mold. Add more water if necessary.) Bake for 2 hours, or until a cake tester inserted into the sides of the dumpling comes out clean. Remove the mold from the water bath and let it sit on the counter for 5 minutes before running a knife around its perimeter. Unmold onto a large, shallow bowl and serve warm with a dollop or two of crème fraîche. It is best eaten the day it is made.

## *Raspberry Buttermilk Muffins*

This recipe is a good standard to use for all kinds of berries. The muffins are moist and tender and a perfect showcase for the fruit.

**MAKES TWELVE 3-INCH MUFFINS OR 9 JUMBO MUFFINS**

**Ground cinnamon for sprinkling**
**½ cup sugar, plus sugar for sprinkling**
**2 cups all-purpose flour**
**1 teaspoon coarse salt**
**2 teaspoons baking powder**
**6 tablespoons cold unsalted butter**
**1 large egg**
**1 cup buttermilk**
**½ pint (1 cup) frozen raspberries, blackberries, blueberries, or huckleberries**

Preheat the oven to 400°F. Grease a muffin tin and sprinkle liberally with cinnamon and sugar.

Sift together 1¾ cups of the flour, the sugar, salt, and baking powder. Cut in the butter with 2 knives or a pastry blender.

Whisk together the egg and buttermilk and blend with the dry ingredients until just combined—it will still be lumpy.

Toss the berries in the remaining ¼ cup flour and fold into the batter. Fill the muffin cup to the top and sprinkle generously with cinnamon and sugar. Pour a little water into the empty cups if you're making 9 larger muffins.

Bake for 20 to 25 minutes, until a cake tester comes out clean. Serve warm.

## *Raspberry–Marcona Almond Coffee Cake*

It has only been in the last few years that Marcona almonds, prized for their large sweet meat, have been imported into the United States from their native Spain. You can buy them in specialty stores, where they are sold both raw and toasted with a sprinkling of sea salt. If you buy the latter, use them as they are; otherwise, lightly roast the raw nuts following the instructions on page 73. Substitute whole or slivered regular (American) almonds if you can't find Marconas.

**MAKES 10 SERVINGS**

CAKE

**¼ pound (1 stick) unsalted butter, melted (warm, not hot)**
**2 large eggs**
**1¼ cups granulated sugar**
**1 teaspoon almond extract**
**1½ cups self-rising flour**
**1½ teaspoons baking powder**
**1 pint (2 cups) frozen raspberries**
**2 tablespoons toasted Marcona almonds, coarsely chopped**

GLAZE

**¼ cup confectioners' sugar**
**1 tablespoon cream or milk**
**¼ teaspoon almond extract**

Preheat the oven to 350°F and grease a 10-inch springform pan.

Put the melted butter, eggs, sugar, and almond extract into a bowl and beat well. Stir in the flour and baking powder and stir until smooth. Spread two-thirds of the batter in the bottom of the pan. The batter will be very thick, so you will have to use either the back of a spoon or your fingers. Sprinkle the raspberries over the top. Using a teaspoon, drop the remaining batter over the berries as evenly as possible—the berries will not be completely covered—and sprinkle with the chopped almonds. The batter will rise as it cooks, covering most of the berries.

Bake for 40 to 45 minutes, until a toothpick stuck in the center of the cake comes out clean. Cool in the pan for 5 minutes.

Stir the confectioners' sugar, cream, and almond extract together until smooth and drizzle over the warm cake. Remove the sides and serve the cake warm or at room temperature.

## *Salmon Street Oatmeal Dried Cranberry Scones*

These intensely flavorful scones are from a recipe used by the main bakery for the Portland public schools. A friend of mine, Sally Schultz, a retired teacher from Portland's Lincoln High School (which is on Salmon Street—named after the salmonberries that used to grow nearby), requested the recipe after eating them every day in the school's cafeteria. Once I made them I knew why they were her favorite. These scones are dense, moist, and a lovely golden brown color.

**MAKES 12 SCONES**

**2 cups stone-ground whole wheat flour**
**1¾ cups old-fashioned oatmeal**
**¾ teaspoon baking soda**
**1½ teaspoons baking powder**
**1½ cup plus 1 tablespoon sugar**
**12 tablespoons (1½ sticks) unsalted cold butter, cut into pieces**
**½ cup sweetened dried cranberries or other dried berries**
**½ cup buttermilk**
**Raw brown sugar (turbinado) for sprinkling**

Preheat the oven to 375°F. Lightly grease a cookie sheet.

Combine the flour, oats, baking soda, baking powder, and sugar in a large bowl. Cut in the butter with 2 knives or a pastry blender until coarse crumbs form. Stir in the dried berries and buttermilk until the mixture is evenly moistened, then knead the dough in the bowl until it holds together. (If you have a food processor, put the flour, oats, baking soda, baking powder, sugar, and butter in the bowl with the steel blade. Pulse 8 to 10 times, until the mixture forms coarse crumbs. With the machine running, add the buttermilk and process just until it forms a ball.) Transfer to a floured surface and work in the dried cranberries by kneading 5 to 6 times. Put the dough on the cookie sheet and shape into a 9-inch disk. Score into 12 wedges and sprinkle with raw brown sugar. Bake for 18 to 20 minutes, until a cake tester poked in the middle comes out clean. Serve immediately or wrap and store at room temperature for 1 to 2 days.

# SOUPS AND SALADS

All four of the berry soup recipes in this chapter are simple to make, and only the Strawberry-Rhubarb Soup requires any cooking. You would never know from their rich, smooth taste that berry soups are merely berry purees with flavorings. The blackberry has a touch of lime for tartness, the mango-raspberry some soothing cream of coconut, and the blueberry a pinch of cardamom for a spicy burst of flavor that lingers on the palate. I like to feature these three soups as a trio for a summer lunch or light summer dinner in little espresso cups or small individual bowls, with a platter of artisanal bread and cheese.

Three other especially good summer dishes are the Summer Fruit Salad with Port-Lime Dressing, which can be served with dinner—it's good with grilled chicken or pork—or as a dessert; the Himalayan Red Rice Salad with Blueberries, which is hearty enough with berries, nuts, and rice that it can be an entree for lunch or dinner; and the Summer Berries and Flowers in White Wine Jelly—a molded salad, a real showstopper.

The Strawberry, Fig, and Spanish Blue Cheese Salad can transition into fall, or try the Hardy Kiwi Fall Salad with Black Currant Dressing. Last Thanksgiving I made the Persimmon, Apple, and Pickled Cranberry Salad using some of the season's best fruit—apples, persimmons, and pomegranate seeds—topped with a few pickled cranberries.

After the holidays I always look for the first fresh spears of asparagus, harbingers of spring. I like them roasted and drizzled with a ruby-red Champagne-raspberry vinaigrette. Once they appear, I eagerly await the arrival of the first fresh strawberries.

## *Blueberry Cardamom Soup*

Marcus Samuelsson, the James Beard award-winning chef from Aquavit restaurant in New York, grew up in Sweden, where chilled blueberry soup is popular as both an appetizer and a dessert. This recipe of his has the most wonderful cardamom aftertaste that gently lingers on the palate. Because the cardamom makes the soup slightly spicy, Marcus suggests serving it hot as a cold-weather appetizer or even as a sauce over ice cream. I also serve it with one or two other berry soups in small espresso cups for a light summer lunch.

**MAKES ABOUT 1 QUART, SERVING 4**

**3 pints (6 cups) fresh blueberries, plus a handful for garnish, rinsed and drained, or frozen blueberries plus fresh mint sprigs or edible flowers for garnish**
**¾ cup sugar**
**2 tablespoons fresh lemon juice (from 1 lemon)**
**1 teaspoon ground cardamom**
**¾ cup mango puree (see Note, page 117)**
**1 cup muscatel, ice wine, or honey wine**
**8 thin slices melon, any kind**

Put the blueberries, sugar, lemon juice, and cardamom in a saucepan over medium heat. Bring the mixture to a boil and cook until the sugar dissolves, about 5 minutes. Let the mixture cool slightly, then puree in a food processor with the mango puree and wine. Strain and chill.

Serve the soup in shallow bowls garnished with a sprinkling of fresh blueberries and 2 melon slices.

### The Woods—Everyone's Garden

Marcus Samuelsson grew up in Göteberg, Sweden, and fondly remembers his country's important berry culture. "Berries are one of the things that we have. There is no private land, so you can walk through the woods and pick anything from anywhere—lingonberries, wild raspberries, bilberries—it is everyone's garden. Growing up there, I didn't realize that was unique until I left. People also have big backyards with their own garden, and berries are a big part of it; they grow apples, plums, pears, and tons of berries. In the kitchen cooks traditionally use the berries with meat—like lingonberries with venison or blackberry jam with duck—as well as for desserts."

### *Chilled Blackberry-Lime Soup*

Chef Philippe Boulot, managing partner of the Heathman Restaurant in Portland, Oregon, created this lovely chilled blackberry soup, which he serves in the heart of berry season. It's simple to make and has a light, refreshing taste that is both complex and satisfying. It can be made up to 3 days in advance or made without the yogurt and frozen up to 1 month ahead.

**MAKES 6 SERVINGS**

**1 cup sugar**
**4 pints (8 cups) fresh marionberries, other blackberries, or raspberries, rinsed and drained, or frozen marionberries, thawed with juice**
**1½ cups plain low-fat yogurt**
**Juice of 1 lime, plus 6 small lime wedges**
**6 fresh mint sprigs**

In a saucepan, combine the sugar with 1 cup water. Bring to a boil and stir until the sugar is dissolved to make a simple syrup. Pour the berries into the saucepan, reduce the heat to simmer, and cook for another 10 minutes, stirring frequently to release the juice from the berries.

#### The World's Berry Gene Bank

The USDA's Agriculture Research Service National Clonal Germplasm Repository in Corvallis, Oregon, collects, maintains, distributes, and evaluates germplasm of temperate fruit, nut, and specialty crops. Included in its collections are international heritage cultivars, diverse global wild-species representatives of strawberries, blackberries, raspberries, blueberries, cranberries, lingonberries, currants, and gooseberries. The research program adheres closely to the practical problems of plant seed storage and maintenance, including in vitro culture and cryopreservation, virus and disease testing, identity verification, and propagation techniques. The NCGR-Corvallis is a gene bank for invaluable plant resources.

Remove the pan from the heat and transfer half of the mixture to a blender or food processor. Puree and strain through a fine strainer into a glass or stainless-steel bowl to remove the seeds. Repeat for the remaining half. Chill in the refrigerator for 3 to 5 hours.

Once the soup is chilled, stir in 1 cup yogurt and the lime juice and divide equally among 6 shallow soup bowls. Garnish with a dollop of the remaining yogurt and a sprig of mint and serve with a small bowl of lime wedges.

## *Mango-Raspberry Summer Soup*

Chilled soups are always refreshing and a welcome addition to any summer menu. I serve this lovely golden-colored mango soup in shallow bowls garnished with sprigs of fresh mint and a few fresh raspberries.

**MAKES 4 SERVINGS**

- **2 cups mango puree (about 1 mango; see Note)**
- **1½ cups fresh orange juice**
- **2 pints (about 4 cups) fresh raspberries, rinsed and drained, or frozen raspberries, thawed with juice**
- **2 bananas, peeled**
- **1 papaya, peeled and seeded**
- **1 cup milk**
- **2 heaping tablespoons canned reduced-fat cream of coconut**
- **4 fresh mint sprigs**

Put the mango, orange juice, raspberries, bananas, papaya, milk, cream of coconut, and ice cubes in a blender and puree until smooth. Pour into 4 shallow soup bowls. Garnish each with a sprig of mint.

*Note:* Make mango pulp by peeling a mango, cutting the fruit off the pit, and then pureeing it in the food processor. When I'm pressed for time, I buy it canned at a market that sells East Indian ingredients. The brand I like is Ratna Alphonso mango pulp (1 pound 14 ounces). You will have some pulp left over, which makes a wonderful sorbet. Just freeze the puree in an ice cream maker following the manufacturer's instructions.

## *Strawberry-Rhubarb Soup*

This cold soup was inspired by a recipe in *Salute to Healthy Cooking,* a cookbook by the French Culinary Institute in New York City. Only the rhubarb needs to be cooked, and that is easily accomplished in the microwave.

**MAKES 4 SMALL SERVINGS**

- **3 stalks rhubarb cut into 1½-inch chunks (about 2 cups)**
- **1 pint (about 2 cups) fresh strawberries, rinsed, drained, and sliced, or frozen strawberries, thawed with juice**
- **¼ cup fresh orange juice**
- **5 tablespoons sugar**
- **½ cup light sour cream**
- **Johnny-jump-ups (pansies) or other edible flowers for garnish**

Put the rhubarb in a small microwave-safe dish and cover with plastic wrap. Microwave on high for 5 minutes or until tender. Let cool slightly.

Transfer the rhubarb to a food processor and add the strawberries, orange juice, sugar, and sour cream. Process until smooth. Serve in individual serving bowls, garnished with edible flowers.

### Strawberries in Carlsbad

Springtime in Carlsbad, California, a small coastal community 20 miles north of San Diego, is a sight to behold. In mid-April the blooming fields of ranunculus and stock are a kaleidoscope of color, surrounded by acres of bright green strawberry plants. The large berries, mostly 'Camarosas', have a long growing season, from February to July, and can be bought on the spot at adjoining roadside stands.

## *Autumn Salad of Arugula, Blueberries, and Smoked Almonds*

Use baby arugula leaves for this colorful salad. Their peppery bite is a lovely contrast to sugary blueberries and smoky almonds. I recently served this salad on an October Indian summer evening when we had family over for grilled cheeseburgers.

**MAKES 4 SERVINGS**

**4½ ounces baby arugula or baby spinach**

**½ pint (1 cup) fresh blueberries, rinsed and drained, or frozen blueberries, thawed in a single layer on a paper towel for 20 minutes**

**¼ cup smoked almonds, coarsely chopped**

**1 Jonagold or Braeburn apple, cored and cut into ½-inch cubes**

**¼ cup olive oil**

**2 tablespoons sherry vinegar**

**¼ teaspoon salt**

**Freshly cracked pepper**

Put the arugula, blueberries, almonds, and apple cubes in a salad bowl.

Whisk together the olive oil, vinegar, salt, and a few twists from a peppermill. Pour over the salad and toss to blend. Serve immediately.

*Variation*: Sprinkle ½ cup crumbled Gorgonzola cheese over all just before serving.

## *Mâche and Blueberry Salad*

Mâche (pronounced "mahsh") is a thumb-size salad green with a sweet, nutty flavor. It's composed of tiny clusters of succulent, deep green leaves that are also called *lamb's lettuce, field greens,* and *corn salad* after the pastures where it grows wild. You'll often see mâche at farmers' markets, and now that it is being grown commercially in the Loire Valley in France and in Salinas, California, it is becoming more readily available in local supermarkets. I like its mild flavor paired with the tangy bite of fresh blueberries, but if you can't find mâche, substitute mesclun.

**MAKES 4 SERVINGS**

**½ pound mâche or mesclun**

**1 large avocado, pitted, peeled, and cut lengthwise into ¼-inch slices**

**2 slices red onion, peeled and broken into rings**

**½ pint (1 cup) fresh blueberries, raspberries, or small to medium strawberries, rinsed and drained**

**2 teaspoons red wine vinegar**

**2 tablespoons extra virgin olive oil**

**Pinch of coarse salt**

**Freshly ground pepper**

Put the mâche, avocado, red onion slices, and blueberries in a salad bowl.

Whisk together the vinegar, olive oil, salt, and pepper to taste and pour the dressing over the salad ingredients. Toss and serve immediately.

## *Himalayan Red Rice Salad with Blueberries*

Himalayan red rice has a wonderful toothsome texture and pleasant nutty flavor that goes well with blueberries. You can buy it at specialty food shops, or substitute half brown and half wild rice.

**MAKES 4 ENTREE SALAD SERVINGS**

**SALAD**

**1 cup Himalayan red rice, washed and drained**
**2 cups chicken stock**
**⅓ cup chopped toasted hazelnuts (page 73)**
**½ cup (about 2 ounces) sweetened dried cranberries**
**¾ cup (about 3 ounces) dried apricots, chopped**
**½ cup chopped red onion**
**½ pint (1 cup) fresh blueberries**
**½ pound mâche, mesclun, or baby spinach**

**DRESSING**

**¼ cup fresh lime juice (from about 2 limes)**
**2 tablespoons honey**
**1½ teaspoons grated ginger (it's not necessary to peel it first)**
**2 teaspoons grated lime zest**
**⅓ cup extra virgin olive oil**
**Pinch of coarse salt**
**Pinch of freshly ground pepper**

Put the rice in a pan with the chicken stock. Cover, bring to a boil, and then reduce the heat to a simmer. Cook for 40 minutes or until it is tender. Drain, if necessary, and let cool.

Add the hazelnuts, cranberries, dried apricots, and red onion and toss.

Whisk together the lime juice, honey, ginger, lime zest, olive oil, salt, and pepper. Pour ½ cup of the dressing over the rice mixture and toss to blend. Gently fold in the blueberries. The salad can be prepared to this point up to 2 days in advance.

Arrange the greens loosely in the middle of 4 dinner plates and drizzle with the remaining dressing. Arrange the rice salad in a mound in the middle of the greens. Serve immediately.

## *Field Mushroom Salad with Raspberries*

Field mushrooms are the common, commercially raised white mushrooms found at supermarkets. Make a special effort to use fresh tarragon; its subtle flavor infuses into the mushrooms and makes this recipe especially memorable.

**MAKES 8 SERVINGS**

**⅓ cup extra virgin olive oil**
**2½ tablespoons fresh lemon juice (from about 1 lemon)**
**2 heaping teaspoons chopped fresh tarragon leaves or ¼ teaspoon dried, crushed**
**⅛ teaspoon freshly grated nutmeg**
**½ to ¾ teaspoon coarse salt, to taste**
**1 pound fresh mushrooms, trimmed and thinly sliced**
**½ pound mesclun or other mixed greens**
**½ pint (1 cup) fresh raspberries, blueberries, marionberries, or other blackberries, rinsed and drained**

Whisk together the olive oil, lemon juice, tarragon, nutmeg, and salt. Put the mushrooms in a shallow dish and pour the dressing over all. Marinate at room temperature for 1 hour or up to 3 days, covered, in the refrigerator, tossing the mushrooms occasionally. Arrange the greens on a large platter or 8 salad plates. Spoon the mushrooms over the greens and sprinkle with the fresh raspberries. Store any extra mushrooms and the dressing in a covered jar in the refrigerator. They will keep for at least 1 week.

## *Fresh Beet and Raspberry Salad*

I like this unusual salad because every bite has something flavorful in it. It's a pretty presentation, too.

**MAKES 4 SERVINGS**

**5 small (about 10 ounces) red and golden beets—about ¼ cup diced beets per serving**
**¼ cup extra virgin olive oil, plus oil for roasting beets**
**Sea salt**
**2 tablespoons Champagne vinegar**
**3 ounces (about 5 cups) mesclun**
**¼ ounce (½ cup) fresh cilantro, main stems removed**
**¼ ounce (½ cup) fresh dill, main stems removed**
**½ pint (1 cup) fresh raspberries, rinsed and drained**
**1 avocado, peeled, pitted, and sliced lengthwise**
**Freshly ground pepper**

Preheat the oven to 350°F.

Trim and scrub the beets to remove any dirt, then rinse them under cold running water. Pat dry with a paper towel and rub with a little olive oil. Wrap the beets in a large piece of foil and roast until the flesh is tender when poked with a fork, about 45 minutes to 1 hour. Let cool in the foil and then peel off their soft skin. Cut the beets into 1-inch cubes and season with a pinch of salt.

Whisk together the vinegar and olive oil and pour 2 tablespoons over the beets. Season them with a pinch of salt and toss. Marinate at room temperature for at least an hour or covered in the refrigerator for up to 3 days.

Put the mesclun, cilantro, and dill in a salad bowl and toss with the remaining dressing and a pinch of salt. Arrange the greens on individual serving plates. Scatter the beets and raspberries over the greens and garnish with the avocado slices. Sprinkle with a pinch of salt and freshly ground pepper and serve immediately.

## *Roasted Asparagus with Raspberry Vinaigrette*

Fresh raspberries make an intensely flavorful salad dressing that goes well with fresh asparagus. I usually serve the asparagus family style, but on occasion I make individual servings. When I do, I arrange the roasted asparagus spears on salad plates and ladle a spoonful of dressing over them just before serving. For another variation, put the asparagus, either individually or family style, on a bed of greens before serving. I use thick asparagus because it has more flavor than the thin spears.

**MAKES 4 SERVINGS**

**1 pound thick asparagus**
**½ cup extra virgin olive oil, plus oil for brushing**
**Coarse salt**
**3 tablespoons raspberry or Champagne vinegar**
**½ pint (1 cup) fresh raspberries or blackberries, rinsed and drained, or frozen berries, thawed in a single layer on a paper towel for 20 minutes**
**Freshly ground pepper**

Preheat the oven to 500°F and set the rack about 6 inches from the top of the oven. Prepare the asparagus by holding the base firmly and bending the stalk. It will snap where it is too tough to eat. Discard the base.

Arrange the asparagus in a single layer on a baking sheet and brush with olive oil. Sprinkle with coarse salt and roast until the spears are tender when pierced with a fork, about 10 to 15 minutes, depending on their thickness. Transfer to a platter and set aside.

For the dressing, puree a heaping ½ cup of the berries and push them through a fine strainer to remove the seeds. Whisk together the ½ cup olive oil, raspberry vinegar, pureed raspberries, ½ teaspoon salt, and pepper to taste.

Ladle a few spoonfuls of the raspberry vinaigrette over the asparagus and pour the rest into a small bowl with a ladle to pass. Sprinkle the remaining raspberries over the asparagus and serve.

### Please Pass the Berry Oil

Scientists have discovered that blackberry and raspberry seeds have exceptional nutraceutical value. They contain polyunsaturated oil that is composed of high levels of two powerful antioxidants—ellagic acid and ellagitannin—and very little saturated fat. Besides their health benefits, when berry oils are cold-pressed they retain some of their aroma and pigment, making them desirable for cooks. What used to be composted or fed to livestock may, in the near future, be a berry oil on your kitchen shelf.

## *Hardy Kiwi Fall Salad with Black Currant Dressing*

Hardy kiwis are available from mid-September to mid-November. They are bite-size and add a bright burst of flavor when paired with pears and pecans. If you can't find them, substitute kiwifruit, cut into quarters, or red grapes, cut in half. I buy black currants in the summer and keep them in the freezer year-round to use in recipes. If you like, substitute blackberries or raspberries for the currants.

**MAKES 4 SERVINGS**

**SALAD**

**¼ pound arugula**
**2 Bosc pears, peeled, cored, and cut in half lengthwise**
**½ lemon**
**½ pint (1 cup) hardy kiwis, rinsed and drained**
**½ cup toasted and chopped pecan pieces (page 73)**
**¼ pound goat cheese**
**Sea salt**

**BLACK CURRANT DRESSING**

**1 tablespoon black currant or other berry puree, such as blackberry or raspberry (see page 70)**
**¼ cup extra virgin olive oil**
**1 tablespoon sherry vinegar**

Divide the arugula among 4 salad plates. For each plate, cut each pear half lengthwise into ¼-inch slices and arrange them over the arugula. Sprinkle a little lemon juice over the pear slices and top with the hardy kiwis, pecans, and goat cheese. Sprinkle each salad with a small pinch of salt.

Make the dressing by whisking the black currant puree, olive oil, and vinegar together. Drizzle the dressing over all. Serve immediately.

## *Persimmon, Apple, and Pickled Cranberry Salad*

Keiko Hayashi, the award-winning author of *Simple & Delicious Japanese Cooking*, came from Japan to teach some cooking classes in Portland last year. One of the dishes she made was a salad similar to this. It's perfect for Thanksgiving if you garnish it with a few pickled cranberries. I like it because it is a refreshing blend of flavors and textures.

**MAKES 4 SERVINGS**

**8 lettuce leaves**
**1 Gravenstein or other tart apple, cored and cut into thin slices**
**1 Fuyu persimmon, peeled, pitted, and sliced**
**½ avocado, peeled, pitted, and cut into lengthwise slices**
**Seeds from ½ pomegranate (see Note)**
**1 teaspoon fresh lemon juice**
**2 tablespoons vegetable oil or mild olive oil**
**Pinch of sea salt**
**⅓ cup pickled cranberries, drained (see page 176)**

Put 2 lettuce leaves on each salad plate. Arrange the apple slices, persimmon, and avocado over the lettuce and sprinkle with the pomegranate seeds.

Whisk together the lemon juice, oil, and sea salt and drizzle it over the salads. Garnish each plate with spiced cranberries.

*Note:* To remove the pomegranate seeds, fill a small bowl with cold water. Immerse the pomegranate half in the water, cut side down, squeeze, and gently shake to loosen the seeds. Strain and pick over.

## *Strawberry, Fig, and Spanish Blue Cheese Salad*

Mint, a small restaurant in northeastern Portland, Oregon, was the inspiration for this strawberry salad, which is a satisfying combination of textures and flavors—highlighted by the piquant, bold taste of Spanish blue cheese. Also known as Picón, this cow's milk cheese is aged in limestone caverns and has characteristic deep blue veining and a crumbly texture. Order it by mail if it's not in your stores or substitute Roquefort or Gorgonzola.

**MAKES 4 SERVINGS** **¼ pound (about 1½ bunches) baby watercress**

**¼ pound dried figs, thinly sliced lengthwise**

**1 pint (2 cups) fresh strawberries, sliced**

**2 ounces Picón cheese**

**3 tablespoons extra virgin olive oil**

**1 tablespoon sherry vinegar**

**Coarse salt**

**Freshly ground pepper**

Trim 4 inches off the stems of the watercress. Rinse and wrap in paper towels or spin dry. Put the watercress in a salad bowl. Toss in the figs and strawberries and crumble the blue cheese on top.

Whisk together the olive oil and vinegar and toss with the salad greens. Sprinkle with salt and freshly ground pepper to taste and toss again. Serve immediately.

## *Pimentón Chicken Salad with Summer Berries*

This salad is not only delectable to eat but also makes a beautiful presentation for a summer buffet. I like to serve it with white cheddar cheese that has been made with layers of chipotle powder in the curds—it looks like a creamy piece of marble with deep red veins—and fresh artisanal bread from the bakery.

I coat the poached chicken thighs with pimentón-flavored mayonnaise to give them additional flavor. Pimentón is an intoxicating spice made from smoked ground pimiento peppers from Spain that adds a complex, dusky taste to food. Three types are available at specialty food stores—bittersweet, sweet, and spicy hot; I prefer the bittersweet, but all three work equally well. Look for La Vera brand, which is regulated by a governing board in La Vera, Spain. Their cans have numbered labels on them guaranteeing quality: La Tienda, 1325 Jamestown Road, Williamsburg, VA 23185-3335; 800-710-4304; www.tienda.com. (pimentón, Marcona almonds, and other Spanish products).

**MAKES 4 SERVINGS** **2 cups chicken stock**

**8 boneless chicken thighs**

**Coarse salt**

**Freshly ground pepper**

**1 cup mayonnaise**

**½ teaspoon fresh lemon juice, plus lemon juice for the greens**

**1 teaspoon pimentón (smoky paprika)**

**8 thin slices prosciutto**

**¼ pound mesclun**

**Extra virgin olive oil**
**1 papaya, peeled, seeded, cut lengthwise into ¼-inch slices**
**½ pint (1 cup) fresh raspberries, rinsed and drained**
**½ cup fresh blueberries, rinsed and drained**
**¾ pound chipotle white cheddar cheese or another interesting cheese**

Put the stock and chicken thighs in a shallow pan over medium heat and bring to a boil. Reduce the heat and simmer until the chicken is almost done, about 15 minutes. Cover and turn off the heat. Let cool in the stock until they are completely cooked.

Remove the thighs from the stock (use the stock for a soup base or store in the freezer) and discard the skin. Season the chicken with salt and pepper.

Blend together the mayonnaise, lemon juice, and pimentón and generously spread over the chicken. Wrap each thigh in a piece of prosciutto. Cover with plastic wrap and store in the refrigerator until serving time. The chicken can be prepared up to a day in advance.

Toss the mesclun with just enough olive oil to lightly coat each leaf and a drizzle of lemon juice. Divide the greens among 4 plates and top each with 2 chicken thighs. Arrange the papaya slices next to the chicken and sprinkle the raspberries and blueberries over all. Put a slice of cheese on each plate and serve immediately, accompanied by a basket of good bread and some more olive oil for dipping.

## *Summer Berries and Flowers in White Wine Jelly*

I found this charming recipe in a nineteenth-century cookbook at the South Carolina Historical Society years ago. I've always regretted that I didn't write down the name of the book, because it's a timeless recipe that makes a lovely addition to any summer table.

When you are assembling it, remember that the top is actually the bottom of the mold, so arrange your fruit and flowers accordingly. You'll be thrilled with the results—this dish has been known to bring applause. Serve it with grilled poultry or light-colored meat, such as pork or veal.

**MAKES 8 TO 10 SERVINGS**

**Three ¼-ounce envelopes unflavored gelatin**
**½ cup sugar**
**1 bottle (750 ml) dry white wine**
**¼ cup fresh lime juice (from about 2 limes)**
**1 cup edible flowers, such as pansies (Johnny-jump-ups), nasturtiums, or calendulas**
**½ pint (1 cup) mixed fresh summer berries, such as blackberries, raspberries, and blueberries, rinsed and drained**

Rinse a 5-cup mold (I use a ring mold, but you can use any shape) with cold water.

In a saucepan, heat the gelatin and 1 cup water over medium heat until the gelatin dissolves. Add the sugar and white wine and continue cooking until the sugar dissolves. Remove from the heat and stir in the lime juice.

Pour 1 cup of the mixture into the mold and set in the freezer until it is just starting to get firm, about 10 minutes. Remove from the freezer and decoratively press the berries and edible flowers into the gelatin. Pour a small amount of the remaining mixture over the flowers and fruit and freeze for 10 more minutes. Pour the remaining gelatin mixture into the mold and refrigerate for 1 hour. When firm, unmold onto a platter by gently dipping the mold in a bowl of warm water. Serve immediately.

## *Summer Fruit Salad with Port-Lime Dressing*

Mario Ferreira works for the Porto Wine Institute in New York. "When I was a kid growing up in Turquel, a little town near Alcobaca, Portugal, I remember seeing older women (my mother included) adding porto wine to big bowls of fruit salad, which would be served to the family as a dessert after a meal," he says.

I also add a little lime juice and honey (add less honey if your fruit is exceptionally sweet). As the fruit sits, the salad becomes pleasantly juicy and sweet.

**MAKES 4 TO 6 SERVINGS**

Salad

**½ pint (1 cup) fresh strawberries, rinsed, drained, and sliced**
**½ pint (1 cup) fresh blueberries, rinsed, and drained**
**½ pint (1 cup) fresh blackberries, rinsed, and drained**
**2 cups cubed Galia, Chanterais, casaba, or other interesting sweet melon**
**8 fresh mint leaves, rolled together lengthwise and finely sliced**
**½ pint (1 cup) fresh raspberries, rinsed and drained**

Dressing

**¼ cup ruby or tawny port**
**1 tablespoon finely grated lime zest**
**4 teaspoons fresh lime juice**
**2 to 4 teaspoons honey, to taste (use 4 teaspoons with tawny port)**

Put the strawberries, blueberries, blackberries, melon, and mint in a glass bowl and toss.

Whisk the port, lime zest, lime juice, and honey together until the honey dissolves. Pour over the berries and toss. Sprinkle the raspberries over all and toss gently to mix.

# MAIN COURSES

Berries add a rich depth of flavor when cooked with poultry and meat or when they are used to enhance their sauces. In braised dishes, such as the Blackberry-Port Lamb Shanks, I add the berries at the beginning of the cooking time so they cook down slowly to create a satisfyingly flavorful sauce. I garnish the finished dish with a few uncooked berries, giving guests a hint of what they are eating. For the other lamb recipe in this chapter—Jalapeño-Stuffed Leg of Lamb—I use berries as a condiment in the Blackberry-Chile-Mint Preserves; the same for the Lingonberry-Ginger Sauce that accompanies the Swedish Meatballs, and the Strawberry-Papaya Relish served with the Curried Halibut.

You have to be careful using berry sauces with fish—their success is a delicate balance between the acidity of the sauce and the fat content of what you are cooking. Sugar is seldom an ingredient, and sweet berries, like strawberries or blueberries, should be used only with plenty of citrus juice, like a relish or salsa, or a splash of vinegar as in the Prosciutto Prawns with Huckleberry Balsamic Glaze.

The old French name for gooseberry is *groseille à maquereau,* derived from the common practice at the time of serving mackerel with a gooseberry sauce, a northern European tradition that made its way south and still appears on European menus. The berries that work best with fatty fish are high-acid berries, like culinary gooseberries or cranberries (see Berry Oils, page 152). You can use other berries judiciously, like the marionberries in the Slow-Roasted Pacific Cod, because marionberries have just enough acid for the fairly lean cod. And, as the recipe says, if you substitute salmon, which has a higher fat content, add vinegar (or lime or lemon juice) to the sauce to cut the richness of the fish.

Dark meats and poultry, including game birds, which can also be rich, are perfect with the intense flavors of dark berries, like blackberries, huckleberries, wild blueberries, and black currants. Just remember that a spoonful or two of an exceptionally fine berry sauce, like the currant sauce served with the Muscovy Duck Breasts, goes a long way.

## *Curried Halibut with Strawberry-Papaya Relish*

When halibut is roasted using extremely high heat, it becomes surprisingly butter-textured and stays perfectly moist. You will need a cast-iron skillet or heavy baking dish that can be preheated safely in a 500°F oven. The halibut absorbs heat from both the preheated pan and the oven. The high heat immediately breaks down the fish's connective tissue, producing moist, buttery flakes that melt in your mouth.

This is an unusually quick recipe if you make the relish ahead of time. It will keep for 3 to 4 days covered in the refrigerator. I serve a simple green salad to accompany the fish.

**MAKES 4 SERVINGS**

STRAWBERRY-PAPAYA RELISH

**½ cup chopped fresh strawberries**
**½ cup peeled, seeded, and chopped papaya**
**2 tablespoons chopped fresh cilantro leaves**
**1 tablespoon chopped red onion**
**1 teaspoon fresh lime juice**
**1 teaspoon mild olive oil**
**Pinch of coarse salt**

CURRIED HALIBUT

**1½ pounds fresh halibut, trimmed of skin and cut into 4 pieces**
**Curry powder**
**Coarse salt**
**2 to 3 teaspoons canola oil**
**One 13½-ounce can reduced-fat coconut milk**
**6 cups cooked basmati rice**
**8 fresh cilantro sprigs**

Put a cast-iron skillet in the oven and preheat to 500°F.

Toss all the relish ingredients together and set aside. Meanwhile, bring the fish to room temperature.

Generously season the halibut with curry powder and coarse salt. Heat the canola oil in a sauté pan over medium-high heat. When the pan is hot, pan-sear the fish on both sides until golden brown, about 45 seconds per side. Transfer the fish to the hot skillet in the oven and roast for 6 more minutes, until the fish is barely cooked throughout.

An instant-read thermometer inserted in the center of each piece should read 135°F, and the flesh will feel firm (not sink in) when pressed with your finger. The fish will continue to cook when it comes out of the oven. Transfer the fish to a warm platter and cover to keep warm.

Heat 4 wide pasta bowls.

Pour the coconut milk into the hot skillet over medium-low heat. Gently scrape the bottom of the pan to release the caramelized cooked bits as the milk heats. Season the milk with a pinch of salt if needed.

Divide the rice among the bowls. Lay the fish on top and ladle the coconut milk over all. Put a spoonful of the relish on top of the fish and sprinkle the cilantro leaves over all. Serve immediately.

## *Prosciutto Prawns with Huckleberry Balsamic Glaze*

If you've ever visited picturesque Mendocino County, you'll know that it's in the heart of northern California's coastal huckleberry country. At the Brewery Gulch Inn on scenic Highway 1, Chef Jeffery Neumeier serves sweet local prawns in a huckleberry glaze. The berries are slightly tart, like lemon, and help to bring out the flavor of other foods. In this dish you have the sweet-and-sour taste from the sauce, a hint of salt from the prosciutto, and the rich meat of the prawns all in one glorious bite. The prawns can be assembled up to 8 hours in advance, and the sauce can be made 2 to 3 days in advance.

**MAKES 12 SERVINGS AS AN APPETIZER**

**¼ cup fresh huckleberries or wild blueberries, rinsed and drained, or frozen berries, thawed in a single layer on a paper towel for 20 minutes**
**¼ cup balsamic vinegar**
**1 pound medium prawns or large shrimp (25 to 30 per pound), peeled, deveined, and rinsed**
**Coarse salt**
**Freshly ground pepper**
**¼ pound prosciutto, extra thinly sliced**

Preheat the oven to 350°F. Lightly grease a 9 × 13-inch baking pan.

Combine the huckleberries and balsamic vinegar in a small saucepan and bring to a boil. Lower the heat and reduce the mixture for about 10 minutes, until it becomes syrupy. You should have about 3 tablespoons. Remove the pan from the heat and strain the glaze, being sure to extract all the liquid.

Lightly season the prawns or shrimp with salt and pepper. Wrap each one in a thin 3 × 1-inch piece of prosciutto. This can be done up to 8 hours in advance.

Arrange the prawns in a single layer in a baking pan and bake for about 12 minutes, or until they turn from translucent to almost white.

Toss in the balsamic huckleberry glaze and serve immediately.

*Variation:* Wrap the prawns in thinly sliced pancetta and bake in a 425°F oven for 8 to 10 minutes, until they turn from translucent to almost white. Toss in the glaze.

## *Slow-Roasted Pacific Cod with Marionberry Sauce*

This wonderful recipe came from Stu Stein, the chef/co-owner of the Peerless Restaurant in Ashland, Oregon, home of the state's Shakespeare Festival. Stu, who previously was the executive chef at the highly regarded Oval Room in Washington, D.C., pairs Pacific cod, a medium-textured white fish, with a fennel sauté and stewed marionberries, a refreshing combination of flavors and textures. He says, "Salmon will also work for this recipe, but add a little white wine vinegar to the braised fennel to help balance the richness of the salmon."

**MAKES 4 SERVINGS**

FENNEL SAUTÉ

**1 fennel bulb**
**2 tablespoons vegetable oil or mild olive oil**
**1 sweet onion (Walla Walla, Maui, Vidalia, or Texas 1015), peeled and thinly sliced**
**1 tablespoon sugar**
**¼ cup dry white wine**
**½ teaspoon hot red pepper flakes or 1 small Thai chile, seeds removed and finely chopped**
**Coarse salt**
**Freshly ground pepper**

MARIONBERRY SAUCE

**1 tablespoon unsalted butter**
**1 shallot, peeled and finely chopped**
**1 cup dry white wine**
**½ cup fresh marionberries or other blackberries, rinsed and drained, or ½ cup frozen berries, thawed in a single layer on a paper towel for 20 minutes**

**1 cup fish or chicken stock**
**Coarse salt**
**Freshly ground pepper**

**Fish**
**Four 4- to 6-ounce cod fillets, or salmon fillets skinned**
**Coarse salt**
**Freshly ground pepper**
**A few marionberries and fennel fronds for garnish**

Core and thinly slice the fennel bulb. Chop enough of the fronds to make 1 tablespoon and save 4 frond sprigs for garnish.

Pour the vegetable oil into a sauté pan over medium heat. Sauté the onion until soft and translucent, about 8 minutes. Add the sugar, wine, sliced fennel bulb, and pepper flakes (plus 1½ tablespoons white wine vinegar if you're using salmon) and simmer until the liquid is completely evaporated, about 10 minutes. Remove from the heat and add the chopped fennel fronds. Season with salt and pepper to taste. This fennel sauté can be made up to 2 days in advance.

For the sauce, melt the butter in a sauté pan over medium heat and sauté the shallot until translucent, about 5 minutes. Add the wine and marionberries and simmer until the liquid is reduced by half, about 5 minutes. Add the stock and simmer again until the liquid is reduced by one-fourth and is fairly thick. Season with salt and pepper to taste. The sauce can be made up to 1 day in advance; add more stock if necessary when it is reheated.

Preheat the oven to 275°F.

Season the fish with salt and pepper to taste and bake for about 12 to 15 minutes, until it is just cooked in the center. To serve, divide the fennel sauté among 4 plates and top each with a fish fillet. Drizzle the marionberry sauce in a circle around the fennel on the plate. Garnish with additional marionberries and a few fennel fronds.

## *Sautéed Chicken Breast with Blueberry Port*

Duck Walk Vineyard in Water Mill, Long Island, makes an impressive port from wild blueberries grown in Maine. My nephew, who lives nearby, gave me a bottle last summer, along with this tasty recipe that is also from the vineyard. I added some fresh berries and chopped rosemary for more flavor. Serve the chicken and sauce accompanied by polenta, risotto, or half wild, half brown rice.

### Forest Gypsies

One morning last fall, my husband and I were in the Elk Pass wilderness area near Mount Adams, in the foothills of the Washington Cascades, picking huckleberries. We were driving down an old dirt logging road when we came upon a tailgate camp set up with bright blue tarps protecting gallon buckets filled to the brim with fresh huckleberries. Two men, with telling purple fingers, walked over to say hello. These were forest gypsies—people who make a living foraging for wild crops, selling their harvest to a wholesaler, then, when the season is over, moving on to another state for another crop. "We may not be rich, but we work for ourselves," they told me. "In April and May we pick morel mushrooms at Fisher Hill near Mount Adams. Then we go to Idaho in June to pick huckleberries for the next two months. After that we come back here to Washington to pick huckleberries in September and wild mushrooms in October. We pick here with the Cambodians. After what they've been through in their country, they love the freedom they feel here in the mountains." I had the feeling that these two free spirits also cherished their freedom.

**MAKES 4 SERVINGS**

**2 teaspoons olive oil**
**1 cup diced yellow onion**
**4 garlic cloves, chopped**
**1 to 2 teaspoons chopped fresh rosemary or ½ to 1 teaspoon dried**
**4 boneless, skinless chicken breasts**
**Coarse salt**
**Freshly ground pepper**
**½ cup Duck Walk blueberry port or tawny port**
**1 cup chicken stock**
**½ pint (1 cup) fresh wild blueberries, huckleberries, or blueberries, or frozen berries, thawed in a single layer on a paper towel for 20 minutes**

Heat 4 plates.

Pour the olive oil into a large sauté pan over medium heat. Sauté the onion and garlic with the rosemary for 3 to 4 minutes, until the onion starts to soften. Season the chicken breasts with salt and pepper to taste and brown on both sides with the onions and garlic. Pour in the port and reduce by half as the chicken continues to cook, turning the pieces frequently. Add the chicken stock and continue cooking for about 10 more minutes, until the juices run clear and the chicken is cooked through. Transfer the chicken breasts to the warmed plates.

Add the blueberries to the sauce and cook for 2 to 3 minutes, until they are warmed through. Season the sauce if necessary and serve it ladled over the chicken.

## *Grilled Paprika Chicken with Blackberry Sauce*

I love the earthy flavor of smoky paprika, a hauntingly delicious spice imported from Spain that goes well with berries. Substitute sweet paprika if you can't find it.

**MAKES 4 SERVINGS**

- **One 3- to 4-pound roasting chicken**
- **2 cups chicken stock**
- **1½ tablespoons bittersweet pimentón (see page 125)**
- **2 teaspoons coarse salt**
- **½ teaspoon freshly ground pepper**
- **6 fresh rosemary sprigs**
- **1 pint (2 cups) fresh marionberries or other blackberries, rinsed and drained, or frozen berries, thawed with juice**

Preheat the oven to 350°F.

Cut off the wing tips and put them, and the neck if there is one, in a small pan with the chicken stock. Set the pan over medium-high heat and reduce to 1 cup. Strain and set aside.

Pat the chicken dry with a paper towel. Blend the pimentón and salt and pepper together and rub the mixture over the bird and inside the cavity. Place 2 rosemary sprigs in the cavity, truss the legs, and put the bird in a roasting pan. Roast for 1 hour and 25 minutes, until the internal temperature is 175°F and the juices run a clear yellow. Remove the bird from the oven and keep warm while you make the sauce.

Puree the blackberries in a food processor or blender and push the puree through a fine strainer or food mill to remove the seeds. Discard the fat from the roasting pan and add the reserved chicken stock, blackberry puree, and another rosemary sprig. Put the roasting pan over medium-high heat and bring the stock to a boil. Cook rapidly for 3 to 4 minutes, stirring and scraping to release the caramelized bits on the bottom of the pan. The sauce will thicken slightly. Add any juices to the pan that may have accumulated from the cooked chicken and remove the rosemary sprig. Season with salt and pepper.

Joint the chicken and put the pieces on a warm platter. Garnish with the remaining rosemary sprigs and pour the blackberry sauce into a small bowl with a ladle to accompany the chicken.

## *Panfried Quail with Sage in Huckleberry Sauce*

Of all the game birds, quail is one of my favorites. Since its succulent dark meat is not overly gamy, and it is always moist and tender, I often serve it to first-time game eaters. In this simple recipe, I accompany the quail with another prized food from the wild, huckleberries. You can buy game meats from Nicky USA, Inc., 223 SE Third Avenue, Portland, OR 97214; 800-469-4162; www.nickyusa.com (wild and farm-raised game, rabbit, buffalo, wild mushrooms, huckleberries, foie gras, and more).

**MAKES 2 SERVINGS**

- **⅓ cup all-purpose flour**
- **½ teaspoon coarse salt**
- **¼ teaspoon freshly ground pepper**
- **4 quail, 4 to 6 ounces each (preferably semiboneless)**
- **3 tablespoons olive oil**
- **2 tablespoons unsalted butter**
- **8 fresh sage leaves**
- **½ cup chicken stock**
- **½ cup dry vermouth or 1 cup dry white wine**
- **½ cup fresh huckleberries or wild blueberries, rinsed and drained, or ½ cup frozen berries, thawed in a single layer on a paper towel for 20 minutes**

Heat 4 plates.

Combine the flour, salt, and pepper in a shallow dish. Dredge the quail through the mixture and set aside. Put the olive oil and butter in a sauté pan and heat to medium-hot. Fry the sage leaves until crisp and drain on paper towels.

Sauté the quail, about 4 to 5 minutes on each side, until the juices run a rosy color when pricked with a fork. Transfer to warm plates while you make the sauce.

Pour the chicken stock, vermouth, and huckleberries into the pan the quail was sautéed in. Put it back over medium-high heat and stir, scraping the bottom of the pan as it cooks to release the caramelized bits. Reduce the sauce until it thickens, about 5 minutes. Season with salt, if necessary, and ladle over the quail. (If the sauce gets too thick, add a little more chicken stock. If it's not thick enough, reduce it further.) Garnish each plate with 2 sage leaves.

### *Slow-Roasted Pheasant with Huckleberry Sauce*

On a recent trip to New York, I enjoyed a memorable meal at Union Pacific, cooked by its talented young chef, Rocco DiSpirito. My favorite dish was his slow-roasted baby pheasant. The birds were served split, crispy golden brown on the outside, with meat so tender you could cut it with a fork. He said, "The secret is cooking the pheasant in the oven at a very low temperature, then sautéing it in butter after it comes out of the oven." This is my interpretation of his dish, served with a huckleberry sauce. Never roast stuffed birds at this low temperature because the dressing might not cook completely, risking bacterial growth.

Always put the pheasant in the oven directly from the refrigerator (leaving it at room temperature can allow dangerous bacteria to grow), and monitor the bird with a meat thermometer to be sure it cooks to a minimum of 160°F.

**MAKES 4 SERVINGS**

**1 cold (directly from the refrigerator) wild or farm-raised pheasant, about 3 pounds (not stuffed)**
**Roasted Fennel-Coriander Rub (recipe follows)**
**½ cup chicken stock**
**½ cup fresh huckleberries, black currants, or wild blueberries, rinsed and drained, or ½ cup frozen blueberries, thawed in a single layer on a paper towel for 20 minutes**
**2 to 3 tablespoons unsalted butter (optional)**

Preheat the oven to 200°F.

Pat the pheasant dry and season inside and out with the rub. Put the bird breast side up in a roasting pan and cover with foil. Bake for about 6½ hours, until an instant-read thermometer reaches 160°F. Transfer to a plate to rest. The bird is ready to be served at this point, but if you like, you can quarter the bird and quickly sauté the pieces in butter to give them a rich golden brown color.

Put the roasting pan (unwashed) over medium-high heat and pour in the chicken stock and huckleberries. Cook rapidly for 3 to 4 minutes, scraping the bottom of the pan with a wooden spoon to release the caramelized bits. Stir in the butter and serve over the pheasant.

### Huckleberry Nights

RAF pilots flew deep into Germany on night maneuvers during World War II, their performance constantly hindered by poor visibility in the dark, gloomy nights. Then an older woman in one of the families suggested the pilots eat bilberry (huckleberry) jam to improve their night vision. It proved to be effective, and bilberry jam became a staple in the RAF diet. Medical research has proven 50 years later that beneficial chemicals (anthocyanosides—powerful antioxidants) in the berries do in fact improve night vision by enhancing retinal function.

*Roasted Fennel-Coriander Rub*

**2 teaspoons fennel seeds**
**2 teaspoons coriander seeds**
**1 teaspoon coarse salt**
**½ teaspoon freshly ground pepper**

Stir in salt and pepper. Makes enough for 3-pound bird, generously seasoned inside and out with the rub.

Toast the fennel and coriander seeds in a small skillet over high heat for 2 to 3 minutes, until they turn a deep golden brown. Transfer to a spice mill (I use an inexpensive coffee grinder I bought just for grinding spices) and process until finely ground—it does not have to be perfectly smooth. Stir in the salt and pepper.

### Indian Legends and Traditions

Several years ago my husband and I met a Yakima Indian woman and her sister, with handmade berry baskets tied to their hips, picking huckleberries near Mount St. Helens. Their families, and other Native Americans from their tribe, have traveled from eastern Washington to the same location to pick berries for centuries. We enjoyed listening to them discuss the legend of the eagle that first brought berries to the mountain when time began centuries ago. Their niece and nephew hadn't come with them that day, so they picked some leafy huckleberry stems to take back to the reservation to teach the younger generation how to make huckleberry tea, a cure they use for an upset stomach. You can buy berry teas from Alaska Spice Company, PO Box 1950, Wasilla, AK, 99687-1950; 877-977-4230; www.alaskaspicecompany.com. (herbal wild berry and berry black teas).

## *Muscovy Duck Breasts with Black Currant Sauce*

Muscovy duck, known in France as *canard de Barbarie*, is becoming more and more popular in the United States. In this recipe from the Genoa Restaurant in Portland, Oregon, chef Molly Schaefer Priest, winner of the 2002 Wild About Game Cook-Off, serves sautéed Muscovy duck breast cloaked in a dusky black currant sauce—a perfect match for this rich and savory meat.

The secret to this dish is to cook the duck breasts slowly, skin side down, until most of the fat is rendered and the skin is a crispy dark golden brown.

If you don't have black currants to make the syrup, Loóza—a Belgian company that specializes in juices—makes black currant nectar (*nectar de cassis*) that can be substituted for the black currant syrup. Look for Loóza products in the juice section at the supermarket. Demi-glace is available at many supermarkets and butcher shops, or you can make your own. If it's not available, the dish will still be tasty without it.

**MAKES 4 SERVINGS**

**DUCK BREASTS**

**4 Muscovy duck breasts**
**Coarse salt**
**Freshly ground pepper**

**BLACK CURRANT SAUCE**

**2 tablespoons peeled and coarsely chopped shallot**
**3 tablespoons sherry vinegar**
**1 tablespoon duck or veal demi-glace**
**1 cup meat or chicken stock**
**3 tablespoons Black Currant Syrup (recipe follows)**
**2 tablespoons Dijon mustard**
**1 tablespoon butter, softened**

Preheat the oven to 150°F (warm). Warm 4 dinner plates.

Pat the duck breasts dry with a paper towel and season with salt and pepper to taste. Heat a large heavy skillet over medium-high heat. (I use a grill pan—the ridges keep the meat from cooking in all the fat.) Put the duck breasts skin side down (no need to add any oil first) in the pan and reduce the heat to medium-low heat. Sauté until the fat is slowly rendered and the skin turns a rich caramel brown, 15 to 20 minutes. Turn the breasts over and brown lightly on the other side, 5 to 7 more minutes. The ducks should be rare to medium-rare—an instant-read thermometer should reach 160°F to 165°F.

Transfer to the warm oven to rest.

Discard all but 2 to 3 teaspoons of the pan drippings. Sauté the shallots in the drippings over medium-high heat until they start to become translucent, about 8 minutes. Whisk in the sherry vinegar, duck or veal glaze, and stock, scraping the bottom of the pan to release the cooked caramelized bits. Stir in 3 tablespoons of the black currant syrup and the Dijon mustard. Cook until the liquid is reduced by half and whisk in the butter.

Thinly slice each duck breast on the bias and arrange on the warmed plates. Ladle a spoonful of sauce over the meat and serve immediately.

### *Black Currant Syrup*

**MAKES ABOUT ⅓ CUP**

**¼ cup fresh black currants, wild blueberries, or huckleberries, rinsed and drained, or frozen berries, thawed with juice**
**¼ cup sugar**

Cook the black currants and sugar together in a small saucepan over medium-high heat until thick and syrupy, about 10 minutes. Strain and set aside. The syrup can be made up to a week in advance. Cool and store covered in the refrigerator until ready to use.

## *White Pekin Duckling with Loganberry-Hoisin Glaze*

There is nothing quite like the mouthwatering aroma of duck roasting to a crisp golden brown. Before cooking it, I coat the bird inside and out with a robust Szechwan peppercorn rub to give it additional flavor. Use regular pepper if you can't find the Szechwan peppercorns. For the sauce, I simply mix blackberry puree with hoisin sauce. Their complex flavor is a perfect complement to the rich duck meat.

**MAKES 2 SERVINGS**

**1 tablespoon whole Szechwan peppercorns (available at Chinese markets)**
**1 tablespoon coarse salt**
**One 5-pound White Pekin duckling**
**2 tablespoons hoisin sauce**
**¼ cup loganberry or blackberry puree (about ½ cup loganberries, crushed and seeded) (see Note)**

Preheat the oven to 500°F.

Toast the peppercorns in a small skillet over high heat for 2 to 3 minutes, until they are hot and fragrant. Grind them with the salt in a grinder (I use an inexpensive coffee mill that I bought just to grind spices) or put the peppercorns and salt in a self-sealing plastic bag and finely crush with a mallet. The mixture doesn't have to be homogenous.

Trim the wing tips and neck fat from the duck and remove the giblets. (You can sauté the liver and serve on crackers while the duck cooks.) Pat the bird dry with paper towels, then rub inside and out with the seasoning.

Put the bird breast side up on a rack in a roasting pan. Roast for 25 minutes. Reduce the heat to 350°F and roast for 40 minutes longer, until a meat thermometer reads 160°F to 165°F. Transfer the duck to a platter and let rest at room temperature for 20 minutes before carving.

Stir together the hoisin sauce and loganberry puree and put it in individual sauce bowls for each plate. Carve the duck into 2 boneless breasts and leg-thigh portions and serve accompanied by the sauce.

*Note:* If you are using blackberries, add a few drops of lemon juice to the sauce.

## *Hot-Smoked Turkey with Blackberry Barbecue Sauce*

Every Thanksgiving, Molly Schaefer Priest, chef at the Genoa Restaurant in Portland, Oregon, and her husband grill a turkey that they marinate the day before in an apple cider brine. It creates a moist, intensely flavorful bird, which I grill with my blackberry barbecue sauce to give it additional flavor. You will need a barbecue with a lid and either a big or spare refrigerator for this recipe.

**MAKES 20 SERVINGS**

**5 quarts apple cider**
**2 cups coarse salt**
**One 20-pound fresh or thawed frozen turkey**
**Apple or hickory chips**
**1 recipe American Barbecue Sauce (page 150)**

Blend together the apple cider and salt in a crock or noncorrosive container large enough to hold the turkey. Remove the giblets, neck, and liver from the cavity of the bird. Discard or put them in your freezer for making stock on another day. Submerge the bird in the marinade, cover with plastic wrap, and store overnight in the refrigerator.

The next day, rinse and pat the bird dry and bring to room temperature. Light the barbecue and soak the chips in water for 15 minutes, then drain. Sprinkle a quarter of the wood chips on the sides of the coals. Put the turkey on the grill and cover with the lid. Cook for 3½ to 4 hours, adding more chips every 45 minutes. Brush liberally with the barbecue sauce after the first 2 hours. Continue grilling, brushing often until the thigh meat registers 170°F. The juices will run clear yellow.

Remove the bird from the grill. Cover loosely with foil and let rest for 20 minutes before carving.

*Note:* For a 10- to 12-pound turkey, use 2½ quarts apple cider and 1 cup coarse salt for the brine and one half the recipe for American Barbecue Sauce. Grill for 1 hour following the above instructions.

## *Blackberry-Port Lamb Shanks*

Loyce Ericson—a sheep rancher in Oregon's Willamette Valley—won third place in the Great Northwest Lamb Cook-Off with this recipe. "These can be baked in the oven or, even better, let your Crock-Pot do the cooking! Serve the shanks accompanied by rice, noodles, risotto, or couscous, with plenty of the juice on the top," she says. They can be cooked up to 2 days in advance.

**MAKES 6 SERVINGS**

**2 teaspoons coarse salt**
**1 teaspoon freshly ground pepper**
**6 lamb shanks**
**½ cup all-purpose flour**
**1 to 2 tablespoons mild or extra virgin olive oil**
**1½ cups tawny port or Madeira**
**2 tablespoons honey (optional)**
**1 tablespoon fresh lemon juice**
**½ teaspoon fresh thyme leaves, crushed**
**12 garlic cloves, peeled**
**¾ pint (1½ cups) fresh marionberries or other blackberries, rinsed and drained, or frozen marionberries, plus a handful for garnish**

Preheat the oven to 275°F.

Rub salt and pepper onto the shanks and dredge them in flour. Heat the oil in a Dutch oven and sauté the shanks over medium-high heat until they are well browned, about 10 minutes. Discard any fat that has accumulated in the bottom of the pan. (If using a Crock-Pot or other slow cooker, transfer the shanks to the Crock-Pot and turn it to high.)

Stir together the port, honey (if using), lemon juice, and thyme and pour over the meat. Sprinkle the garlic and marionberries over all. Cover and bake for 6 to 6½ hours (cook in the Crock-Pot for 6 hours), until the meat is tender and falls off the bone. Discard any fat that has accumulated and season the cooking juices with salt and pepper if needed.

Serve the shanks in a large, shallow serving bowl with some of the sauce ladled over the top and garnished with a handful of fresh blackberries. Pass any remaining sauce along with the shanks.

## *Jalapeño-Stuffed Leg of Lamb with Blackberry-Chile-Mint Preserves*

Chefs James Keeney and Jim Borovicaka from Blinn's Boathouse in Lake Oswego, Oregon, took first place in the 2002 Lamb Cook-Off contest with this mouthwatering recipe that uses a savory blackberry-chile-mint preserve to accompany a leg of lamb. The robust flavor of smoked lamb, fresh mint, chiles, and blackberries is a winning combination that brings out the best in all of the ingredients. I have simplified the chefs' rub using only coarse salt, freshly ground pepper, and pimentón (smoked paprika). Once the lamb is seasoned and stuffed, the chefs refrigerate it for 48 hours. You can stuff and cook it all the same day if you are short of time, and it will still be good. I hot-smoked the meat instead of cold-smoking it. I've also made this without any smoke at all, and that's good, too.

Don't let the chiles keep you from trying this recipe. It's surprisingly *not* hot, and the lamb's rich flavor will keep you coming back for more.

**MAKES 8 SERVINGS**

**1 bone-in leg of lamb, 6 to 8 pounds**

**1 teaspoon pimentón (preferably bittersweet, see page 125), or sweet paprika**

**1 teaspoon coarse salt**

**½ teaspoon freshly cracked pepper**

**½ bunch fresh mint, chopped (about ⅓ cup)**

**3 to 5 jalapeño peppers, quartered and seeded**

**2 cups hickory, mesquite, or other wood chips**
**Blackberry-Chile-Mint Preserves (page 172)**

Unroll the lamb and trim out as much interior fat as possible. Mix together the pimentón, salt, and pepper and rub it into both sides of the meat. Sprinkle the leg with a thin layer of mint and peppers. Roll the meat up lengthwise (so it still resembles a leg of lamb) and tie with string. Refrigerate for at least 2 and up to 48 hours to let the flavors permeate the meat.

Light the barbecue (you will need one with a cover) and soak the wood chips in water for 15 minutes. Let the meat come to room temperature. Drain the chips and sprinkle them over the coals. Put the meat on the grill, cover, and hot-smoke the meat until an instant-reading thermometer reads 140°F, about 1½ hours. Transfer the lamb to a warm platter and let the meat rest for 15 to 20 minutes before carving. Serve accompanied by a bowl of the preserves.

## *Pork Tenderloin Salad with Warm Strawberry Dressing*

This is a good recipe for early-season strawberries when they aren't at their best. When they are sautéed, they absorb the balsamic vinegar and cooking juices, and their flesh becomes sweet and flavorful. If they are exceptionally large berries, cut the slices in half.

**MAKES 4 TO 5 SERVINGS**

**1 tablespoon chopped fresh rosemary**
**1 tablespoon chopped garlic**
**1 teaspoon coarse salt, plus a pinch for seasoning the salad**
**½ teaspoon freshly ground pepper**
**1½ pounds pork tenderloin**
**⅓ cup balsamic vinegar**
**1 pint (about 2 cups) fresh strawberries, sliced**
**2 tablespoons extra virgin olive oil**
**¼ pound mixed fresh greens, such as baby lettuce, spinach, and arugula**
**1 avocado, peeled, pitted, and sliced**

Preheat the oven to 325°F.

Mix the rosemary, garlic, salt, and pepper together. Pat the meat dry with paper towels and rub with the rosemary-garlic mixture. Put the seasoned tenderloin in a small, flame-proof roasting pan. Brown the meat on all sides. Transfer the meat to the oven and roast for 15 to 20 minutes, until it reaches an internal temperature of 150°F on an instant-read thermometer. Remove the tenderloin from the pan and wrap in foil to keep it warm while you prepare the sauce. The meat will be slightly pink, but it will keep cooking as it rests.

Put the roasting pan over medium-high heat and pour in the balsamic vinegar. Use a wooden spoon to loosen the caramelized bits on the bottom of the pan. After 1 to 2 minutes, when the vinegar has been reduced by not quite half, gently add the strawberries and olive oil and toss. Remove the pan from the heat and set aside.

Carve the meat into ½-inch slices. Pour any collected juices in the pan and stir to blend with the dressing.

Spread the greens out on a rectangular platter and arrange the meat on top; tuck the avocado slices around the meat. Drizzle with the warm strawberry dressing. Sprinkle with a pinch of sea salt and serve immediately. Alternatively, serve on individual salad plates.

## *Swedish Meatballs with Lingonberry-Ginger Sauce*

A Swedish neighbor of ours used to invite us over for cocktails and her mother's savory meatballs. You'll be surprised how fast six dozen will disappear at a party. Serve them with a bowl of lingonberry-ginger sauce for dipping. These meatballs will keep in the freezer for up to 3 months.

**MAKES 6 DOZEN**

**2½ pounds ground chuck**
**1 pound ground pork**
**1 tablespoon salt**
**1½ tablespoons dry mustard**
**2½ teaspoons ground coriander**
**2½ teaspoons ground allspice**
**3 large eggs, beaten**
**¾ cup fresh bread crumbs**
**¾ cup diced scallion**
**Lingonberry-Ginger Sauce (recipe follows)**

Preheat the oven to 350°F. Line 2 baking sheets with parchment paper to keep the bottom of the meatballs from becoming too brown. If you don't have parchment paper, lightly oil the baking pans. Heat a serving bowl or platter.

Put everything but the sauce in a large bowl and thoroughly mix together. Form the mixture into 1-inch balls and put them on the baking sheet ½ inch apart. Bake for

20 minutes or until the meat is lightly browned on the outside and no longer pink in the center. Serve on a platter accompanied by a bowl of the sauce and a box of toothpicks.

### *Lingonberry-Ginger Sauce*

Use this simple but tasty dipping sauce at room temperature (not warm, or it will become too thin) as an accompaniment for Swedish meatballs or grilled poultry or pork.

**MAKES 2 CUPS**

**One 18-ounce jar apple jelly**
**1 tablespoon peeled and grated fresh ginger**
**¼ cup peach or mango chutney**
**1 tablespoon fresh lemon juice**
**½ cup wild lingonberries in sugar or whole cranberry sauce (see Note)**

Stir all the ingredients together and serve in a bowl to accompany Swedish meatballs, poultry, or pork.

*Note:* Jars of lingonberries are sold as sweetened preserves.

### Jewels of the Siberian Tundra

"The time of red cloudberries arrives in the tundra at the end of summer. Until that time the berries lie quietly in the softly glittering palms of the green leaves, hard purple, with protruding black hairs, bitter and tart to taste. They are avoided not only by people, but by birds and animals, and ripen in silence yet a long time. But already the days are gradually shortening, mixing sunny hours with rain and sometimes with heavy snow, bending foliage to earth, where the moss still harbors the reserves of warm summer days. The cloudberries were strewn like brilliant corpuscles among green but already slightly yellow-spotted leaves, down in the grass, on the silver reindeer moss, inviting and tempting you to stoop down and gather a handful to put in your mouth, the berries taut, cool, but already filled with sweet aromatic juice."

—From *Journey in Youth or, the Time of Red Cloudberries* by Yuri Rritkheu

## *Beef Tenderloin with Lingonberry Cream Sauce*

When we were in Alaska last year, we stayed at Tangle Lakes Lodge, about seven hours south of Fairbanks. While we were picking wild blueberries, we were particularly impressed with the vast number of lingonberries growing in the mossy tundra. The lodge's chef told us his favorite way to prepare them was in a cream sauce over caribou, a meat I love for its exquisite flavor.

Don't worry if you don't have caribou—although it is available and often sold online by its European name, reindeer—I have substituted beef in this recipe, but it works with pork tenderloin or rabbit loin, too.

For the cream sauce, I use Lingonberry Danish Spread, a low-sugar jam imported from Denmark that I buy at my grocery store during the holidays. Once it's opened, keep it in the refrigerator and it will last all year. You can use it on biscuits or scones or mix it with a little French-style mustard and a pinch of cinnamon and nutmeg as a glaze for ham. Import markets carrying Scandinavian products have it year-round. You can order lingonberry spread from Berry Bazaar (Micosta Enterprises), 3007 Route #20, Hudson, NY 12534; 518-822-9708; www.micostaent.com.

**MAKES 4 SERVINGS**

**Four 1½-pound beef tenderloin or pork loin**
**Pinch of coarse salt**
**Freshly ground pepper**
**Mild olive oil**
**¼ cup beef stock**
**¼ cup heavy cream**
**2 tablespoons lingonberry spread**
**1 tablespoon red wine**

Preheat the oven to 160°F to 200°F. Put a platter and four plates in the oven.

Pat the meat dry with paper towels and remove any silver skin. Rub the flesh with salt and pepper and slice into ⅓-inch-thick medallions.

Heat 1 to 2 tablespoons of oil in a sauté pan over medium-high heat. Cook the medallions for about 2 minutes on each side—they should still be rare in the center. Transfer the meat to the warm platter and put it in the oven while you prepare the sauce.

Put the unwashed pan back over medium-high heat. Pour in the stock, cream, lingonberry spread, and red wine and gently scrape the bottom of the pan to release any caramelized bits. Reduce the liquid until it thickens—it will coat the back of a spoon. (You need only enough sauce to pour a few spoonfuls over the meat. Remember: the more concentrated the sauce, the more intense its flavor will be. If you reduce it too much, stir in a little more cream or chicken stock.)

Ladle the sauce over the meat and serve immediately.

### Alaska Berries by the Bucketful

Tangle Lakes, Alaska, gets its name from the abundance of lakes that dot the alpine tundra, the remains of an enormous glacial lake. North America's oldest archaeological sites are found here, inhabited by man more than 10,000 years ago. On the weekend we were there, 500 caribou were passing through on their annual fall migration, and loons serenaded us every evening at dusk. But the highlight of our trip was picking berries on the mossy slopes that offered wild blueberries, lingonberries, and bearberries by the bucketful. You can buy Alaskan berry products at Alaska Wild Berry Products, 5225 Juneau Street, Anchorage, AK 99518; 800-280-2927; www.alaskawildberryproducts.com (large selection of Alaskan wild berry preserves).

## *Venison Tenderloin with Horseradish–Sour Cream Sauce and Blackberry Preserves*

Ashley Perdue Ratcliffe grew up in Mobile, Alabama, where her father, a world-class marksman, kept their larder stocked with game. She now lives in the quaint coastal town of Bolinas, California, where game is still a treasured meal, although the meat sometimes comes to her in a curious manner.

Her home, the oldest in the village, has an enclosed back porch, complete with a sink for washing vegetables from the adjoining garden. One morning she found a note on her front door from a hunter friend telling her to look in the sink in the back. She was astonished but delighted to find a deer leg wrapped in newspaper! Ashley prepared it just as her mother had cooked venison in the South.

"Cook the meat fast over high heat and only to rare," she says. "Slice it and ladle the sauce over the top. Alongside, serve sour cream mixed with horseradish to taste and blackberry jam or conserve. Each plate should have a small amount of both—

touching, but not mixed—so that the diner may decide how he wants to include them with each bite."

**MAKES 4 SERVINGS**

**¼ cup olive oil plus extra**
**¾ cup red wine**
**½ onion, cut into quarters**
**1 carrot, sliced into thick coins**
**1 celery rib, cut into thirds**
**2 garlic cloves, coarsely chopped**
**12 juniper berries, smashed**
**10 peppercorns**
**1½ pounds venison, pork, or beef tenderloin**
**1 cup sour cream**
**1 to 2 tablespoons creamy horseradish**
**Coarse salt**
**Freshly ground pepper**
**½ jigger gin**
**1 tablespoon heavy cream**
**Blackberry preserves**

Make the marinade by putting the olive oil and wine in a shallow dish and whisking together. Add the onion, carrot, celery, garlic, juniper berries, and peppercorns and stir to mix. Put the tenderloin in the marinade and roll it to coat all sides. Cover and marinate in the refrigerator for 24 hours.

Heat 4 dinner plates. Combine the sour cream and horseradish and set aside.

Remove the meat from the marinade and reserve the marinade. Pat the tenderloin dry with paper towels and season generously with salt and pepper.

Drizzle the oil into a large skillet and put it over medium-high heat. Quickly sauté the meat for 3 to 4 minutes, until it is browned on all sides but still deep pink in the center. Transfer the meat to a warmed plate and set aside while you make the sauce.

Pour the marinade into the same saucepan the meat was cooked in and turn the heat to medium-high. Reduce the marinade by half. "Add a splash of gin (about half a jigger), cook a moment—and then add a bit of cream, just to bring it to a silken finish. Serve the venison sliced, with a ladle of sauce, and accompanied by a dab of horseradish-flavored sour cream and blackberry preserves," says Ashley.

# SAUCES

There is nothing more wonderful than the penetrating taste of a good berry sauce. Many berries, like raspberries and strawberries, don't need much more than a pinch of sugar and a few drops of lemon or lime juice to enhance their flavor, while others, like huckleberries and wild blueberries, require a little heat to unlock their magic. Blackberries can be used either way. For something different, try Stewed Blackberries, made with a split vanilla bean and a cinnamon stick, served over vanilla ice cream, or a blackberry coulis over pound cake. Raspberries can go either way, too. Warmed with plump Juneberries and flavored with a few drops of almond extract, raspberries make a fine sauce, or simply serve them all by themselves spiked with a splash of framboise.

But don't use berry sauces only for desserts. Their earthy, intense character and mild acidity makes them ideal for meats and poultry, too. I have given two recipes for barbecue sauce, one Asian, the other American, both made with blackberries. Their complex flavor can stand up to the powerful smoky taste of grilled meats.

Always make berry sauces with high-quality fresh or frozen berries. For dessert sauces, add the sugar judiciously. Nothing ruins a sauce more than making it too sweet. How do you know when it's sweet enough? The best way is to add just a little sugar. The first flavor to hit your palate should be the fruit, then the sugar, not the other way around. For many berries, acid is essential, too, to maximize the berries' naturally good taste. (It's like the salt of the entree world.) Add lime or lemon juice, drop by drop, until the berry flavor bursts in your mouth.

In the summer I stock my freezer with peak-of-the-season berries for the rest of the year. I use one-pint freezer bags for raspberries, strawberries, and currants specifically for making sauces. When I need them, I simply thaw the berries on a paper towel for 20 minutes and puree the berries in my food processor.

One last tip: never use berry sauces straight from the refrigerator. They should be served either heated or at room temperature so you can fully experience their pure, exquisite taste.

## *American Barbecue Sauce*

Use this sauce on barbecued ribs or chicken and brush it on toward the end of the cooking time.

**MAKES ABOUT 3 CUPS**

**1 pint (2 cups) fresh marionberries or other blackberries, rinsed and drained, or frozen marionberries, thawed with juice**
**3 garlic cloves, peeled**
**¼ cup red wine vinegar**
**½ cup light or dark brown sugar (not packed)**
**¼ cup light or dark corn syrup**
**1 cup ketchup**
**¼ teaspoon hot red pepper flakes**
**1½ teaspoons pimentón (see page 125)**
**1½ teaspoons coarse salt**
**½ teaspoon coarsely ground pepper**
**1 tablespoon unsalted butter (optional)**

Puree all the ingredients in a food processor. Transfer to a small saucepan and simmer for 1 hour or until the sauce has thickened slightly. Let cool and store in a covered jar in the refrigerator for up to 1 month.

*Note:* To use this recipe with brined poultry or rabbit, make a salt solution by mixing together 1 quart cold water with ½ cup coarse salt in a 9 × 13-inch glass pan (use a deep, noncorrosive bowl for whole chickens). Soak for 30 minutes. For ribs, add 2 cups red wine vinegar to the brine. Rinse and pat dry. Grill and use the sauce as directed.

## *Asian Blackberry Barbecue Sauce*

Use this Asian-style barbecue sauce on grilled chicken, duck, quail, turkey, or pork. Brush it on toward the end of the cooking time and once again when the meat comes off the grill. Beware: there is a lot of sugar in this sauce, which means that it will burn easily, so use it only over medium or low heat.

**MAKES A SCANT 2 CUPS**

**1½ pints (3 cups) fresh marionberries or other blackberries, rinsed and drained, or frozen marionberries, thawed with juice**
**3 garlic cloves, peeled**
**2 tablespoons chopped fresh ginger (about 4 slices)**
**½ cup rice vinegar**
**½ cup Vietnamese sweet chili sauce for chicken (I like the Caravelle brand)**
**½ cup packed dark brown sugar**
**1 teaspoon coarse salt**

Puree all the ingredients in a food processor and store in a covered jar in the refrigerator for up to 1 month.

## *Berry Coulis (Sauce)*

Sauces don't have to be complex to taste good, especially when they are made with berries. Most berries are best left uncooked and simply sweetened with a pinch of sugar and enhanced with a few drops of lemon juice. The exceptions to this rule are black currants, wild blueberries, saskatoon berries, green gooseberries, cranberries, and huckleberries, which all need heat to bring out their flavor, and berries of not-peak-season quality. Simply heat these berries in a saucepan over medium heat for 3 to 4 minutes, until their juices start to run.

Adding 2 to 3 teaspoons of framboise, cassis, or berry dessert wine to berry sauces intensifies their delectable flavor and complexity even more. Or you can add them to deglaze a pan for a sauce. To order berry dessert wines, contact Hood River Vineyards, 4693 Westwood Drive, Hood River, OR 97031; 514-386-3772; hoodriverwines@gorge.net.

**MAKES ABOUT 1½ CUPS**

**1 pint (2 cups) fresh berries, rinsed and drained, or frozen berries, thawed with juice**
**¼ to ⅓ cup sugar, to taste**
**1 to 2 teaspoons fresh lemon juice**

Put all the ingredients together in a food processor fitted with the steel blade or a blender and puree until smooth. If the berries have large seeds, remove them by pushing the puree through a fine strainer with the back of a spatula. Purees will keep covered for up to a week in the refrigerator.

*Note:* If you prefer, puree only 1 cup of berries, then carefully stir the remaining cup of whole berries into the puree to finish the sauce.

*Variations:* Try a combination of berries for an interesting sauce:

**1 cup marionberries or other blackberries and 1 cup raspberries, plus a splash of framboise**

**1 cup boysenberries and 1 cup loganberries**

**½ cup red currants and 1½ cups raspberries**

## *Berry Oils*

Several years ago *Saveur* magazine ran a short story on cranberry oil, an idea I've adopted for my own kitchen. These jewel-colored oils are simple to make, healthy to eat, and add a unique touch to what could otherwise be an ordinary dish. You can make them with any berries, but I like to use berries with a higher acid content—loganberries, most varieties of the green gooseberries, cranberries, lingonberries, raspberries, red and black currants, and marionberries—because they take the place of lemon juice.

Berry oils can be whisked with a few drops of lemon or lime juice and used as a salad dressing or drizzled over grilled fish (like salmon), poultry, rabbit, or roasted or steamed vegetables. Let your imagination be your guide.

**MAKES ½ CUP**

**1 cup fresh cranberries, rinsed and drained**

**½ cup high-quality extra virgin olive oil**

Put the cranberries and olive oil in a food processor and process for 30 seconds or until the cranberries are chopped. Pour into a small bowl, cover, and macerate in the refrigerator for at least 8 hours and up to 2 days. Strain the mixture and discard the pulp. Store in a covered jar in the refrigerator for up to 1 month.

### Birth of the West Coast Cranberry Industry

The commercial cranberry industry began on the West Coast in 1885, when Charles McFarlin planted along the southern Oregon coast vines that he had brought from Cape Cod. The cultivar was named 'McFarlin' in his honor, and it is still the primary cranberry cultivar grown in Oregon. Today the Coquille Indians are growing lovely organic cranberries near the same area with plantings of the 'Stevens' cultivar. These dark purple cranberries are not only larger than other types of cranberries but sweeter, too, making them perfect for fresh eating, such as in a tossed green salad.

## *Bing Cherry–Raspberry Sauce with Cinnamon Schnapps*

Fresh raspberries and cherries are both at the peak of their season in early to midsummer. When they are cooked together with a splash of cinnamon schnapps, they make a sassy sauce that elevates plain pound cake with vanilla ice cream to another level.

**MAKES 3 CUPS**

**2 cups (1 pint) fresh Bing cherries or other dark, sweet cherries, pitted and coarsely chopped**
**1 pint (2 cups) fresh raspberries, rinsed and drained**
**¼ cup sugar**
**2 tablespoons cinnamon schnapps**

In a medium saucepan, stir together the Bing cherries, 1 cup of the raspberries, and the sugar. Bring to a boil, then reduce the heat to simmer. Cook until the cherries begin to soften, about 20 minutes. Remove from the heat and stir in the remaining cup of raspberries and the cinnamon schnapps. Serve warm or at room temperature over ice cream or pound cake (or both).

## *Black Currant Coulis*

I learned how to make black currant coulis from Tommie van de Kamp, who owns Queener Fruit Farm with her husband, Peter. They raise currants, which Tommie sells locally and by mail order. Black currants can be overpowering raw, but heating them magically mellows out the fruit's fine flavor and creates a complex sauce that is divine. Use it over red meat, duck, or other game birds, poached pears, drizzled on panna cotta (page 243), cheesecake, ice cream, or custard. See Raspberry Russian Cream (page 246). But remember, a little bit goes a long way. You can buy black currant coulis from Queener Fruit Farm, 40385 Queener Drive, Scio, OR 97374; 888-593-3637; pvdkfarm@wvi.com (black currant coulis, red and black currant jelly, black currant jam and spread, and frozen black currants).

**MAKES ABOUT 1 CUP**

**1 pint (2 cups) fresh black currants, rinsed and drained, or frozen black currants (it's not necessary to remove them from the strig because the sauce is strained after it is cooked)**
**4 to 5 tablespoons sugar, to taste**

Put the black currants and 1 cup water in a small saucepan and bring to a boil. Reduce the heat to medium and gently crush the berries with the back of a spoon as they simmer. Cook for about 10 minutes, until the sauce thickens. Puree the mixture by pushing it through a fine strainer with the back of a spoon. Stir in the sugar while the mixture is still warm. Cool and store covered in the refrigerator for up to 2 weeks.

## *Boysenberry Applesauce*

Berry applesauce is intensely flavorful and a good dish to accompany pork or game meats, such as quail or venison. I love the flavor of boysenberries, but they have large seeds, making it necessary to seed the berries before adding them. The other berries have seeds, too, but they are smaller and not noticeable. Serve warm or at room temperature.

**MAKES 4 SERVINGS**

- **½ pint (1 cup) fresh boysenberries, rinsed, drained, pureed, and seeded (see page 70), or other fresh blackberries, such as marionberries, loganberries, or black currants, rinsed and drained, or frozen berries**
- **2½ pounds Golden Delicious apples, peeled, cored, and cut into eighths**
- **1 to 2 tablespoons honey, to taste**
- **2 lemon slices**

If you're using boysenberries, put all the ingredients in a medium pot over medium-high heat with ½ cup water. Bring to a boil, then reduce the heat to simmer, cover, and cook until the apples are soft, about 15 minutes. For other fresh or frozen berries, gently stir them in at the end of the cooking time. Heat frozen berries until they are completely thawed. If there is still a lot of liquid with the apples, remove the lid and raise the heat for a few minutes, but watch that the mixture doesn't burn. Remove the lemon slices just before serving.

## *Cumberland Sauce*

Cumberland sauce is a classic British accompaniment for wild game, especially birds. It is especially good on any type of poultry, domestic or wild, and ham.

**MAKES ABOUT 1¼ CUPS**

- **½ cup red currant jelly or other berry jelly**
- **⅓ cup fresh orange juice**
- **2 tablespoons fresh lemon juice**
- **1 teaspoon cornstarch**
- **½ cup Madeira or port**
- **1 tablespoon grated orange zest**
- **1 tablespoon Grand Marnier**

Combine the jelly, orange juice, and lemon juice together in a saucepan over low heat. Stir the cornstarch into ¼ cup of the Madeira and whisk into the jelly mixture. Continue stirring until the mixture starts to thicken. Stir in the remaining Madeira, the orange zest, and the Grand Marnier. The sauce will keep covered in the refrigerator for up to 1 week.

*Variation:* Substitute ¾ cup whole cranberry sauce for the berry jelly. Serve with turkey or other poultry dishes.

## *Huckleberry Sauce with Lime Juice*

There are few things better than eating homemade pancakes, slathered in butter and topped with a warm huckleberry sauce. This recipe is just right—not too thick and not too sweet, with a perfect acid balance from the fresh citrus juices. It is also scrumptious warmed and poured over vanilla ice cream. The recipe makes a lot, but remember: it is also the ultimate hostess gift.

**MAKES ABOUT 3 PINTS**

**1½ cups sugar**
**¼ cup cornstarch**
**2½ pints (5 cups) fresh huckleberries or wild blueberries, rinsed and drained, or frozen huckleberries**
**2 tablespoons fresh orange juice**
**2 tablespoons fresh lime juice (from 1 lime)**

Blend the sugar and cornstarch together in a medium saucepan until the mixture is smooth. Stir in 2 cups water and put the pan over medium heat. Add the berries and citrus juices and bring the mixture just to a boil, stirring gently. Immediately turn the heat down and cook for a few more minutes, until the sauce thickens slightly. It should be the consistency of maple syrup.

Store any leftover sauce in a covered container in the refrigerator for up to a week. Pour into pint jars, adjust the caps, and process in a boiling water bath for 10 minutes.
I have frozen this sauce for up to a month, but it's so easy to make I usually prepare it fresh as I need it.

### Good Berries, Squishers, and Pruners

Eric Schramn lives in Mendocino, California, where for the past 20 years he and his crew have picked coastal huckleberries from August 15 to December 15. They average 5,000 to 6,000 pounds a year, selling some of the berries locally, while shipping the bulk of them to restaurants in San Francisco, New York, and Los Angeles.

"It's not much different than the 1800s," he told me, "except schooners hauled the huckleberries from Mendocino to San Francisco in those days. Now I put them in my truck and deliver them."

He describes huckleberries as either "good" berries, ones that are firm and full without cracks or discoloration; "squishers," which are soft and old and will make your fingers purple; or "pruners," shriveled huckleberries that have dried up on the bush like raisins. Naturally, when you are picking huckleberries the goal is to get a bucketful of "good berries." Leave the rest for the birds.

## *Juneberry-Raspberry Ice Cream Topping*

Dan and Betty Kelner, major suppliers of Juneberry stock for growers, make this sauce to serve over ice cream. I have added a little fresh lime juice to intensify the flavors.

**MAKES ABOUT 2 CUPS**

- **2 pints (4 cups) fresh Juneberries, blueberries, or huckleberries, rinsed and drained, or frozen Juneberries**
- **½ pint (1 cup) fresh raspberries, rinsed and drained, or frozen raspberries**
- **1½ tablespoons cornstarch**
- **1½ cups sugar**
- **2 tablespoons fresh lemon juice**
- **1 teaspoon fresh lime juice**
- **1 teaspoon almond extract**

Put the Juneberries in a saucepan with 2 cups water and bring to a boil. Cook for 3 minutes, then add the raspberries and cook for another 3 minutes. Turn the heat down to simmer.

Blend the cornstarch and sugar and slowly stir it into the berries. Continue cooking until thick and clear, about 3 minutes. Stir in the lemon and lime juice and almond extract and let cool. Store covered in the refrigerator for up to 1 week.

## *Raspberry Chipotle Sauce*

Chipotles are smoked jalapeño peppers with characteristic fruity undertones that complement the dusky flavors of many berries. I use the sauce as a glaze for grilled meat, including game and game birds, chicken, and turkey. It's also good spooned over cream cheese and served on crackers for an appetizer. I've even used it on a breakfast burrito with scrambled egg and smoky bacon.

**MAKES 1½ CUPS**

**1½ to 2 pints (3 to 4 cups) fresh raspberries or blackberries, rinsed and drained, or frozen raspberries, thawed with juice**
**1 to 3 chipotles packed in adobo sauce, plus 1 teaspoon of the sauce**
**2 tablespoons fresh lemon juice**
**2 tablespoons powdered pectin**
**¾ cup sugar**
**1 to 2 teaspoons unsalted butter**
**¾ teaspoon baking soda**

Heat a ¾- to 1-pint glass bottle.

Puree 3 cups of the berries with the chiles and sauce. You will need 1½ cups puree. If you are short, puree more berries and add to the mixture until you have 1½ cups.

Pour the puree and lemon juice into a large, nonreactive pan. Add the pectin and mix thoroughly. Put the pan over high heat and bring to a full rolling boil, stirring constantly. Stir in the sugar, mix well, and bring back once again to a full rolling boil. Stir in the butter and baking soda. If there is foam, it will disappear in a few minutes. Fill the bottle using a funnel. Store in the refrigerator for up to 1 month or, for storing in your pantry, process in a boiling water canner (see page 161) for 10 minutes.

## *Savory Boysenberry-Juniper Vinegar*

This blackberry vinegar is full bodied and complex flavored. I use it for deglazing the pan when I'm cooking game, as well as for whisking with extra virgin olive oil (3 parts oil to 1 part vinegar) when I want a hearty salad dressing. Cabernet Sauvignon vinegar makes an especially flavorful berry vinegar. I buy it at the grocery store.

**MAKES ABOUT 3 CUPS**

**2 cups red wine vinegar**
**1½ pints (3 cups) fresh boysenberries or other blackberries, rinsed and drained, or frozen boysenberries**
**½ teaspoon cracked black pepper**
**1 teaspoon cracked juniper berries**

Have a 1-quart bottle ready.

Put all the ingredients in a nonreactive saucepan and bring to a boil. Turn the heat to medium and simmer for another 5 minutes. Remove from the heat and let cool. Strain and pour the vinegar through a funnel into the bottle and attach the lid. It will keep indefinitely.

## *Stewed Blackberries with Vanilla and Cinnamon*

Pat Fusco grew up in Georgia, enjoying the fruits of labor from her grandfather's garden. "Blackberries were a sign of high summer. Boppa grew large ones called 'dewberries' at the back of his garden, and there were patches of smaller wild berries in vacant lots and along country roads all around us. When they weren't made into cobblers, jam, or jelly, they were enjoyed in a kind of compote referred to as *stewed blackberries.* This method of gentle cooking enhances their dusky sweetness. The compote is a delicious simple dessert served warm with some cookies or plain cake or cold over ice cream or fruits. It is especially lovely over sliced ripe peaches," she said. Try using other berries as well.

**MAKES 4 SERVINGS**

**¼ to ¾ cup sugar, to taste**
**1 pint (2 cups) fresh marionberries or other blackberries, rinsed and drained, or frozen marionberries, thawed in a single layer on a paper towel for 20 minutes**
**1 half vanilla bean, split**
**One 2- to 3-inch cinnamon stick**

Mix 1 cup water and the sugar in a saucepan, bring to a boil, and boil for 10 minutes. Add the berries, vanilla bean, and cinnamon stick to the syrup. When the mixture almost returns to a boil, turn the heat down and simmer for 10 minutes. Remove the spices before serving.

## *Tomatillo Salsa*

Tomatillos look like green cherry tomatoes in a brown, papery husk. In Mexico, where they are called *tomate verde,* tomatillos have been a kitchen staple for centuries. Their tart flavor makes a perfect accompaniment to seafood and grilled meats. In this recipe I poach them first with the garlic to slightly mellow out their flavors.

**MAKES 1½ CUPS**

**½ pound (about 8) tomatillos**
**1 garlic clove, peeled**

**3 tablespoons chopped sweet onion such as Walla Walla**
**⅓ cup lightly packed cilantro leaves**
**1 jalapeño pepper, seeded and finely chopped**
**½ teaspoon coarse salt**

Peel the paper husk off the tomatillos and rinse the fruit. Put the tomatillos in a saucepan with the garlic clove and cover completely with cold water. Bring to a boil. Reduce the heat to simmer and cook for 5 to 7 minutes or until the tomatillos turn olive colored and become slightly tender. Drain and chop the tomatillos and garlic.

Toss together the tomatillos and garlic with the onion, cilantro, jalapeño, and salt. Serve as a sauce to accompany seafood, grilled meats, or Mexican dishes, such as tacos or huevos rancheros. Serve immediately or up to 3 hours later. After that the salsa loses its bright color and flavor.

## *Triple Red Berry Sauce*

The combination of these three jewel-colored berries produces a brilliant crimson sauce with a flavor so intense it almost sparkles on the plate. Serve it over vanilla ice cream, Raspberry Russian Cream (page 246), or Lemon Curd Cake (page 232).

**MAKES ⅔ CUP**

**¼ cup fresh cranberries, rinsed and drained, or frozen cranberries, thawed**
**½ cup fresh raspberries, rinsed and drained, or frozen raspberries, thawed with juice**
**Heaping ½ cup fresh strawberries, rinsed and drained, or frozen strawberries, thawed with juice**
**2½ teaspoons sugar**
**1 teaspoon framboise**

Puree the cranberries, raspberries, strawberries, sugar, and framboise together in a food processor or blender until smooth. Store covered in the refrigerator for 3 to 4 days.

# PUTTING BERRIES BY

Stocking my pantry shelves with homemade preserves is one of the most satisfying things I do in the kitchen. But to make good preserves it's essential to know a little bit about pectin, a naturally occurring chemical in many fruits and an important constituent in berries. Pectin is soluble fiber in the berries' juices and contributes to their firmness; the harder the berry, the higher the pectin level. Raspberries, for instance, have a lower pectin content than blackberries and consequently are much softer. Berries high in pectin include green gooseberries, underripe blackberries and boysenberries, cranberries, and currants. These high-pectin berries make thick and luscious jams when they are cooked down slowly with sugar.

For the best results, blend these high-pectin berries with sugar and let the mixture sit at room temperature for at least 1 hour or even overnight. This important step releases the berries' juices ahead of cooking, which helps maintain the fine flavor that can easily be destroyed by high heat.

Other fruits, like raspberries, elderberries, and strawberries, need additional pectin, either by being mixed with high-pectin fruit, such as red currants or underripe blackberries, or through the addition of commercial pectin, in liquid or powdered form. Carefully follow the instructions that come with the package of pectin to ensure success. Success with jams and jellies depends on a delicate balance among the fruit, pectin, sugar, and acid. The commercial packages of pectin are formulated to work with the quantities of sugar and fruit they call for, and there is not a lot of room to deviate.

Note also that powdered and liquid forms of pectin do not have interchangeable recipes.

Freezer jam is another alternative for berry cooks. It has the advantage of preserving the natural taste of the fruit because little, if any, cooking is required, so the heat can't destroy the fruits' fine flavor. The downfall has always been that freezer jams used large quantities of sugar in proportion to fruit. Ball has recently developed a new freezer jam pectin (Fruit Jell Freezer Jam Pectin) that requires no cooking and only 1½ cups of sugar for 4 cups berries. Look for it at the grocery store with the canning jars and other commercial pectins.

Whichever method you choose, remember, the secret to making blue-ribbon preserves is to buy only peak-of-the-season berries, which will produce the best color, flavor, and consistency. Capturing that little bit of summer in a jar goes a long way in the dark days of winter.

## PROCESSING PRESERVES

Making preserves is not difficult, but it's essential to be organized before you start. Wash the required amount of jars in the dishwasher or by hand (it's not necessary to sterilize them if the preserve is going to be processed at least 10 minutes). Keep the rinsed jars warm in the dishwasher or inverted on a towel-lined cookie sheet in an oven set on the lowest setting.

Prepare the lids according to the manufacturer's directions—they vary.

Fit a large, lidded pot with a wire rack, or use a water canner. Add approximately enough water to come up 2 inches above the tops of the jars. Bring the water almost to a boil.

Using a wide-mouth funnel, ladle the hot preserves into the jars, leaving ¼-inch head space to allow for expansion during processing. Attach the lids and screw bands. Place the filled and covered hot jars onto the rack. (A jar lifter, available at cookware shops and at groceries during canning season, is helpful for safely moving the jars to and from the hot water.) If necessary, add more water to cover the jars by 2 inches. Cover the pot and bring to a full boil. Begin timing for 10 minutes. If preserves have been put into sterilized jars, the processing time is 5 minutes. Turn the heat off and carefully remove the jars from the canner using the jar lifter. Place the jars on a cookie rack or towel to cool with at least an inch of space between the jars. Cool the jars away from drafts for 12 to 24 hours.

When the jars are cool, check the seal. The center of the lid should have been pulled down by the vacuum created during processing, and will be slightly concave. Remove the screw bands, wash off the outside of the jar, and store in a cool, dark, dry place.

## TESTING JAMS AND JELLIES

So much of making preserves is trial and error because all berries are different. Some have more sugar, others more pectin, and some berries react differently when cooked earlier in the season than later. Strawberries, for instance, have more pectin when they first come to the market in the springtime than later in the season because the plants are older and weaker. The good news is that even if your preserves are a little runny, you can use them for syrup. Here are two standard rules to help guide you:

1. **Chill a small plate in the freezer or refrigerator. Pour a small amount of boiling jelly onto the cold plate and put it back in the freezer for a few minutes. If the mixture becomes thick, it is done.**
2. **Or dip a cool metal spoon into the boiling jam mixture. Raise it 12 inches or so above the pot and out of the steam and turn it so the jam runs off the side. If the jam forms two drops that flow together and fall off the spoon as one sheet, it should be done.**

### *Blueberry-Loganberry Ginger Jam*

Blueberries and loganberries just seem to complement each other, the tartness of the loganberries bringing out the best in the mild-flavored blueberries. The ginger adds a subtle, pleasing taste to this jam.

**MAKES THREE 8-OUNCE JARS**

**1 pint (2 cups) fresh loganberries or other blackberries, rinsed and drained, or frozen loganberries, thawed with juice**
**1 pint (2 cups) fresh blueberries, rinsed and drained, or frozen blueberries, thawed with juice**
**2 cups sugar**
**1½ teaspoons ground ginger**
**2 teaspoons unsalted butter**

Have hot and washed three 8-ounce jars. Prepare the lids according to the manufacturer's directions.

Combine the fruit, sugar, and ginger in a medium saucepan. Use a potato masher to crush the fruit thoroughly. Let sit at room temperature for 1 to 2 hours, stirring occasionally to help the sugar dissolve.

Add the butter, and bring to a boil, stirring often to prevent burning. Reduce the heat to medium-low and simmer for 30 to 40 minutes, until the jam thickens. (To test, see page 162.)

Ladle the jam through a wide-mouth funnel into jars. Attach the lids and process in a boiling water canner for 10 minutes (see page 161).

## *Raspberry–Red Currant Jam*

Cooked red raspberries and red currants produce a magnificent crimson red jam that is flavorful without being overly sweet. Red currants look like clusters of ruby pearls, and though they have little flavor, their high acid content intensifies the raspberry taste, and their high pectin level produces a thick, delicious jam. I seed half of the mixture, but you can seed all of it if you like.

**MAKES TWO 8-OUNCE JARS**

**1½ pints (3 cups) fresh red currants, rinsed and drained, or frozen currants, thawed with juice**
**1 pint (2 cups) fresh red raspberries, rinsed and drained, or frozen raspberries, thawed with juice**
**1¼ cups sugar**
**1½ tablespoons fresh lemon juice**
**2 teaspoons unsalted butter**

Have washed and hot two 8-ounce jars. Prepare the lids according to the manufacturer's directions.

Crush half of the fruit and push it through a fine strainer with the back of a spatula to remove the seeds. Combine the seedless berry puree, the remaining berries, sugar, and lemon juice in a heavy, nonreactive skillet. Let the mixture stand for at least 1 hour and up to 2 hours.

Add the butter and bring the mixture to a boil, stirring often to prevent burning. Reduce the heat to medium-low and simmer for 35 to 40 minutes, until the jam thickens. (To test, see page 162.) Ladle the jam through a wide-mouth funnel into the jars. Attach the lids and process in a boiling water canner for 10 minutes (see page 161).

## *Strawberry-Rhubarb Cardamom Jam*

Cardamom is an ancient spice with an exotic flavor that binds the fruitiness of the strawberries and the tangy sweet-and-sour taste of the rhubarb in this jam recipe.

## Bar-le-Duc Jelly

In the fourteenth century, nuns in the French village of Bar-le-Duc, near the German border, made the town famous by selling their white currant jelly. They painstakingly removed the seeds by hand, using the sharpened tip of a goose feather. The jelly was so expensive that only the nobility enjoyed it. Today Bar-le-Duc jelly is still being produced in the same town. Order it from Crossings, 4 New Street, Worcester, MA 01605; 800-209-6141; www.crossingsfrenchfood.com.

**MAKES THREE 8-OUNCE JARS**

**1½ pints (3 cups) fresh strawberries, rinsed and drained, or frozen strawberries, thawed with juice**
**½ pound rhubarb, chopped (2 cups)**
**2 cups sugar**
**1¼ teaspoons ground cardamom**
**1 teaspoon unsalted butter**

Have washed and hot three 8-ounce jars. Prepare the lids according to the manufacturer's directions.

Combine the fruit, sugar, and cardamom in a heavy, nonreactive skillet. Use a potato masher to crush the fruit thoroughly. Let sit at room temperature for 1 to 2 hours, stirring occasionally to help the sugar dissolve.

Add the butter and bring the mixture to a boil, stirring often to prevent burning. Reduce the heat to medium-low and simmer for 30 to 40 minutes, until the jam thickens. (To test, see page 162.)

Ladle the jam through a wide-mouth funnel into jars. Attach the lids and process in a boiling water canner for 10 minutes (see page 161).

## *Strawberry–Sweet Plum Jam*

Marie Simmons, author and columnist for *Bon Appétit,* gave me this tasty jam recipe. Strawberries and plums are cooked down into a thick, deeply flavorful preserve that is just right for English muffins or homemade biscuits.

**MAKES FIVE 8-OUNCE JARS**

**1 pound ripe red plums, halved, pitted, and cut into ½-inch pieces**
**2 pints (4 cups) ripe fresh strawberries, rinsed and drained, or frozen strawberries, thawed with juice**
**2½ cups sugar**
**¼ cup fresh lime juice (from about 2 limes)**
**1 teaspoon unsalted butter**

Have washed and hot five 8-ounce jars. Prepare the lids according to the manufacturer's directions.

Combine the plums, strawberries, sugar, and lime juice in a heavy, nonreactive skillet. Use a potato masher to crush the fruit thoroughly. Let the mixture stand for at least 1 hour and up to 2 hours, stirring occasionally.

Add the butter and bring the mixture to a boil, stirring often to prevent burning. Reduce the heat to medium-low and cook for 30 to 40 minutes, until the jam thickens. (To test, see page 162.)

Ladle the jam through a wide-mouth funnel into the jars. Attach the lids, leaving ¼-inch headspace, and process in a boiling water canner for 10 minutes (see page 161).

## *Sunshine Berry Preserves*

This age-old method for making preserves was a favorite of the early Oregon settlers. The berries are cooked briefly and then set out in the sunshine. The intense summer heat evaporates the juices, concentrating their penetrating flavor and creating a preserve that is unrivaled. If the preserves don't thicken after 7 or 8 hours, put the berries in a shallow pan or ovenproof platter and place in the oven at 200°F. Stir every 20 to 30 minutes, until thickened. This recipe works only when there is low humidity and with fresh berries; frozen berries are too juicy.

**MAKES ABOUT SIX 8-OUNCE JARS**

**1½ pints (about 3 cups) berries, rinsed and drained**
**2½ to 3 cups sugar, to taste**
**2 tablespoons fresh lemon juice (from 1 lemon)**

Put the berries, sugar, and lemon juice in a saucepan and stir gently to mix. Cover and let stand for 1 hour at room temperature. Set the pan over medium-high heat and bring to a boil. Remove the lid and boil vigorously for 8 minutes. Remove the pan from the heat and let sit for 30 minutes uncovered.

Pour the mixture into a 9 × 13-inch pan and cover with plastic wrap, leaving a small opening along one side. Put the pan in a sunny spot and stir the mixture every hour.

Remove the preserves from the sun when the mixture has thickened to about the consistency of maple syrup. It will take from 5 to 10 hours, depending on how hot it is and the type of berries you are using.

Wash six 8-ounce jars and lids (see page 161).

Store preserves in covered jars in the refrigerator for up to 1 month or pack in freezer containers to within 1 inch of the top. Cover and freeze for up to 1 year, or process following the directions on page 161.

### Muir's Manzanitas

"The manzanita never fails to attract particular attention. The species common in the Valley is usually about six or seven feet high, round-headed with innumerable branches, red or chocolate-color bark, pale green leaves set on edge, and a rich profusion of small, pink, narrow-throated, urn-shaped flowers, like those of arbutus. The knotty, crooked, angular branches are about as rigid as bones, and the red bark is so thin and smooth on both trunk and branches, they look as if they had been peeled and polished and painted. In the spring large areas on the mountain up to a height of eight or nine thousand feet are brightened with the rosy flowers, and in autumn with their red fruit. The pleasantly acid berries, about the size of peas, look like little apples, and a hungry mountaineer is glad to eat them, though half their bulk is made up of hard seeds. Indians, bears, coyotes, foxes, birds and other mountain people live on them for weeks and months."

—John Muir, 1912

## *Deer Isle Wild Blueberry Preserves*

Brooke Dojny is a columnist for *Bon Appétit* and the author of about a dozen cookbooks, including *The New England Cookbook,* the source of this recipe. She is a native

New Englander who divides her time between Connecticut and her lovely home overlooking Eggemoggin Reach, near Deer Isle, Maine. When she makes preserves with the succulent wild blueberries from the nearby barrens, she uses her sister Martha's recipe, cooking the berries with cinnamon to enhance their flavor. You can buy wild blueberries from the Wild Blueberry Association of North America, P.O. Box 100, Old Town, Maine 04468-0100; 207-581-3499; www.wildblueberries.com.

**MAKES ABOUT TWELVE 8-OUNCE JARS**

**2 quarts (8 cups) wild or cultivated blueberries or huckleberries, rinsed and drained, or frozen wild blueberries, thawed with juice**
**7 cups sugar**
**3 tablespoons fresh lemon juice**
**½ teaspoon unsalted butter**
**One 2- to 3-inch cinnamon stick, broken in half or thirds**
**Two 3-ounce pouches liquid fruit pectin**

Have washed and hot twelve 8-ounce jars and lids.

Put the berries in a large pot and crush with a potato masher. Add the sugar, lemon juice, butter, and cinnamon stick and bring to a boil, stirring constantly. Add the pectin and return to a boil. Boil for 1 minute, stirring constantly. Remove from the heat and discard the cinnamon stick. Ladle the blueberry mixture through a wide-mouth funnel into the jars. Attach the lids and process in a boiling water canner for 10 minutes (see page 161).

## *Bumbleberry Jam*

This recipe comes from a friend of mine, Shannon Robbins, who is a passionate gardener and cook. Shannon and her grandmother have every berry known that is grown in Oregon (and that's a lot) stashed away in the freezer for making preserves when fresh berries aren't available. Her recipe is called Bumbleberry Jam because it's made with a mixture of berries.

**MAKES EIGHT 8-OUNCE JARS**

**½ pint (1 cup) fresh raspberries, rinsed and drained, or frozen raspberries, thawed with juice**
**¾ pint (1½ cups) fresh marionberries or other blackberries, rinsed and drained, or frozen marionberries, thawed with juice**
**¾ pint (1½ cups) fresh strawberries, rinsed and drained, or frozen strawberries, thawed with juice**
**7 cups sugar**

**1 tablespoon fresh lime juice (from about 1 lime)**
**¼ teaspoon freshly ground pepper**
**One 3-ounce pouch liquid fruit pectin**

Have washed and hot eight 8-ounce jars. Prepare lids according to the manufacturer's directions.

Put the fruit in a nonreactive pot with the sugar, lime juice, and pepper. Stir to blend and let sit at room temperature for 15 minutes. Put the pot over medium heat and bring to a boil. Stir in the pectin and bring back to a boil. Cook for 1 minute. Remove from the heat and skim off any foam.

Ladle the jam through a wide-mouth funnel into jars. Attach the lids, leaving ¼-inch headspace, and process in a boiling water canner for 10 minutes (see page 161).

## *Blueberry–Toasted Walnut Conserve*

In Russia this is one of the popular methods for preserving the golden sea buckthorn berries. The toasted walnuts add a rich, complex taste that complements the berries. I use blueberries and I have added a cinnamon stick and cloves for additional flavor.

**MAKES THREE 8-OUNCE JARS**

**1 cup (about 6 ounces) walnuts, toasted (see page 73) and finely ground**
**2 cups sugar**
**1 cinnamon stick**
**5 cloves**
**1½ pints (3 cups) fresh blueberries, wild blueberries, huckleberries, or sea buckthorn berries, rinsed and drained, or frozen berries, thawed with juice**

Have washed and hot three 8-ounce jars. Prepare lids according to the manufacturer's directions.

Put the ground walnuts in a pan with the sugar, cinnamon stick, and cloves. Stir to mix and bring to a boil. Turn the heat down to simmer and cook for 20 to 25 minutes. Remove the cinnamon stick and cloves with a spoon. Add the berries and continue cooking, stirring frequently, for 15 to 20 more minutes, until the conserve has thickened. (To test, see page 162.)

Ladle the conserve through a wide-mouth funnel into jars. Attach the lids, leaving ¼-inch headspace, and process in a boiling water canner for 10 minutes (see page 161).

*Savannah Pyracantha Jelly*

Pyracantha, which grows wild in the South, makes a fine jelly. This recipe comes from the kitchen of Jane Rainey, who lives in Savannah and makes it every year.

**MAKES ABOUT SEVEN 8-OUNCE JARS**

**2 pints (4 cups) fresh pyracantha berries, rinsed and drained, or frozen pyracantha berries, thawed with juice**
**⅓ cup fresh lemon juice**
**1 cup fresh grapefruit juice**
**One 1.75-ounce box powdered pectin**
**7 cups sugar**

Have washed and hot seven 8-ounce jars. Prepare lids according to the manufacturer's directions.

Bring 1 quart water to a boil in a large pot. Add the berries, bring back to a boil, and boil for 20 minutes, crushing the berries with a potato masher or large wooden spoon as they cook.

Strain through 4 to 6 layers of cheesecloth or through a fine-mesh strainer into a bowl to catch the liquid and let stand until cool. Discard the berries and refrigerate the juice overnight. Strain again the next day. You should have about 2¾ cups juice. (Add a little water if you are short.)

Put the juice in a nonreactive pot with the lemon juice, grapefruit juice, and powdered pectin. Bring to a boil and add the sugar all at once. Return to a rolling boil, stirring constantly, and boil for 1 minute. Remove from the heat and skim off the foam.

Ladle the jelly through a wide-mouth funnel into the jars. Attach the lids and process in a boiling water canner for 10 minutes (see page 161).

### No Funerals Yet

Pyracantha jelly is popular in the South, where several varieties of pyracantha grow wild. When I e-mailed Dr. Jerry Parsons, a horticulture specialist with the Texas Extension Service in San Antonio and professor at Texas A&M University, about the rumors I'd heard about pyracantha berries being inedible, this is what he emphatically wrote back: "The pyracantha is nothing more than a small apple; it is not on any poisonous plant list. Hundreds of people, including me, have made the jelly from this recipe and no funerals yet. You have my permission to use this recipe, which has been used in Texas for over 50 years that I know of myself. To extract the juice, boil 1 pound of berries in ¾ cup of water for 1 minute. Strain the juice through a clean cloth. To 1 cup juice add 1 teaspoon lemon juice and a package of powdered pectin. Bring it to a hard boil; add ¾ cup sugar and continue the rolling boil for 1 minute, stirring constantly. Pour into hot jars. Process in a hot water canner for 10 minutes."

## *Mayhaw Jelly*

Mayhaws are the bright red fruit of the mayhaw tree, which grows in the South. Their flesh produces a delicate-tasting reddish orange jelly the color of fire opals.

**MAKES ABOUT SIX 8-OUNCE JARS**

**3 pounds fresh mayhaw berries, rinsed and drained, or frozen mayhaw berries, thawed with juice**
**One 1.75-ounce box powdered pectin**
**5½ cups sugar**

Have washed and hot six 8-ounce jars. Prepare lids according to the manufacturer's directions.

To make the juice, put the berries in a deep pot and crush with a potato masher. Pour in 6 cups water. Cover and bring to a boil. Reduce the heat to simmer and cook for 20 minutes. Strain through 3 layers of cheesecloth or a fine-mesh strainer. You will need 4 cups juice. (Add water if you don't have quite enough.)

Pour the mayhaw juice into a noncorrosive pan and combine with the pectin over medium heat. Bring to a hard boil, stirring occasionally. Add the sugar all at once. Continue stirring, and when the mixture returns to a full rolling boil, cook for 5 more minutes, stirring constantly. Remove from the heat and skim off the foam with a metal spoon.

Ladle the jelly through a wide-mouth funnel into jars. Attach the lids and process in a boiling water canner for 10 minutes (see page 161).

## An Enterprising Mayhaw Business

Joy Jinks is a social worker who lives in Colquitt, a rural agricultural community in the far southwest corner of Georgia. In 1991 she and three of her friends each put in $300 to help the local economy to develop some regional food products.

One of their ideas was to start a mayhaw jelly business. Mayhaws are the fruit of the may hawthorn tree, which grows in the bogs and swamplands of the southern United States from east Texas to Florida. It grows abundantly in Colquitt and the surrounding area of Miller County, where mothers and grandmothers have been making jellies with these prized tart red fruits for years.

When the berries were ripe in May, the enterprising foursome put the word out, and soon townsfolk began delivering mayhaws to their doorstep by the bucketfuls. They paid the pickers, many of them previously unemployed, with two-dollar bills, and it didn't take long for the business community to see the impact of this start-up business on the local economy.

The following Christmas they printed a flyer touting their jelly and sent it to local companies listed in the telephone directory. The women were amazed when, in just a few days, they were overwhelmed with orders for mayhaw jelly.

With the road to success just around the corner, they headed to New York in January to market their products at the Fancy Food Show. When they arrived at the Javits Center to set up their booth, they were heartbroken to discover their boxes had not arrived.

Not to be defeated, they made a cardboard sign and sat it on the table. It said, "Our product is lost on a truck in New York City." You can imagine their husbands' surprise that night in Colquitt when they turned on the NBC national news and saw their wives and their sign! "When we started, all we had was sheer audacity. We were a great team because we brought out each other's strengths and creativity. We didn't know it couldn't be done," Joy told me.

After nine years they sold their business, but the new owners have kept the same name. The Mayhaw Tree, 105 Mitcham Circle, Tiger, GA 30576; 800-2Mayhaw; www.mayhawtree.com.

## *Black Currant Conserve*

Darra Goldstein, a professor of Russian at Williams College, shared this recipe from her fascinating cookbook *A Taste of Russia.* Darra lived and studied in Moscow for a year. She says, "Black currant conserve was one of my favorite things to eat during those long Russian winters when there was virtually no fresh fruit to be had. The Russians love the dusky flavor of the currants. Many people grow them at their country dachas and put them up for the winter. Mounds of currants are also for sale at green markets throughout the city. The proportions to use for this relish are one part black currants to two parts sugar—or less, as the Russians have a notorious sweet tooth."

**MAKES THREE 8-OUNCE JARS**

**½ pint (1 cup) fresh or frozen black currants, rinsed and drained**
**2 cups sugar**

Have sterilized three 8-ounce jars. Prepare lids according to the manufacturer's directions.

Put the currants and sugar in a food processor fitted with the steel blade. Pulse 10 to 12 times to grind coarsely together. Pack into sterilized jars and store in the refrigerator for 1 month before eating. This conserve will keep for about 3 months.

## *Blackberry-Chile-Mint Preserves*

Next time you grill a leg of lamb, make this spicy preserve as an accompaniment in place of mint jelly. The recipe comes from chefs James Keeney and Jim Borovicaka, who served it with their Jalapenó-Stuffed Leg of Lamb (page 142) when they won first place in the 2002 Lamb Cook-Off contest held in Canby, Oregon. The pleasing mint and pepper flavors are perfect for cutting through the richness of the meat. Try it with grilled lamb chops and duck, too.

**MAKES SEVEN TO EIGHT 8-OUNCE JARS**

**4 pints (8 cups) fresh marionberries or other blackberries, rinsed and drained, or frozen mari onberries, thawed with juice**
**7 cups sugar**
**3 jalapeño peppers, seeded and finely chopped**
**1 serrano pepper, seeded and finely chopped**
**1 teaspoon unsalted butter**
**⅓ cup loosely packed fresh mint leaves**
**One 3-ounce pouch liquid fruit pectin**

Have washed and hot eight 8-ounce jars. Prepare lids according to the manufacturer's directions.

Combine the berries and sugar in a pot and let macerate for 15 minutes at room temperature. Set the pot over medium heat and, when the mixture is warm, add the peppers. Bring to a boil, stirring constantly, and add the butter to stop the foaming. When the mixture reaches a rolling boil (one that can't be stirred down), stir in the mint and pectin. Return to a rolling boil and cook for 1 more minute. Ladle the jam through a wide-mouth funnel into the hot jars. Process in a boiling water canner for 10 minutes (see page 161).

*Note:* If you don't have time to make the preserves from scratch, try the following. The chipotles will add a rich, smoky flavor.

**1 cup blackberry jam**
**2 chipotle chiles packed in adobo sauce, finely chopped**
**1 teaspoon finely chopped fresh mint**

Stir the jam, chiles, and mint together and let sit for at least 1 hour before serving.

## *Gooseberry Cheese*

Gooseberry cheese is the result of an ancient method of preserving. The berries are cooked with sugar until most of the water evaporates, leaving a thick, concentrated pulp, traditionally called a cheese. In England these were kept in the pantry in wide-mouth oiled jars, and a slice was commonly served as an accompaniment to meats. While gooseberry cheese is no longer common, I wouldn't be without it anymore. The gooseberry season is short, so this way I can enjoy them all year long.

I make gooseberry cheese once a summer when gooseberries are at their peak and keep the jar in the refrigerator. I use it as an alternate filling in Sautéed Filo Pastry Stuffed with Blackberries and Mascarpone (page 239) and as a condiment with game meats, smoked poultry, and aged hard cheese, like white cheddar.

**MAKES ONE 8-OUNCE JAR**

**1 pint (2 cups) fresh gooseberries, rinsed and drained, or frozen gooseberries thawed with juice**
**1 cup sugar**

Have washed one 8-ounce jar and lid. Put the gooseberries and sugar in a saucepan and cook over medium heat until the mixture pulls away from the sides of the pan and has been reduced to about 1 cup. Pour into a small jar and cover. It will keep in the refrigerator for up to a year.

> "The running blackberry would adorn the parlors of heaven."
>
> —Walt Whitman

## *Aunt Jennie's Blackberry Syrup*

My aunt Jennie and her husband, Lee, make berry syrups with the magnificent blackberries and strawberries they grow in the field next to their house in Arcata, California. When I asked for the recipe, Lee sent me the following e-mail: "Jennie wants me to tell you about our great attachment for our KitchenAid. It fits the grinder and removes all the seeds and bulk from our blackberries. Sure beats the hand method, and there is no need for a cloth bag. Of course, the easiest part is that she gets me to do it."

If you don't have the attachment, crush the berries and push them through a fine strainer with the back of a spatula. (If you use the KitchenAid Fruit/Vegetable Strainer, available at cookware shops, you'll end up with juice; if you push the crushed berries through a strainer with the back of a spatula, you'll have more of a puree—both will work for this recipe.)

**MAKES FIVE 8-OUNCE JARS**

**¼ cup fresh lemon juice (from about 2 lemons)**
**2 to 2½ pints (4 to 5 cups) fresh blackberries, rinsed and drained, or frozen blackberries, thawed with juice, pureed and seeded (see page 70) to make 3 cups seedless puree**
**One 1.75-ounce box powdered pectin**
**4½ cups sugar**
**1 teaspoon unsalted butter**
**1½ teaspoons baking soda**

Have washed and hot five 8-ounce jars. Prepare lids according to the manufacturer's directions.

Pour the lemon juice and blackberry puree into a large, nonreactive pan. Add the pectin and mix thoroughly. Put the pan over high heat and bring to a full rolling boil, stirring constantly. Stir in the sugar, mix well, and bring once again to a full rolling boil. Add the butter and baking soda, stirring constantly. Immediately fill the jars using a wide-mouth funnel and attach the lids. Process in a boiling water canner for 10 minutes (see page 161).

### Nectar of the Gods

Marlene Parrish, who lives in the black raspberry country of western Pennsylvania, keeps a bucket with a handle in the trunk of her car from the last week of June through the second week of July. She gave me her prized recipe for black raspberry syrup. When she picks the berries and they are "too dry and seedy for pies, make syrup—it's the food of the gods," she says. "Weigh the berries and use an equal amount of sugar. Cook until it thickens slightly (not too thick as you would jam) and put it through cheesecloth to get the syrup. Jar the syrup and seal. Pour it only on state occasions over pound cake or ice cream. This method works equally well for elderberries."

## *Strawberry–Rose Geranium Syrup*

Homemade berry syrups are easy to make and handy to have on hand for guests or to give as hostess gifts. One of my favorites is this Strawberry–Rose Geranium Syrup with its delicate pink color and exotic fruit flavor. Try it drizzled over Dutch Pancakes (page 103) or French toast.

**MAKES FIVE 8-OUNCE BOTTLES**

**2 to 2½ pints (4 to 5 cups) fresh strawberries, rinsed and drained, or frozen strawberries, thawed with juice and pureed (see page 70), to make 3 cups puree**
**¼ cup fresh lemon juice (from about 2 lemons)**
**5 unsprayed rose geranium leaves, torn in half**
**One 1.75-ounce box powdered pectin**
**4½ cups sugar**
**1 teaspoon unsalted butter**
**1½ teaspoons baking soda**

Have washed and hot five 8-ounce bottles. Prepare lids according to the manufacturer's directions.

Put the strawberries, lemon juice, and rose geranium leaves in a large, nonreactive pan. Bring the mixture to a boil and immediately remove from the heat. Let cool and discard the leaves. Add the pectin and mix thoroughly with the fruit puree. Put the pan over high heat and bring to a full rolling boil, stirring constantly. Stir in the sugar, mix well, and bring once again to a full rolling boil. Add the butter and baking soda, stirring constantly. Immediately fill the jars using a funnel and attach the lids. Process in a boiling water canner for 10 minutes (see page 161).

## *Inn at Little Washington's Pickled Cranberries*

"Pickled cranberries can be kept for several months in the refrigerator and improve with age," says Patrick O'Connell, chef and co-owner of the Inn at Little Washington. "These effortless little pickles make a perfect garnish for roast goose, pork, duck, ham, or turkey and add a festive touch to holiday martinis." Or try them on a toothpick in a Cosmopolitan (page 90) or rolled up in filo with mascarpone (page 239).

**MAKES ABOUT EIGHT 8-OUNCE JARS**

**One 12-ounce bag fresh cranberries, rinsed and drained, or frozen berries**
**1¼ cups sugar**
**1¼ cups cider vinegar**
**½ cup apple cider**
**5 to 6 cloves**
**¼ teaspoon whole allspice**
**¼ teaspoon black peppercorns**
**One 2- to 3-inch cinnamon stick**
**1 teaspoon peeled and roughly chopped fresh ginger**

Have washed and hot eight 8-ounce jars and lids. Combine all of the ingredients with ½ cup water in a large saucepan and bring to a rolling boil. Remove from the heat and allow to cool.

Pour the pickled cranberries into decorative glass jars or plastic containers. Cover with the remaining liquid and attach lids. Store in the refrigerator for up to 6 months. They get better the longer you keep them.

## *Spicy Horseradish-Cranberry Relish*

Helen Judd, the mother of one of my good friends, has always loved to cook. When her own mother died in 1973, Helen inherited the oldest restaurant west of the Mississippi, the Hays House in Council Grove, Kansas. (Daniel Boone's cousin Seth Hays started the restaurant in 1857.) Helen and her husband ran the restaurant for the next 20 years. This is one of her favorite cranberry recipes. I particularly like this cranberry relish after it's been frozen and slightly thawed, which makes it convenient for serving at Thanksgiving because it can be prepared weeks in advance. It takes just an hour at room temperature to thaw.

| | |
|---|---|
| **MAKES ABOUT 1 PINT, SERVING 8** | **½ pound (2 cups) fresh cranberries, rinsed and drained**<br>**½ cup (1 small) chopped onion**<br>**⅓ cup sugar**<br>**¾ cup sour cream**<br>**1 to 2 tablespoons prepared horseradish, to taste**<br>**Pinch of coarse salt** |

Put all the ingredients in a food processor or a blender and puree until smooth. Serve immediately or put in a plastic container and freeze for up to 1 month. Thaw 1 hour before serving.

## *Berry Leathers*

Fruit leathers are pliable sheets of pureed fruits that are slowly dried in the sun, the oven, or a food dehydrator. The drying process evaporates the water in the berries, concentrating their intense flavor and creating a naturally nutritious snack. Fruit leathers are loaded with vitamin C and health-benefiting anthocyanins. Stored in plastic wrap, they will keep for up to a year in the refrigerator.

The secret to making fruit leathers successfully is to use perfectly flat cookie sheets so the puree will dry evenly. (This is the voice of experience speaking here. I once made them using an old, uneven pan. The leather dried in some areas and remained thick in others, and I ended up throwing half of it out.)

Keep in mind that the water content of berries varies widely. In Oregon where I live, our local strawberries are grown for processing and are exceptionally juicy, so it takes longer to make fruit leather because there is more liquid to evaporate. Start drying berry leathers in the morning to allow plenty of time.

The leather is completely dried when it pulls away from the plastic wrap easily and holds its shape.

| | |
|---|---|
| **MAKES 2 SHEETS APPROXIMATELY 12 × 17 INCHES** | **Vegetable spray**<br>**8 pints (16 cups) fresh berries, rinsed, drained, pureed, and seeded (see page 70), to make 4 cups seedless puree**<br>**2 to 3 tablespoons honey, to taste** |

If you're using the oven, preheat it to 140°F. If your oven isn't calibrated this low, set it on the lowest setting and prop open the door. Use an oven thermometer to maintain the heat at 140°F to 145°F. Wet 2 cookie sheets with water, line them with plastic wrap, and lightly spray them with vegetable oil. If you are using a dehydrator, follow the manufacturer's instructions.

Thoroughly combine the berry puree and honey. Using a spatula, spread the mixture ⅛- to ¼-inch thick over the plastic wrap, starting at the center and working out to within 2 inches of the edge. Repeat for the second pan. Put the pans in the oven and start checking every 25 minutes after they have been in the oven for 3½ hours. The leather should be dry in 4 to 6 hours, depending on the berries. Leave the door slightly ajar to allow the moisture to escape. Since the leather dries from the edges inward, always test by gently pushing down on the leather in the center of the pan—your finger should not leave an indentation. The dried leather should also be pliable, stretching when it is torn, and will not feel sticky.

To dry in the sun, protect the fruit from insects by covering it with cheesecloth, being careful not to let it touch the fruit. It will take about 24 hours (bring the fruit in at night). Pasteurize the leather in a 140°F oven for 30 minutes.

Loosely roll the fruit leather and wrap in plastic wrap. It will keep for several months at room temperature and up to 1 year in the freezer.

## *Boysenberry Honey*

Any berry will work for this simple recipe, which makes a great gift in a decorative jar.

**MAKES TWO 8-OUNCE JARS**

**2 cups mild-flavored honey, such as clover**
**1 pint (2 cups) fresh boysenberries, rinsed and drained, or frozen boysenberries, thawed with juice**

Wash two 8-ounce jars with lids.

Put the honey and berries in a small saucepan and mash the berries with the back of a spoon. Heat just to boiling, then immediately remove from the heat and pour through a fine strainer into a small jar. Will keep for 1 year at room temperature.

### Manzanita Berries

One fall several years ago, we hiked Yosemite's high country with a group of friends. On the ride to the trailhead, I chatted with our bus driver, whose family homesteaded in the valley. She and her daughter continue to make preserves with many of the berries that grow in the region, just as her mother and grandmother did. "The manzanita berry is one of our favorites," she told me. "We pick them for jelly in the fall when the small clusters turn a beautiful golden bronze, almost like a piece of jewelry you'd like to wear. In the springtime they have small pink blossoms that make wonderful honey. My grandfather always used to take our bees to a manzanita grove by our house after the flowers opened."

## *Strawberry-Balsamic Mustard*

Mostarda di fragole, an intensely flavored, strawberry-mustard-balsamic vinegar Italian condiment, often accompanies meats and game birds. I liked it so much I created my own version, which I serve with smoked birds and pork.

Fresh or frozen strawberries are simmered with balsamic vinegar and a little smooth French-style mustard and sugar until the vinegar is reduced and the fruit breaks down, producing a thick, jamlike conserve that is aromatic with strawberries but not too sweet. Substitute blueberries for the strawberries if you wish. Blackberries and raspberries also work; add more sugar if necessary.

**MAKES ABOUT THREE 8-OUNCE JARS**

**3 pints (6 cups) fresh strawberries, rinsed and drained, or frozen strawberries, slightly thawed with juice**
**One 8½-ounce bottle balsamic vinegar**
**1 tablespoon Dijon mustard**
**2 tablespoons sugar**

Wash three 8-ounce jars. Prepare the lids according to the manufacturer's directions. Put the strawberries (if your strawberries are bigger than a golf ball, cut them into quarters first), vinegar, mustard, and sugar in a nonreactive pan over medium-high heat. Bring to a boil, then reduce the heat to simmer. If the berries are not breaking down, mash them 3 to 4 times with a potato masher. The mixture is done when it is thick and homogeneous, about the consistency of jam—it will also thicken some as it cools. Store in jars in the refrigerator. It will keep for up to 1 month.

### *Raspberry Pastilles*

In Europe, a tiny plate of fruit pastilles—small, soft, intensely flavorful gumdroplike candies—is often sent to the table after dinner. These sweets, popular in England in the fifteenth century, were traditionally served cut into different shapes. During the winter they were stored in the pantry and eaten when fresh fruits were not available.

Like all classical recipes that have withstood the test of time, pastilles are incredibly delicious, and every good berry cook should know how to make them. The sweetened fruit is slow-cooked over low heat, which concentrates the flavor and forms a soft candy with the pure essence of the berry. (It's just like making jam, but you cook it longer.) If the pastilles are covered tightly, they will keep at room temperature for years, although in our house they've never lasted longer than a week.

Once they are coated in sugar, they can also be rolled in grated sweetened coconut or dipped in bittersweet chocolate.

**MAKES ABOUT 36 CANDIES**

**1⅓ cups sugar, plus ¼ cup for coating the fruit**

**2 pints (4 cups) fresh raspberries, rinsed and drained, or frozen raspberries, thawed with juice, pureed and seeded (see page 70), to make 2 cups seedless puree**

Preheat the oven to 300°F. Butter an 8-inch-square pan. Put ¼ cup of the sugar in a small bowl. Combine the berries and 1⅓ cups sugar in a wide saucepan over medium-high heat. Bring to a boil and cook for 2 minutes. Reduce the heat to low and simmer gently for 20 minutes, until the mixture almost leaves the sides of the pan and a spoon drawn through the mixture leaves a trough. Pour into the pan and bake for 10 minutes—the fruit will be bubbling rapidly. Let cool in the pan.

When the candy is completely cool, cut into squares. To remove the pieces from the pan, rub a little oil on the lip of a table knife or small spatula and dip it in the remaining sugar. Pick up one piece of candy and completely coat it in sugar. Repeat for the remaining pieces. Store covered in plastic wrap in a decorative tin or box.

*Variation I:* Roll individual sugared pastilles in a bowl of grated coconut, pressing the coconut into the candy.

*Variation II:* Dip individual sugared pastilles in melted high-quality bittersweet chocolate (such as Scharffen Berger).

# ICE CREAMS, SORBETS, AND OTHER FROZEN TREATS

Berries make delightful frozen desserts however you choose to use them. The fruit can be served fresh, accompanied by a frozen topping, like the Late-Harvest Riesling Ice, for a fancy adult version of a snow cone, or sprinkled over a berry-flavored or specialty ice cream. For these desserts, always use peak-of-the-season berries and serve them in glass bowls or stemmed glasses to showcase their lovely colors.

For sorbets, pureed and sweetened berries are frozen either in an ice cream maker or by the still-freeze method. A small scoop of this intensely flavored sorbet goes a long way, and it's fun to serve two or three of these sorbets at the same time, as restaurants often do, for contrasting flavors to dazzle the palate. Or you can transform sweetened berry purees into old-fashioned popsicles, an exceptionally healthy treat. But remember, as with all foods that are served cold, freezing masks flavors so you will need to add more sugar to enhance the fruit than if you were serving the berries at room temperature.

Frozen berries make surprisingly good frozen desserts, but always start with high-quality individually quick-frozen whole fruit, known in the trade as IQF. These berries can be served frozen, cloaked in a hot caramel sauce (page 193), or, if you have a food processor, made into berry-flavored frozen yogurts, sorbets, or ice creams in just minutes.

A wide selection of ice cream makers is available on the market, from the old-fashioned hand-cranked types to more modern electric versions that make two quarts at a time. If you don't have one, whip the cream first and then add the rest of the ingredients and freeze.

Berry ice creams are best if eaten within several hours of being made, or they will deflate and become too firm. Start the ice cream maker as soon as your company arrives for dinner. It's festive to watch the process and equally pleasurable to anticipate eating homemade ice cream. If it is ready before you are ready to eat, remove the paddle, cover the canister with plastic wrap, and set it in the freezer until you are ready to serve it. Store any remaining ice cream in a covered plastic container in the freezer.

### *Rose Geranium Ice Cream with Raspberries*

Rose geranium leaves have an exotically seductive flavor that goes particularly well with raspberries and strawberries. I buy scented rose geraniums at the nursery in the springtime, and occasionally I can get them to winter over.

I infuse milk and cream with the leaves for the ice cream. When the mixture is almost frozen, I fold in the whole raspberries.

**MAKES 1 QUART**

- **2 cups heavy cream**
- **2 cups milk**
- **½ cup unsprayed rose geranium leaves, washed and torn or coarsely chopped**
- **½ cup sugar**
- **1 pint (2 cups) fresh raspberries, rinsed and drained, or frozen raspberries, thawed in a single layer on a paper towel for 20 minutes**

Pour the cream and milk into a saucepan with the rose geranium leaves and bring to a boil. Remove the pan from the heat and let it sit at room temperature for 2 to 3 hours, until the milk-cream mixture is infused with the rose geranium flavor. Strain and discard the rose geranium leaves. Stir the sugar into the flavored milk-cream mixture and freeze in an ice cream freezer according to the manufacturer's instructions. Add the raspberries during the last 5 minutes of freezing time.

Serve in bowls or stemmed glasses accompanied by a plate of cookies.

### *Loganberry-Buttermilk Ice Cream*

Susan VandeKerk is the chef-owner of the Oyster Catcher Restaurant in Coupeville, Washington, an area that was once known for the excellent loganberries grown there. "My mother grew up on a dairy farm here, and she always made this wonderful loganberry-buttermilk ice cream. It's a simple recipe that works well for raspberries, loganberries, or marionberries."

**MAKES ABOUT 2 QUARTS**

**1 quart (4 cups) fresh loganberries, rinsed, drained, and pureed (see page 70), or frozen loganberries, thawed with juice and crushed**

**3 to 3½ cups sugar, to taste**

**1 quart buttermilk**

**½ cup heavy cream**

Stir all the ingredients together in a large bowl. Transfer the mixture to an ice cream maker and freeze according to the manufacturer's instructions. Serve in bowls or stemmed glasses accompanied by a plate of cookies.

*Note:* If using wild blueberries, huckleberries, or gooseberries, they need to be cooked first. Put the berries in a shallow pan and sprinkle them with a little sugar (from the allotted 3 cups in the recipe) and a sprinkling of lemon juice to bring out their flavor. Cover the pan and bring to a boil. Immediately take the pan off the burner and remove the cover. Let the berries cool and use in the recipe.

## *Christmas Snowballs with Triple Red Berry Sauce*

One of my many fond memories of growing up in Arcata, California, was during the Christmas holidays, when a local dairy sold individual "snowballs"—vanilla ice cream rolled in moist, shredded coconut and topped with a candle that was lit when the lights were dimmed. Eating this frozen treat was always a festive occasion, especially in the temperate coastal redwood country, where children could only dream of playing in the snow. I have re-created this dessert, complete with a brilliant triple red berry sauce flavored with a splash of framboise, for your holiday menu.

**MAKES 8 SERVINGS**

SNOWBALLS

**1 quart high-quality vanilla ice cream**

**1 cup reduced-fat canned coconut milk**

**1½ teaspoons coconut flavoring (optional)**

**4 cups (about 12 ounces) sweetened shredded coconut**

**24 frozen raspberries rolled in sugar for garnish**

SAUCE

**¼ cup fresh cranberries, rinsed and drained, or frozen cranberries, thawed**

**½ cup fresh raspberries, rinsed and drained, or frozen raspberries, thawed with juice**

**Heaping ½ cup fresh strawberries, rinsed and drained, or frozen strawberries, thawed with juice**
**2½ teaspoons sugar**
**1 teaspoon framboise**

For serving, have on hand 8 red or green birthday candles. Soften the ice cream and stir in the coconut milk and coconut flavoring. Freeze until firm enough to form into balls.

Put the coconut in a shallow dish. Use an ice cream scoop to dish up 1 large scoop of the coconut-flavored ice cream and roll it in the coconut, pressing it into a ball. Repeat for the other 7 snowballs and refreeze. When they are completely frozen, wrap the balls individually in plastic wrap, then in foil, or put them in a freezer container with a lid.

Prepare the sauce by pureeing the cranberries, raspberries, strawberries, sugar, and framboise together in a food processor or blender until smooth.

Ladle a tablespoon of sauce in the center of 8 dessert plates and spread it out with the back of a spoon so it's a little bigger than the snowball. Put one snowball on each plate and let sit at room temperature for 10 minutes before serving. Garnish each with three sugar-coated raspberries, placed in the center with stem sides down and a candle in the middle. When the candles are lit, dim the lights and serve.

### The Spirit of Going Berrying

Every child should experience firsthand the joy and adventure of going berry picking—smelling the fragrant aroma of the berry patch in the hot summer sun, hearing the plinking sound of the first berry falling into an empty bucket, and feeling the deep satisfaction of eating a warm, juicy berry right off the bush. The whole spirit of picking berries—whether in the wild or a U-pick farm—and learning at a young age the difference between food picked at the source and that bought at the grocery store, is crucial to keeping our children connected to the land.

In *Wild Fruits: Thoreau's Rediscovered Last Manuscript,* Henry David Thoreau said, "The value of these wild fruits is not in the mere possession or eating of them, but in the sight and enjoyment of them. The very derivation of the word 'fruit' would suggest this. It is from the Latin *fructus,* meaning 'that which is *used* or *enjoyed.*' If it were not so, then going a-berrying and going to market would be nearly synonymous experiences."

## *Double-Hit Strawberry Ice Cream*

Strawberry ice cream is the all-American classic dessert. I add pureed and sliced strawberries to give it an intense strawberry flavor.

**MAKES 1 QUART**

**2 cups milk**
**2 cups cream**
**½ cup sugar**
**1 teaspoon vanilla extract**
**½ pint (1 cup) fresh strawberries, rinsed, drained, and pureed, or frozen strawberries, thawed with juice and pureed (see page 70)**
**½ pint (1 cup) fresh strawberries, rinsed, drained, and sliced**

Blend the milk, cream, sugar, vanilla, and strawberry puree together. Pour the mixture into an ice cream freezer and freeze according to the manufacturer's instructions. Add the sliced strawberries during the last 5 minutes.

Serve in bowls or stemmed glasses accompanied by a plate of cookies.

## *Frozen Strawberry Yogurt*

Frozen berries make excellent frozen yogurts, ice creams, and sorbets in just minutes if you have a food processor. If you want to make ice cream instead of frozen yogurt, simply substitute heavy cream for the yogurt. And if you prefer a sorbet, use more berries in place of the dairy. Frozen yogurts and sorbets are best served as soon as they are made.

### South America's Johnny Appleseed

"The parish records from Huachi Grande Catholic Churchy near Ambato, Ecuador, in combination with local oral tradition, offer a colorful record of the introduction of *F. chiloensis* to the Ecuadorian Andes. According to these sources, Jose Antonio Blanco Antorvoz de Salinas set out across the Andes from Chile to Ecuador in the late 1500s, planting runners of *F. chiloensis* as he traveled. When this 'Johnny Appleseed' of the strawberry finally arrived at Huachi Grande, the plants flourished, and he traveled no farther, as he had found the perfect combination of soils and environment. Huachi Grande later developed a countrywide reputation for its strawberries and was billed as 'La Tierra de las Fruitillas' by the Spanish."

—From "Notes on the Strawberry of Ecuador," by Chad Finn, Jim Hancock, and Chris Heider, in *Journal of the American Society for Horticulture Science*, vol. 33(4)

**MAKES 1 PINT**

**One 16-ounce package frozen whole strawberries or other berries**
**½ cup plain yogurt**
**⅓ cup confectioners' sugar**

Put the berries in a food processor bowl and pulse 3 times. Turn the machine on and finely chop the fruit. Scrape down the sides of the bowl as needed.

Add the yogurt and sugar and process until creamy and smooth. Add more sugar if it's not sweet enough and process to blend. Serve immediately.

*Variations:* To make ice cream, substitute ⅓ cup cream for the yogurt. To make sorbet, thaw a fifth (about 3 ounces) of the fruit in the refrigerator and omit the yogurt.

## *Red Currant Sorbet*

This recipe comes from Ed Mashburn, who grows red and black currants and gooseberries in Pennsylvania—the Northumberland Berry Works. A small scoop of this intensely flavorful sorbet accompanied by a cookie or two is a perfect summer dessert. Use this recipe for black currants and for other berries, too.

**MAKES 6 SERVINGS**

**2 pints (4 cups) fresh red or black currants, rinsed and drained, or frozen currants, thawed with juice**
**¼ cup fresh orange juice**
**½ cup confectioners' sugar**

Put the currants and orange juice in a food processor and puree. Strain by pushing the fruit through a fine strainer with the back of a spatula. Stir in the sugar and freeze in an ice cream freezer according to the manufacturer's instructions. Or follow the still-freeze method (see Note).

*Note:* To use the still-freeze method, pour the sorbet mixture into an 8-inch-square pan or small metal bowl and put it in the freezer. Scrape the edges of the pan to release the frozen particles and stir them into the puree every 40 to 50 minutes, until it forms a firm slush. Pour the mixture into a plastic container, cover tightly, and freeze. If the sorbet has been frozen overnight, let stand at room temperature for about 25 minutes before serving.

## *Blood Orange Vodka Berry Sorbet*

Mustards Grill, a fine Napa Valley restaurant, makes this intensely flavored sorbet with fresh strawberries and Charbay Blood Orange vodka (see box). Liquor stores carry a variety of berry vodkas, so if you can't find the Charbay, try another one, such as Absolut Mandrin from Sweden.

**MAKES ABOUT 1½ QUARTS**

**3 tablespoons blood orange vodka**
**4 pints (8 cups) fresh strawberries, rinsed, drained, and pureed, or frozen strawberries, thawed with juice, pureed (see page 70)**
**2 cups Simple Syrup (see page 69)**
**2 tablespoons fresh lime juice**

Stir all the ingredients together and freeze in an ice cream freezer according to the manufacturer's instructions.

### The Karakasevic Family, Winemakers and Master Distillers

In Vienna, in 1751, the House of Karakasevic, makers of wines and brandies, was recognized by the Austrian-Hungarian imperial court of Empress Maria Theresa. More than 250 years later, the same family is still carrying on the family tradition as the thirteenth continuous generation of winemakers and distillers in the business. After leaving their Yugoslavian homeland in 1962, the family eventually settled in St. Helena in the Napa Valley. They built a winery and a distillery and opened business as Domaine Charbay. Try their flavored vodkas sprinkled on fresh berries or use them to make great mixed drinks. Contact Domaine Charbay, 4001 Spring Mountain Road St. Helena, CA 94574; 800-634-7845; www.charbay.com (flavored vodkas and other spirits).

## *Creamy Lemon Sherbet*

After looking for years for the perfect lemon ice cream to serve with berries, I had almost given up when I ate a bowl of this decadently rich and creamy sherbet one night at Paley's Place in northwest Portland. It is the creation of the talented pastry chef, Jennifer Flanagan. I find it the ideal base for perfectly ripe berries at their peak of sweetness or to accompany the Fallen Lemon Cake with Melba Sauce (page 230). Other dessert possibilities are limitless.

**MAKES 1 QUART**

**Zest of 2 large lemons**
**1 cup sugar**
**¼ cup fresh lemon juice (from 2 lemons)**
**1 cup milk**
**1 cup heavy cream**

Put the lemon zest and sugar in a food processor and pulse twice to blend.

Pour in the lemon juice, milk, and cream and process for 10 to 15 seconds (no longer, or you'll get whipped cream) to dissolve the sugar. Transfer the mixture to an ice cream maker and freeze according to the manufacturer's instructions. (If you don't have an ice cream maker, whip the cream and fold it into the other ingredients. Freeze in a container with a tight-fitting lid.)

## *Berries with Late-Harvest Riesling Ice*

Late-harvest Rieslings are wines made from grapes left on the vine and picked at the end of the harvest, when they have developed a high sugar content, often from the fungus botrytis. The lovely floral and honeysuckle flavors of these wines are perfect partnered with sweet summer berries. I've made this dessert for years, and I'm always thrilled with how good it tastes. Serve it in stemmed glasses accompanied by a plate of butter cookies.

**MAKES 12 GENEROUS SERVINGS**

**¾ cup sugar**

**1½ cups late-harvest Riesling**

**3 pints (6 cups) mixed fresh berries, such as raspberries, blueberries, strawberries, and marionberries or other blackberries, rinsed and drained**

Pour 3 cups water into a small pot with the sugar. Heat gently to dissolve the sugar and let cool. Stir in the Riesling and pour into a 9 × 13-inch pan. Freeze for 4 to 6 hours, until firm.

Divide the berries among 12 stemmed glasses or small serving bowls. With a spoon, scrape ¼ to ½ cup of the ice over each bowl of berries. Serve immediately.

## *Blueberry-Peach Tequila Pops*

These are adult pops, but to make them kid-friendly, just omit the tequila.

**MAKES 4 POPSICLES**

**Blueberry Layer**

**1 pint (2 cups) fresh blueberries, rinsed and drained, or frozen blueberries, thawed with juice, pureed and pushed through a fine strainer (see page 70), to make about 1 cup puree**

**2 tablespoons sugar**

**1½ teaspoons fresh lemon juice**

**1 tablespoon tequila (I use Cuervo Especial)**

**Peach Layer**

**2 heaping cups peeled and pitted fresh peaches (about 3 peaches), or frozen peaches, thawed with juice, pureed and pushed through a strainer (see page 70) to make about 1½ cups puree**

**3 tablespoons sugar**

**1 tablespoon fresh lemon juice**

**2 tablespoons tequila**

Have ready four 5-ounce paper cups and four popsicle sticks (available at craft shops).

Blend together the blueberry puree, sugar, lemon juice, and tequila and divide the mixture equally among the four cups. Freeze for 2 to 3 hours, until the mixture is starting to get firm—it will still be slightly slushy. Poke a popsicle stick into the center of each cup.

Blend the peach puree, sugar, lemon juice, and tequila together. Top each blueberry cup with a generous ⅓ cup of the peach mixture. Cover with plastic wrap and freeze until firm, about 3 more hours. Peel off the paper and serve immediately. Or, for a party, serve the popsicles in a bucket of ice.

*Mango-Raspberry Popsicles:* Substitute raspberries for the blueberries and framboise for the tequila, and pureed mango with 2 tablespoons lime juice for peach layer.

Substitute 2 cups pureed and seeded raspberries, blueberries, blackberries, or strawberries, for the blueberries and peaches (you will need about 2 pints berries), 3 to 4 tablespoons of sugar, and 1 tablespoon fresh lime juice.

### An Eskimo Woman's Memories of Berry Picking

"I am Eskimo. I was born at Mountain Village on the banks of the Yukon River about 85 miles from the mouth. Two hundred inhabitants lived there at that time. Then we didn't have electricity, didn't know anything about it, so we didn't miss it. We lived like they did a long time ago.

"In the village we did our preserving in the fall. We always picked berries at traditional sites. We'd go way down on the Yukon River, about 35 miles away. My dad pitched a tent, and we stayed for as long as a week. We had this huge thing we sat on for a bench that at first we thought was a log. One day my father told me it was from a big animal—it was a mastodon tusk. I was just a little girl, and it was so big my feet dangled because they couldn't reach the ground. I remember it being so huge, and year after year we'd go to that same spot for our berries.

"My mother would buy gum and save it for berry season so we wouldn't eat the berries as we picked.

"When my grandmother was young—before we had salt and sugar—the berries were preserved in seal oil, but we stored everything in keg barrels that we got butter in from Seattle. When we went out for berries, such as blueberries, our grandmother always came with us. She took care of the sugar and things that needed to stay dry. She would pour the berries into the barrel and knew exactly how much sugar to put in—otherwise the berries would ferment. We always stayed at camp until our barrel was full—that was tradition. My dad would cover the barrel with wax from a candle. We opened it around Thanksgiving, so we always looked forward to that day.

"We also opened barrels at Christmas and Easter, and if you were really lucky you'd have Eskimo ice cream for your birthday. It's called *agutuq* (pronounced 'a goo duck'), which means 'something that has been stirred.' To make it, boil fish in chunks for 20 minutes or longer. After it cools down, remove the scales and bone. Take the meat and squeeze the juice out of it. Put it in a bowl and flake like cornmeal. Then—in the old days we stirred reindeer tallow until it was fluffy, but now we use shortening or Wesson oil—add sugar and stir in the flaked fish and add fresh or from-the-barrel berries. I use cloudberries and crowberries because it makes your mouth water it tastes so good."

—Aggie Bostrom, North Pole, Alaska

## *Blackberry-Cabernet Sorbet with Summer Berries*

Linda Wisner once served this exquisite dessert at an August garden party for the Portland Culinary Alliance. She filled a large shallow white bowl with an assortment of fresh berries—strawberries, marionberries, boysenberries, raspberries, and blueberries—then scooped mounds of this blackberry-Cabernet sorbet on top. It was stunning. She served it with a platter of butter cookies, and nothing could have been simpler or tasted any better.

Substitute or add other berries as they come into season.

**MAKES 8 SERVINGS**

**½ cup sugar**

**4 pints (8 cups) fresh marionberries, rinsed and drained, or frozen marionberries, thawed with juice 1 cup Cabernet Sauvignon**

**1 pint (2 cups) fresh boysenberries, rinsed and drained**

**1 pint (2 cups) fresh raspberries, rinsed and drained**

**1 pint (2 cups) fresh blueberries, rinsed and drained**

**½ pint (1 cup) strawberries, sliced, rinsed, and drained**

**8 fresh mint sprigs**

Stir the sugar together with 1 cup warm water until the sugar dissolves. Puree 2 pints of the marionberries and push them through a strainer with the back of a spatula to remove the seeds and pulp. Stir the blackberries and wine into the sugar water and freeze in an ice cream maker according to the manufacturer's instructions.

Put the remaining marionberries, the boysenberries, raspberries, blueberries, and strawberries in a large, shallow bowl and toss gently to blend. Top with scoops of the sorbet and garnish with sprigs of fresh mint.

## *Frozen Cranberries with Hot Caramel Sauce*

Beatrice Ojakangas, a first-generation American, is the author of 22 cookbooks, many of them on the foods of Scandinavia. When I asked her what her favorite way to use lingonberries was, she said, "One of the best things I remember is a dessert made by a Finnish friend. In Finland, people can buy fresh lingonberries by the liter at the open market. She simply froze the berries so that they were separate—like small marbles. Then she tossed them with a bit of sugar and served them with a hot caramel sauce (Finns call the sauce *kinuskikastike*). It is a simple sauce made by boiling equal measures of sugar and whipping cream until the sauce is a pale caramel color. A bit of dark syrup will enhance it, and I always add vanilla and just a tiny pinch of salt to bring out the flavor. The hot sauce is poured over the frozen berries, making quite a nice contrast."

Fresh or frozen lingonberries are almost impossible to buy (though that's slowly changing) in most of the United States, but chopped cranberries work equally well, or you can use a mixture of frozen berries.

This recipe is one of my favorites—I love the combination of the rich and creamy hot caramel sauce with the icy crunch of the tart cranberries. And it's a perfect dessert for entertaining, because all the ingredients can be prepared in advance.

**MAKES 4 TO 6 SERVINGS**

**SAUCE**
**1 cup heavy cream**
**1 cup sugar**
**1 teaspoon dark corn syrup**
**1 teaspoon vanilla extract**
**Pinch of coarse salt**

**2 pints (4 cups) frozen cranberries or lingonberries or a combination of frozen berries (see Note)**

Combine the cream and sugar in a deep, heavy saucepan and place over medium-high heat. Bring the mixture to a boil and boil for 5 minutes or until the sauce turns a pale golden color (the sauce will get darker when you add the corn syrup and vanilla and thicker as it cools). Don't cook the sauce too long, or you will make a taffy! Stir in the corn syrup, vanilla, and salt. Keep hot until served. (The sauce can be made up to a week in advance if stored covered in the refrigerator. Reheat it gently over low heat.)

Just before serving, coarsely chop the frozen cranberries (leave lingonberries whole) and divide them equally among 6 dessert bowls—not glass. Pour the hot caramel sauce over the berries and serve immediately.

*Note:* One New Year's Eve I made this dessert for 16. I used a mixture of frozen berries: two 12-ounce bags cranberries (very coarsely chopped), 2 cups blueberries, 2 cups raspberries, and 3 cups huckleberries. I doubled the sauce recipe with the exception of the sugar—I used only 1½ cups sugar.

# PIES, TARTS, COBBLERS, AND SUCH

For pie lovers, I've included blackberry, huckleberry, strawberry-rhubarb, blueberry, black raspberry, Juneberry, and gooseberry pies. They can be made with either fresh or Individually quick-frozen (known commercially as IQF) berries. Pies made with the latter will be juicier than those made with fresh berries because ice crystals break down the fruit and release their juices. You can ignore it, as I do, or add an extra teaspoon or two of thickener to your filling.

I use an assortment of thickeners—flour, tapioca, and cornstarch. They all work—it's a matter of what you are used to.

If you like, you can make fresh berry pies and freeze them unbaked. Don't cut the slits, and wrap the pies in plastic wrap and double-wrap in foil. They will keep frozen up to 4 months. Remove the wrappings and bake them in a preheated 425°F oven for 15 minutes. Cut slits in the top and bake another 40 to 50 minutes, until the juices are bubbly. If the top is getting too brown, cover it lightly with foil. Bake pies and tarts on a foil-lined baking sheet to catch any juices that might bubble over, and it will also help cook the bottom crust.

For luscious, peak-of-the-season fresh fruit, I've included several of my favorite tarts to show off the berries, plus some old-fashioned Oregon cobbler recipes. When fruit isn't perfect but just good, they are simply fun to make and scrumptious to eat.

## *Almond Gooseberry Cream Pie*

My mother-in-law taught me how to make this gooseberry pie that is an old family favorite. It has a dense, rich, cream-colored, almond-flavored filling that comes from the addition of eggs, not cream. If you are a gooseberry fan, you will love this old-fashioned dessert.

**MAKES 6 TO 8 SERVINGS**

**Basic Pie Crust (page 211) for a double crust**
**2 pints (4 cups) fresh gooseberries, rinsed and drained, or frozen gooseberries, thawed in a single layer on a paper towel for 20 minutes**
**1¾ cups sugar, plus sugar for sprinkling**
**2 tablespoons cornstarch**
**1 teaspoon ground cinnamon**
**1⅛ teaspoons freshly grated nutmeg**
**2 large eggs, beaten**
**½ teaspoon almond extract**
**2 tablespoons milk**

Preheat the oven to 425°F. Line a baking sheet with foil.

Flour a clean surface and roll out the smaller piece of dough ⅛-inch thick into a 10-inch circle. Line a 9-inch pie pan with the pie crust, leaving a 1-inch overhang.

Put the gooseberries in a bowl and toss with the sugar, cornstarch, cinnamon, nutmeg, eggs, and almond extract. Pour the filling into the pastry-lined pan.

Roll out the top crust into an 11-inch circle. Fold the pastry over the rolling pin and ease it over the filling. Tuck the edge of the top crust under the edge of the bottom crust and crimp. Brush the top (not the edges) with milk and sprinkle with the remaining sugar. Cut slits to release steam and cover the edges of the pie with foil or a pie shield.

Transfer the pie to the baking sheet and bake for 35 to 40 minutes or until the top of the pie is golden brown and the filing is bubbly. For frozen berries, bake the pie for 35 minutes at 400°F, then reduce the heat to 375°F and bake for 15 minutes. Cool on a wire rack.

Serve warm with vanilla ice cream.

## *Damn Good Western Pennsylvania Black Raspberry Pie*

Black raspberries grow in abundance in the tristate region of western Pennsylvania, Ohio, and West Virginia, where Marlene Parrish, columnist for the Los Angeles Times Syndicate, lives. She comes from an old Pennsylvania family whose motto has always been "Black raspberry pie for the Fourth of July." According to Marlene, "We also eat them on cereal and plain with milk and sugar. I used to go picking as a kid in my dad's long shirtsleeves so the thorns (we called them 'jaggers') didn't scratch us too much. You have to get out early in the morning, or the birds will beat you every time." She uses this recipe for blueberry, black raspberry, and elderberry pie.

**MAKES 6 TO 8 SERVINGS**

**Basic Pie Crust (page 211) for a double crust**

**2 pints (4 cups) fresh black raspberries, rinsed and drained, or frozen black raspberries, thawed in a single layer on a paper towel for 20 minutes (see Note)**

**3 tablespoons cornstarch**

**1 cup sugar, plus sugar for sprinkling**

**Pinch of freshly grated nutmeg**

**Pinch of freshly grated cinnamon**

**Pinch of coarse salt**

**1 tablespoon unsalted butter**

Preheat the oven to 425°F. Line a baking sheet with foil.

Flour a clean surface and roll out the smaller piece of dough ⅛-inch thick to a 10-inch circle. Line a 9-inch pie pan with the pie crust, leaving a 1-inch overhang. Chill the prepared bottom crust in the refrigerator.

Toss the berries with the cornstarch, sugar, nutmeg, cinnamon, and salt. Allow the berries to macerate while you prepare the lattice top. Roll out the remaining dough to ⅛-inch thickness. Using a ruler and a pizza cutter or knife, cut the dough into strips ½-inch wide.

Pour the filling into the shell and dot with butter. Moisten the rim of the bottom crust with water and lay half of the strips over the pie filling 1 inch apart. Repeat with the remaining strips, laying them perpendicular, to create a lattice pattern. Trim the strips even with the outer rim of the pan. Fold the bottom crust up and over the strips and flute the edge.

Transfer the pie to the prepared baking sheet and bake for 15 minutes. Lower the heat to 375°F and bake for 45 to 50 minutes or "until the pie has bubbled and burped for about 10 minutes," says Marlene. Cool on a wire rack.

Serve warm with vanilla ice cream.

*Note:* Wild black raspberries can often be dry and seedy in hot, dry summers. To remedy this, add ⅓ to ½ cup blueberries to the filling mixture. Their flavor is undetectable, but their juice adds moisture.

## *Peak-of-the-Season Blueberry Pie*

What I like most about this pie is that only a cup of the berries are cooked—the rest are folded in at the end of the cooking time. Before serving, the top is completely covered in a deep, decadent mound of whipped cream. Use this recipe only when you have sweet, peak-of-the-season fresh fruit—it's one of the premier pie recipes for letting the good flavors of the berries speak for themselves. (Frozen just won't do.) Use it for fresh strawberries, blackberries, and raspberries, too. This recipe is often called *strawberry or raspberry glace pie.*

**MAKES 6 SERVINGS**

**¾ cup sugar**

**2½ tablespoons cornstarch**

**¼ teaspoon coarse salt**

**1½ pints (3 cups) fresh, peak-of-the-season cultivated blueberries, strawberries, or raspberries, plus a handful for garnish**

**2 tablespoons unsalted butter**

**1½ tablespoons fresh lemon juice**

**1 baked 9-inch deep-dish pie shell made with Basic Pie Crust (page 211)**

**1 cup heavy cream**

**2 to 3 tablespoons confectioners' sugar**

**½ teaspoon vanilla extract**

Combine the sugar, cornstarch, and salt in a medium saucepan. Put the pan over medium heat and add 1 cup of the berries and ⅔ cup water. Bring to a boil, stirring constantly until the mixture thickens and turns clear instead of cloudy looking, about 2 minutes. Remove from the heat and stir in the butter, lemon juice, and the remaining 2 cups blueberries. Pour the filling into the prepared pie shell and refrigerate until firm, about 2 hours.

Before serving, whip the cream with the confectioners' sugar and vanilla until stiff peaks form, and spread on top of the filling. Sprinkle a handful of blueberries on top of the whipped cream.

## *Juneberry-Raspberry Pie*

Betty Kelner and her husband, Dan, operate the Juneberry Patch in North Dakota. Juneberries are native to the plains, and they are working with the state to help establish a commercial industry there. When she needs to make a pie to show off the fruits of their labor, Betty makes this intensely flavorful recipe combining Juneberries and raspberries.

**MAKES 8 SERVINGS**

**Basic Pie Crust (page 211) for a double crust**
**2 pints (4 cups) fresh Juneberries or blueberries, rinsed and drained, or frozen Juneberries, thawed in a single layer on a paper towel for 20 minutes**
**½ pint (1 cup) fresh raspberries, rinsed and drained, or frozen raspberries, thawed in a single layer on a paper towel for 20 minutes**
**⅔ cup sugar, plus sugar for sprinkling**
**2 tablespoons all-purpose flour**
**1 teaspoon ground cinnamon**
**1 tablespoon fresh lemon juice**
**2 tablespoons milk**

Preheat the oven to 375°F. Line a baking sheet with foil.

Flour a clean surface and roll out the smaller piece of dough ⅛-inch thick into a 10-inch circle. Line a 9-inch pie pan with the pie crust, leaving a 1-inch overhang. Chill the crust while you prepare the filling.

Put all of the remaining ingredients except the milk together in a medium bowl and toss to coat the berries. Transfer the mixture to the prepared pie shell.

Roll out the top crust into an 11-inch circle. Fold the pastry over the rolling pin and ease it over the filling. Tuck the edge of the top crust under the edge of the bottom crust and crimp. Brush the top (not the edges) with milk and sprinkle with the remaining sugar. Cut slits to release steam and cover the edges of the pie with foil or a pie shield.

Transfer the pie to the baking sheet and bake for 35 to 45 minutes or until the top of the pie is golden brown and the filling is bubbly. Cool on a wire rack.

Serve warm with vanilla ice cream.

## *Mount Adams Huckleberry Pie*

There is nothing fancy about this pie; there doesn't need to be. Huckleberries are so good they don't need anything but a little sugar, a splash of lemon juice to intensify their wildly complex flavor, and tapioca for thickening their flavorful juice. I use the same standard berry pie recipe, which cooks have used for years, for blackberries, blueberries, boysenberries, loganberries, and raspberries. It's simple and straightforward, but when you have fruit this good, the less you do to it, the better.

**MAKES 6 TO 8 SERVINGS**

**Basic Pie Crust (page 211) for a double crust**

**2 pints (4 heaping cups) huckleberries, rinsed and drained, or frozen huckleberries, thawed in a single layer on a paper towel for 20 minutes**

**1 cup sugar, plus sugar for sprinkling**

**1 teaspoon fresh lemon juice**

**3 tablespoons quick-cooking tapioca**

**2 tablespoons milk**

Preheat the oven to 400°F.

Flour a clean surface and roll out the smaller piece of dough ⅛-inch thick into a 10-inch circle. Line a 9-inch pie pan with the pie crust, leaving a 1-inch overhang.

Put the huckleberries in a bowl and toss with the sugar, lemon juice, and tapioca. Let the berry mixture macerate at room temperature for 15 minutes. Transfer the filling to the prepared pie shell.

Roll out the top crust to an 11-inch circle. Fold the pastry over the rolling pin and ease it over the filling. Tuck the edge of the top crust under the edge of the bottom crust and crimp. Brush the top (not the edges) with milk and sprinkle with the remaining sugar. Cut slits to release the steam.

### Save Your Fork

When Queen Elizabeth and Prince Philip visited Saskatchewan, Canada, several years ago, they attended a dinner put on by the Blaine Lake Ukrainian women in the basement of their church. As the women were clearing the table, one of them told Prince Philip, "Keep your fork; there's pie." That would be saskatoon pie, of course.

Transfer the pie to the baking sheet and bake for about 1 hour, until the top crust is golden brown and the filling is bubbling. Cool on a wire rack.

Serve warm with vanilla ice cream.

### The Handshake Treaty of 1933

The Native Americans have picked huckleberries in the national forest at the base of Mount Adams in the Washington Cascades—aptly called Indian Heaven—for centuries. But during the Depression they were overwhelmed with the arrival of jobless whites from Portland. The September 4, 1932, *Oregonian* reported on 5,000 city dwellers who arrived in "rickety cars and wagons, afoot and pack-a-back, they are swarming into the high, clean country where bushels of berries are to be had for the gathering."

They turned this peaceful mountain meadow into a small city complete with a stage and nighttime entertainment. After the wrestling match on a blanket, "lanterns are added for footlights and two little ladies, twins, did a clever tap dance to roars of applause from the 400 or 500 crowding the opening and peering from 'box seats' in the tall trees. Men, women and children had come from all the camps for the evening. ... Another little lady exhibited some acrobatics. ... Then the 'Howling Coyotes' unlimbered violin, guitar and wind instrument. Thunderous applause. ... No actor could ever ask a more spontaneously appreciative audience, starved for something to laugh about. There were other features, too. Everywhere berries are used for barter. The milk man makes a trip out from town every day, the butcher, the baker and sundry peddlers all wind their way through the chain of camps trading berries for tobacco and salt. They in turn sell the berries in Portland and other cities or ship them to the middle west and east."

This was a disturbing invasion for the Native Americans. In a meeting with the Park Service, Chief Yallup said, "This is my land. I own it. Time beyond time, long as the old men remember, my young men have come here to hunt the deer and the bear. My old squaws have gathered the berries. When whites came, still we hunted here and picked the huckleberries. Whites gave us a treaty that it should be so. Our lodges stood alone. Now in the last two years whites thick as the needles on the firs have driven our old squaws from the berry fields."

In the end, a new treaty was signed, the Handshake Treaty of 1933. It guaranteed the Indians the sole right to pick berries in the area on the left side of the road that divides Indian Heaven. Everyone else picks on the right side. That treaty is still upheld today.

## *Old-Fashioned Blackberry Pie*

For many pie lovers like me, blackberry pie is at the top of the dessert list. A hundred years ago cooks were making the same simple recipe (except they used lard for their crust), and it's every bit as good today as it was then. Homemade blackberry pie is especially tasty for breakfast, but don't ever admit you even think about it. Use this basic recipe for all berries and adjust the sugar according to their tartness.

**MAKES 6 TO 8 SERVINGS**

**Basic Pie Crust (page 211) for a double crust**
**2 pints (4 heaping cups) Pacific dewberries, marionberries, or other blackberries, rinsed and drained, or frozen blackberries, thawed in a single layer on a paper towel for 20 minutes**
**⅔ to ¾ cup sugar, to taste, plus sugar for sprinkling**
**3 tablespoons quick-cooking tapioca**
**1 tablespoon unsalted butter**
**2 tablespoons milk**

Preheat the oven to 400°F. Cover a baking sheet with foil.

Flour a clean surface and roll out the smaller piece of dough ⅛-inch thick into 10-inch circle. Line a 9-inch pie pan with the pie crust, leaving a 1-inch overhang.

Put the berries in a bowl and toss with the sugar and tapioca. Let macerate at room temperature for 15 minutes. Pour the filling into the prepared pie shell and dot with butter.

Roll out the top crust to an 11-inch circle. Fold the pastry over the rolling pin and ease it over the filling. Tuck the edge of the top crust under the edge of the bottom crust and crimp. Brush the top (not the edges) with milk and sprinkle with the remaining sugar. Cut slits to release steam and cover the edges of the pie with foil or a pie shield.

Transfer the pie to the baking sheet and bake for 50 minutes or until the top of the pie is golden brown and the filling is bubbly. Cool on a wire rack.
Serve warm with vanilla ice cream.

## *Rustic Strawberry-Rhubarb Pie*

This free-form pie resembles a tart with a top crust and looks like something you'd find on the sideboard in a little country inn in France. It's a specialty of my husband Gary's—in both making and eating. I'm especially fond of his aromatic filling—a mixture of strawberries, rhubarb, cardamom, cinnamon, and sugar.

**MAKES 10 SERVINGS**

- **Favorite Tart and Cobbler Pastry (page 213) for a double crust**
- **1 pint (2 cups) fresh strawberries, rinsed, drained, and sliced**
- **2 rhubarb stalks, cut in half lengthwise, then cut crosswise into ½-inch pieces (1½ cups)**
- **½ cup sugar, plus sugar for sprinkling**
- **2 teaspoons all-purpose flour**
- **½ teaspoon ground cinnamon**
- **½ teaspoon ground cardamom**
- **2 tablespoons milk**

Preheat the oven to 400°F. Line a baking sheet with foil.

Toss together the strawberries, rhubarb, sugar, flour, cinnamon, and cardamom and set aside.

Flour a clean surface and roll out the larger piece of dough into an 11-inch circle. Transfer to a cooking sheet.

Mound the fruit onto the dough on the cookie sheet, leaving a 1-inch border all around. Roll out the top crust into a 10-inch circle. Fold the pastry over the rolling pin and ease it over the filling. Brush the top pastry with milk. Fold the bottom pastry over the top pastry and crimp the edges (the milk helps to seal it). Cut vents in the top crust and sprinkle with the remaining sugar. Bake for 40 minutes, until the rhubarb is tender and the top crust is golden brown. Serve warm with vanilla ice cream or crème fraîche (see page 73).

## *Loganberry Chiffon Pie with Lemon Cookie Crust*

Chiffon pies were popular in the fifties and sixties, and I still like to make them with berries. The intense flavor of the fruit is a pleasing contrast to the light and airy filling. I use Dave's Crème au Citron lemon sandwich cookies, which I buy at my grocery store, for the crust.

**MAKES 8 SERVINGS**

**One and a half ¼-ounce envelopes unflavored gelatin**
**1 package (12.3 ounces) lemon sandwich cookies with filling**
**¼ pound (1 stick) unsalted butter, melted**
**4 large eggs, separated**
**1 tablespoon fresh lemon juice**
**¾ cup sugar**
**2 pints (4 cups) fresh loganberries or other blackberries, rinsed and drained, a handful reserved for garnish**
**Pinch of coarse salt**
**1 pint heavy cream, whipped**

In a small bowl, sprinkle the gelatin over ½ cup cold water to soften.

Put the cookies and butter in a food processor and process until the cookies are finely crushed. Press the mixture onto the bottom and sides of a 9-inch pie pan.

Combine the egg yolks, lemon juice, and ½ cup of the sugar in a nonreactive saucepan over medium-low heat. Heat gently, stirring constantly, until the mixture thickens slightly and coats the back of a spoon. Remove from the heat and stir in the softened gelatin. Set aside.

Puree and seed 2 cups of berries (see page 70). Fold the puree into the gelatin mixture and chill until it mounds slightly when dropped from a spoon, 5 to 10 minutes. Don't let it get too firm.

Beat the egg whites with the salt until frothy. Gradually beat in the remaining ¼ cup sugar until the mixture is stiff but not dry. Gently fold the egg whites into the berry mixture, then fold in 1 cup of the whipped cream and the 2 remaining cups loganberries. Pour the filling into the prepared pie shell and smooth the top with the back of a spoon. Chill for 2 hours. Before serving, spread the remaining whipped cream on top of the pie and garnish with fresh berries.

### Clémentine's Perfect Strawberry Tart

"Wild strawberries were at their peak in the adjacent forests at this particular moment, and we bought baskets of them daily from the picturesque old denizens of the woods who picked them in the early dawn and hawked them from door to door. Clementine's Tarte aux Fraises des Bois was one of the classics of her repertoire, and we enjoyed them almost daily during those last two weeks. Her trick, first of all, was to make beautiful, rich, tender (but not too short) pastry shells. I've watched her do it often, but my attempts to imitate her have been woeful, and I just don't feel qualified to pass on the secret. Five minutes before we were ready for dessert she would fill the cold pastry shells with the uncooked wild strawberries. Over them she poured moderately thick raspberry syrup. Into a hot oven she popped them, and when they came out two or three minutes later they defied description. The strawberries had become partially cooked. The pastry was hot and crisp, and the whole thing was permeated with a mysterious perfume, which could be traced to the raspberry syrup. Accompanied by a cool Vouvray, usually a Château Moncontour, these wild strawberry tarts brought an indescribable sense of well-being to our little family and its guests sitting in the long June twilight. In fact, they usually called for another bottle or two of Chateau Moncontour from the cave."

—From *Clémentine in the Kitchen* by Phineas Beck
(Samuel Chamberlain)

## *Berrissimo*

This recipe came from Cathy Whims when she was chef-owner of the highly regarded Genoa Restaurant in Portland, Oregon, where Berrissimo is a popular dessert on the summer menu. It's Italian for "the most berries," and this delectable tart lives up to its name. It's loaded with a mound of berries baked slowly in a rich and creamy custard filling.

**MAKES 10 TO 12 SERVINGS**

**TART**

**2 cups all-purpose flour**

**⅔ cup plus 2 tablespoons sugar**

**1 teaspoon grated lemon zest**

**½ teaspoon coarse salt**

**½ pound (2 sticks) cold unsalted butter, cut into bits**

**1 large egg**

**1 teaspoon vanilla extract**

**¾ teaspoon ground cinnamon**

**2 pints (4 cups) fresh marionberries or other blackberries, rinsed and drained**

**TOPPING**

**1 cup sour cream or crème fraîche (see page 73)**

**3 large egg yolks**

**2 tablespoons honey**

**Dash of vanilla extract**

Preheat the oven to 400°F degrees.

Put the flour, 2 tablespoons sugar, lemon zest, and salt in a food processor and pulse 3 to 4 times to blend. Add the butter, egg, and vanilla and process until just blended. Press the dough, using your fingertips, into an 11-inch tart pan. Chill.

Mix together the remaining ⅔ cup sugar with the cinnamon. Sprinkle a little of the cinnamon sugar over the tart shell and bake it for 15 minutes. Fill the shell with the berries and sprinkle with the rest of the cinnamon sugar. Bake for another 15 minutes.

Whisk together the sour cream, egg yolks, honey, and vanilla and pour it over the berries. Bake for 15 minutes longer, until the topping is set and just starts to turn golden brown around the edges. A knife inserted in the center should come out clean. Serve warm or at room temperature for breakfast, brunch, lunch, dinner, or a snack.

## *Fresh Raspberry Tart*

Award-winning food writer and *Bon Appétit* columnist Marie Simmons gave me this raspberry tart recipe. "For years I made this only with blueberries, but I have also made it with raspberries, apricots, peaches, and figs. It is a family favorite, and usually I make two at a time, as one is never quite enough. The crust is made in the food processor and isn't rolled out. Instead you use your fingertips to gently press the dough into a tart pan. It couldn't be easier. And every time the crust is as tender as a butter cookie."

**MAKES 8 TO 10 SERVINGS**

**CRUST**

**1½ cups all-purpose flour**
**2 tablespoons sugar**
**¼ pound (1 stick) cold unsalted butter, cut into ½-inch pieces**
**1 large egg yolk**
**1 teaspoon vanilla extract**

**FILLING**

**¼ cup sugar**
**2 tablespoons all-purpose flour**
**2½ pints (5 cups) fresh raspberries, blueberries, or high-quality strawberries, rinsed and drained**
**Sifted confectioners' sugar**
**Vanilla ice cream or lightly sweetened whipped cream (optional)**

Preheat the oven to 425°F. Wipe an 11-inch tart pan with a removable rim with a paper towel dipped in a flavorless oil if the surface isn't well seasoned.

Combine the flour and sugar in a food processor. With the motor running, gradually add the butter through the feed tube. Process until thoroughly incorporated.

Stir the egg yolk and vanilla together in a cup. With the motor running, gradually add egg mixture through the feed tube. Pulse the mixture until it begins to pull together. If the mixture seems too dry, add 1 to 2 tablespoons ice water and process until a dough forms. The dough should be crumbly but not dry.

Turn the dough out directly into the tart pan. Press it up along the sides and on the bottom of the pan in a relatively even layer; the dough will have a rough surface.

(Note: While the crust can be made ahead and refrigerated until ready to be baked, it tastes best when it is baked right away.)

To make the filling, stir the sugar and flour together in a large bowl until blended. Add half of the raspberries and toss to coat with the sugar mixture. Spoon into the prepared crust and top with any sugar left in the bottom of the bowl.

Bake for 15 minutes. Reduce the oven temperature to 350°F. Bake until the edges are golden brown and the berries are hot and bubbly, 30 to 40 minutes, running a spoon through the berry mixture to turn over any berries that still have flour on them a halfway through the cooking time. Remove the pan from the oven. Carefully arrange the remaining berries, stem ends down, close together all over the surface of the tart, pressing them down gently into the hot berry mixture. Cool the tart on a wire rack.

Before serving, push the tart up out of the pan. Sprinkle with the confectioners' sugar. Cut into wedges and serve with a spoonful of whipped cream or a scoop of softened vanilla ice cream if desired.

## *Marionberry Streusel Tart*

Papa Haydn's Restaurant in Portland, Oregon, is legendary for its luscious desserts. The proprietor, Evelyn Franz, is a sculptor by profession, and all her kitchen creations reflect her artistic style. This tart is no exception. The extravagant streusel topping is piled high above the berries, making a dramatic presentation and a tart so rich it's best to serve small slices.

**MAKES 10 TO 12 SERVINGS**

**TART**

**2 pints (4 cups) plus ½ cup marionberries or other blackberries, rinsed and drained, or frozen marionberries, thawed in a single layer on a paper towel for 20 minutes**

**6 tablespoons granulated sugar**

**¾ tablespoon quick-cooking tapioca**

**3 tablespoons fresh lemon juice (from 1 or 2 large lemons)**

**1 tablespoon grated lemon zest**

**1 partially baked 11-inch tart shell (page 214)**

**TOPPING**

**2¼ cups all-purpose flour**

**1 cup packed light brown sugar**

**¼ teaspoon coarse salt**

**½ pound (2 sticks) plus 4 tablespoons (½ stick) unsalted butter**

Preheat the oven to 325°F.

Toss the berries with the granulated sugar, tapioca, lemon juice, and zest. Let the berry mixture sit at room temperature for 15 minutes. Pour into the pastry shell.

To make the topping, put the flour, brown sugar, salt, and butter in a food processor and pulse for 10 to 12 seconds or until the mixture forms pea-size crumbs. Sprinkle the topping over the berries—it will be a dramatic heap—and bake for 25 to 30 minutes, until the topping is a rich golden brown. Serve warm or at room temperature.

## *Red Currant Curd and Raspberry Tart*

Ellen McFarland is the co-owner of Park Kitchen restaurant. Prior to that she was the pastry chef at Higgins restaurant in Portland, Oregon. She pairs two of my favorite red berries—currants and raspberries—in this unusual tart. The red currant curd is also good as is, unbaked, topped with the fresh raspberries.

**MAKES ONE 10-INCH TART OR EIGHT 4-INCH TARTS**

**RED CURRANT CURD**

**1 pint (about 2 cups) fresh red currants, rinsed and drained, or frozen red currants, thawed in a single layer on a paper towel for 20 minutes**

**1¼ cups sugar**

**Pinch of coarse salt**

**8 large egg yolks**

**¼ pound (1 stick) unsalted butter at room temperature**

**Fresh lemon juice, to taste (optional)**

**PASTRY**

**1½ cups all-purpose flour**

**2 tablespoons sugar**

**¼ pound (1 stick) cold unsalted butter, cut into ½-inch pieces**

**1 large egg yolk**

**1 teaspoon vanilla extract**

**½ cup strained raspberry or red currant jelly, warm**

**1 pint (2 cups) fresh raspberries, rinsed and drained**

To make the curd, cook the currants in ¼ cup water in a nonreactive saucepan over low heat until they are very soft, about 10 minutes. Press the solids through a fine strainer or strain using a food mill. This should yield about 1 cup of puree. Let cool.

Put the puree in the top of a double boiler and stir in the sugar, a pinch of salt, egg yolks, and butter. Cook the mixture over simmering water (do not let the water boil), stirring constantly until thickened (about 190°F). Strain and correct the seasoning with a few drops of lemon juice and another pinch of salt if necessary. Let cool.

Preheat the oven to 425°F. Spray an 11-inch tart pan with a removable rim with a flavorless oil if the surface isn't well seasoned.

Combine the flour and sugar in a food processor. With the motor running, gradually add the butter through the feed tube. Process until thoroughly incorporated.

Stir the egg yolk and vanilla together in a cup. With the motor running, gradually add egg mixture through the feed tube. Pulse the mixture until it begins to pull together. If the mixture seems too dry, add 1 to 2 tablespoons ice water and process until a dough forms. The dough should be crumbly but not dry.

Turn the dough out directly into the prepared tart pan. Press it up along the sides and on the bottom of the pan in a relatively even layer; the dough will have a rough surface. (Note: While the crust can be made ahead and refrigerated until ready to be baked, it tastes best when baked right away.)

Prick the entire surface with the tines of a fork. Chill in the refrigerator for 15 minutes. Set the tart on a cookie sheet (it helps the bottom of the crust to brown) and bake for about 15 minutes, until the crust is golden brown. Let cool.

Lightly brush the cooled tart shell with about 3 tablespoons of the warm jelly. This will preserve its crispness. Let cool. Fill the shell with the red currant curd and arrange the raspberries on top, fitting them close together. Brush the remaining jelly lightly and evenly over the berries. The tart can be assembled up to 3 hours prior to serving and kept in the refrigerator. Bring to room temperature before serving. Lightly sweetened, softly whipped cream is the nicest accompaniment.

## *Wild Blueberry Galette*

Galettes are rustic, free-form pastries that are ideal for small batches of berries because you can make them as small or as large as you like. They somehow seem fitting for wild fruit, perhaps picked on an outing. I roll out my pastry on a cookie sheet so I don't have to move it once it's filled. Serve the galette warm with a mound of vanilla ice cream.

**MAKES 4 SERVINGS**

**½ recipe Favorite Tart and Cobbler Pastry (page 213)**
**1½ pints (3 cups) wild blueberries or huckleberries, rinsed and drained, or frozen wild blueberries or huckleberries**
**⅓ cup plus 1 teaspoon sugar**
**2 tablespoons quick-cooking tapioca**
**1 tablespoon fresh lemon juice**
**2 tablespoons cream, half-and-half, or milk**
**½ cup crème fraîche (see page 73) or 1 pint vanilla ice cream**

Preheat the oven to 400°F.

Flour a clean surface and roll out the pastry ⅛-inch thick into a 12-inch circle. Transfer the pastry to a cookie sheet. Put the blueberries in a bowl with ⅓ cup of the sugar, the tapioca, and the lemon juice and toss. Arrange the mixture in an even layer on top of the dough, leaving a 4-inch border all around. Carefully lift up the outer edges of unfilled pastry and fold them in over the top of the berries. Some of the berries will still be showing.

Brush the top of the pastry with cream and sprinkle with the remaining teaspoon sugar. Bake for 45 to 50 minutes or until the top of the galette is golden brown and the berries are bubbly.

Serve with a dollop of crème fraîche or a scoop of vanilla ice cream.

## *Basic Pie Crust*

This old-fashioned pastry is both flaky and tender. It makes enough dough for 2 double-crust pies, and you can make it in either your mixer or food processor. This dough also freezes well for several months and will keep in the refrigerator for up to 2 weeks. During berry season, I always have this pastry on hand.

**MAKES ENOUGH FOR 2 DOUBLE-CRUST PIES**

**3 cups all-purpose flour**
**1½ teaspoons coarse salt**
**1¼ cups vegetable shortening, chilled**
**1 large egg**
**1 tablespoon white vinegar**

Combine the flour and salt in a mixing bowl and cut in the shortening. Whisk the egg and vinegar with ¼ cup cold water. Using an electric mixer at low speed, gradually add the egg mixture to the dry ingredients until it forms a ball. Gather the dough and shape into a smooth disk. Double-wrap any unused pastry in plastic wrap or put in a plastic bag and store in the refrigerator for up to 2 weeks or the freezer for up to 2 months.

**TO PREPARE A BAKED PIE SHELL**

Flour a clean surface and roll out the dough ⅛-inch thick into a circle 1½ to 2 inches larger than the pie pan. Lay the rolling pin in the center of the crust, fold the pastry over it, and transfer it to the pie pan. Gently press the dough into the pan. Fold under the edge of the pastry and crimp. Prick the entire surface, including the sides, with a fork. Refrigerate for ½ hour.

Preheat the oven to 450°F. Set the pie pan on a baking sheet and bake for 10 to 15 minutes or until the crust is golden brown. Cool before filling.

## *Canola Oil Pastry*

The advantage of this pastry is that it contains virtually no saturated fat. This pastry dries quickly and works best if used immediately.

**MAKES ENOUGH FOR 1 DOUBLE-CRUST PIE OR ONE 9 × 13-INCH COBBLER**

**2 cups all-purpose flour**
**1 teaspoon coarse salt**
**½ cup canola oil**
**¼ cup cold milk**

Moisten a surface about 18 inches square with water and cover with a piece of wax paper.

Mix the flour and salt together in a bowl and stir in the oil and milk until the dough is smooth. Gather the dough and press into a disk for a cobbler or divide in half for a double-crust pie.

For a cobbler, put the filling in the pan. Transfer the disk to the wax paper and put a second piece of wax paper on top of the dough. Roll it out about ⅛ -inch thick to the desired size and remove the top piece of wax paper. Carefully pick up the bottom piece of wax paper with the rolled-out dough and lay it on top of the filling. Carefully peel off the paper, gently pressing the dough onto the filling and into the corners. Trim the pastry 1 inch from the edge of the pan and roll the pastry under and flute.

For a pie, ease the pastry loosely into the pan, paper side up, and carefully pull off the paper. Using your fingers, gently push the crust into the pan. Trim the edges, leaving a 1-inch overhang. Add the filling. Repeat for the second crust. Roll the pastry under and flute. Cut slits.

*Variation:* For a single-crust pie, use 1½ cups flour, ¾ teaspoon salt, ⅓ cup oil, and 3 tablespoons cold milk. Mix and roll out as directed, transfer to the pan, overhang under the rim and flute. Prick with a fork and bake at 425°F for 12 to 15 minutes.

## *Favorite Tart and Cobbler Pastry*

I've made this tart pastry with its perfect buttery short crust for years. I also use this recipe as a topping for a 9 × 13-inch berry cobbler. You can cut the butter in by hand or do as I do and make it in the food processor in about 30 seconds.

**MAKES TWO 8- OR 9-INCH TART SHELLS OR ONE 11-INCH SHELL WITH A LITTLE DOUGH LEFT OVER**

**2 cups all-purpose flour**
**½ pound (2 sticks) cold unsalted butter, cut into 1-inch pieces**
**1 large egg**
**1 tablespoon heavy cream**
**1 tablespoon fresh lemon juice**
**1 teaspoon sugar**
**½ teaspoon coarse salt**

Put all the ingredients in a food processor and process until the dough starts to form a ball.

Roll out the dough ⅛-inch thick on a floured surface. Fold the dough over the rolling pin and transfer the pastry to the tart pan. When you have pushed the dough into the pan with your fingers, firmly run the rolling pin over the top of the tart to remove excess dough. Prick the bottom and sides of the crust with a fork. Chill for 30 minutes.

Preheat the oven to 400°F.

Grease the shiny side of a piece of foil and line the pan, going up and over the edges. Fill with raw rice or beans (this helps to keep the sides from sagging and the bottom from popping up). Bake for 15 minutes, remove the foil and filling, and bake for another 5 to 10 minutes. Remove from the oven and let cool before filling.

*Note:* Since this pastry has a lot of butter in it, the crust is slightly hard when it is served directly from the refrigerator. Let cobblers and tarts warm up to room temperature or warm them for 10 minutes in a 250°F oven before serving them.

### Container Gardening with Berries

Berries are easily grown in containers and provide good summer patio nibbling. Many berries stay on the plant during the winter and fall, attracting birds and providing, along with their lovely foliage, a colorful backdrop to liven up drab winter gardens. Plant berries that grow as shrubs and on canes in half whiskey barrel–size containers with potting soil and timed-release fertilizer. Try blueberries, blackberries, huckleberries, cranberries, currants, gooseberries, lingonberries, raspberries, or strawberries. Raintree Nursery in Morton, Washington, has an enormous selection of berry plants and ships throughout the U.S. (Imagine 42 cultivars of blueberries, 19 of strawberries, 19 of blackberries, 13 of raspberries, five of cranberries, and six of lingonberries.) All the different cultivars are listed on their Web site with individual photos: Raintree Nursery, 391 Butts Road, Morton, WA 98356-1700; 800-391-8892; www.raintreenursery.com.

## *Press-In Butter Pastry*

**MAKES ONE 11-INCH TART SHELL (SEE NOTE)**

**1½ cups all-purpose flour**
**2 tablespoons sugar**
**¼ pound (1 stick) cold unsalted butter, cut into ½-inch pieces**
**1 large egg yolk**
**1 teaspoon vanilla extract**

Preheat the oven to 425°F. Spray an 11-inch tart pan with a removable rim with vegetable oil if the surface isn't well seasoned.

Combine the flour and sugar in the bowl of a food processor. With the motor running, gradually add the butter through the feed tube. Process until thoroughly incorporated.

Stir the egg yolk and vanilla together in a cup. With the motor running, gradually add the egg mixture through the feed tube. Pulse the mixture until it begins to pull together. Stop the machine. If the mixture seems dry and is not starting to form a ball, add 1 to 2 tablespoons ice water and process until a dough forms. The dough should be crumbly but not dry.

Turn the dough out directly into the prepared tart pan. Press it up along the sides and on the bottom of the pan in a relatively even layer; the dough will have a rough surface. (Note: While the crust can be made ahead and refrigerated until ready to be baked, it tastes best when baked right away, making chilling unnecessary.)

To bake the crust blind, prick the entire surface with the tines of a fork and refrigerate for 15 minutes. Bake for about 15 minutes, until the crust is golden brown.

*Note:* To make by hand, combine the flour and sugar in a medium bowl. Cut in the butter with 2 table knives or a pastry blender until the mixture forms coarse crumbs. In a small bowl, stir together the egg yolk and vanilla and drizzle over the flour mixture. Using your hands, shape the dough into a ball. Add 1 to 2 tablespoons ice water if the dough seems dry.

## *Black Currant and Apple Crumble*

Tommie van de Kamp and her husband, Peter, own Queener Fruit Farm, located in the heart of the fertile Willamette Valley near Scio, Oregon, one of the world's premier berry-growing regions. Among other fruits, they have five acres of currants, which they sell to local chefs and through mail order (see page 153).

This is Tommie's crumble recipe. She says, "When I was growing up in Wales, my mother would make a black currant pie just like an apple pie, but I prefer to make this quicker, though just as delicious, crumble."

**MAKES 4 SERVINGS**

**½ cup fresh black currants, rinsed and drained, or frozen black currants, thawed in a single layer on a paper towel for 20 minutes**

**⅓ cup plus 3 tablespoons sugar**

**4 (about 2 pounds) large, mildly tart, firm apples, such as 2 Granny Smith or Newtown Pippin and 2 Rome**

**1 cup all-purpose flour**

**4 tablespoons (½ stick) unsalted butter**

**Vanilla ice cream (optional)**

Preheat the oven to 400°F. Grease an 8- or 9-inch square glass baking dish.

Gently toss the currants with 1 tablespoon of the sugar. Peel, core, and slice each apple into 6 pieces. Make 2 layers of apples and currants in the pan, sprinkling each with a tablespoon of sugar.

Combine the flour and butter with a pastry cutter or your hands until the mixture forms pea-size crumbs; work in the remaining ¼ cup plus 1 tablespoon sugar. Sprinkle the topping evenly over the fruit.

Bake for 35 minutes, until the topping is golden brown and the fruit is bubbly. Serve warm with a scoop of vanilla ice cream if desired.

## *Boysenberry-Loganberry Cobbler*

These are two of my favorite blackberries. Boysenberries are perfectly sweet with an intense blackberry flavor, while loganberries have a tart raspberry taste. When the two are baked together, their flavors and acidity balance each other perfectly. A scoop of vanilla ice cream is a must when it comes time to dish up this dessert.

**MAKES 6 SERVINGS**

**½ recipe Favorite Tart and Cobbler Pastry (page 213)**
**1½ pints (3 cups) fresh boysenberries, rinsed and drained, or frozen boysenberries, thawed in a single layer on a paper towel for 20 minutes**
**1½ pints (3 cups) fresh loganberries, rinsed and drained, or frozen loganberries, thawed in a single layer on a paper towel for 20 minutes**
**½ to ⅔ cup sugar, to taste, plus sugar for sprinkling**
**3 table spoons all-purpose flour or quick-cooking tapioca**
**1 tablespoon unsalted butter (optional)**
**2 tablespoons milk**

Preheat the oven to 400°F.

Flour a clean surface and roll out the dough ⅛-inch thick into a 9-inch square. Put the berries into an 8-inch square baking dish and toss with the sugar and flour. Dot with butter. Fold the pastry over the rolling pin and ease it over the filling. Gently press down on the crust, pushing it into all the corners. Tuck the edge of the pastry over, toward the sides of the pan, and crimp, sealing in the berries. Brush the top with milk, sprinkle with sugar, and cut vents to release the steam. Bake for 45 minutes (50 for frozen berries), until the crust is golden brown and the juices are bubbly. Serve warm with vanilla ice cream.

*Note:* For 12, use the full crust recipe, 12 cups of berries, 1 cup sugar, 6 tablespoons flour or ½ cup quick-cooking tapioca, 1 to 2 tablespoons butter (optional), and ¼ cup milk.

## *Cannon Beach Blackberry Cobbler*

Kathy Allcock, a friend of mine who is a great cook, says, "This old cobbler recipe came from my grandmother, who got it from an older woman across the street, and we always make it in the summer with blackberries we pick at Cannon Beach."

It's an unusual recipe—all the ingredients are mixed together and put into a buttered baking pan, then a cup of hot water is poured over the top. As the batter cooks, it absorbs the water while rising to the surface, producing a memorable moist and berry-laden cobbler that just begs for some good old-fashioned vanilla ice cream to go with it.

**MAKES 6 SERVINGS**

**1 cup all-purpose flour**
**½ cup sugar, plus ½ to 1 cup sugar, to taste, for the berries**
**½ teaspoon baking powder**
**2 tablespoons unsalted butter, softened**
**½ cup milk**
**1 pint (2 cups) fresh marionberries or other blackberries or frozen marionberries, thawed in a single layer on a paper towel for 20 minutes**

Preheat the oven to 350°F. Grease an 8-inch square baking dish.

Stir together the flour, ½ cup sugar, baking powder, butter, and milk. Toss the berries with the remaining sugar and stir into the batter. Spoon the batter into the baking dish. Pour 1 cup hot water over all and bake for 45 minutes (50 for frozen berries), until the batter rises to the surface around the edges of the pan and is light golden brown. Serve warm.

## *Mother's Day Blackberry Cobbler*

Pete Peterson, a Portland friend whose specialty is organic produce, got this recipe from his grandmother, Marie Peterson, who used to make it for their threshing crew on land she and her husband homesteaded in North Dakota in the 1920s. Years later the family moved to a small farm in rural Washington, where they raised strawberries. Pete fondly remembers helping his grandmother make this cobbler with his cousins, and he highly recommends letting little hands help. "It's a perfect cobbler for kids to make for a Mother's Day breakfast in bed," Pete says. "A good fruit combination that time of the year is strawberries and rhubarb. Sprinkle the rhubarb with 1 to 2 tablespoons of sugar and let it sit 10 to 15 minutes before mixing it with the strawberries to sweeten it."

**MAKES 6 SERVINGS**

**2 to 3 tablespoons unsalted butter**
**3 pints (6 cups) fresh berries, rinsed and drained, or a combination of berries and fruit (see Note)**
**⅔ cup sugar**
**1 cup all-purpose flour**
**1 teaspoon baking powder**
**⅔ cup milk**
**Vanilla ice cream or sweetened whipped cream**

Preheat the oven to 375°F.

Put the butter in an 8-inch square glass baking pan and melt it in the oven, being careful not to let the butter burn. Remove from the oven and let cool. (Dad helps here.)

If the fruit is tart, toss it with 1 to 2 tablespoons of the sugar. Add the fruit to the baking pan and spread it out evenly to fill it no more than two-thirds full.

Stir together the flour, remaining sugar, and the baking powder. Pour in the milk and stir until just blended. Do not overmix. Spoon the batter over the fruit—do not mix it in.

Bake for 35 to 40 minutes or until the crust is golden brown. Serve warm or with vanilla ice cream or sweetened whipped cream.

*Note:* For best results, use two or more types of fruit; for stone fruit, peel, remove the pits, and cut into thin slices.

## *Apple-Huckleberry Crisp*

This recipe was inspired by Anna Thomas, author of *The Vegetarian Epicure.* I have made and enjoyed her apple crisp recipe for more than 30 years. This is my version with fresh huckleberries from the mountains.

**MAKES 8 SERVINGS**

- **2 pounds Golden Delicious apples, peeled, cored, and cut into ¼-inch-thick slices (about 5 cups)**
- **1 pint (2 cups) fresh huckleberries or wild blueberries, rinsed and drained, or frozen huckleberries or blueberries**
- **¾ cup packed dark brown sugar**
- **½ teaspoon freshly grated nutmeg**
- **¾ teaspoon ground cinnamon**
- **¼ teaspoon coarse salt**
- **¾ cup all-purpose flour**
- **¼ pound (1 stick) unsalted butter**

Preheat the oven to 350°F. Butter a shallow 3-quart dish (I use a gratin dish) and add the apples and huckleberries. Pour ½ cup water over the fruit and smooth the top to make it level.

In a food processor, pulse the sugar, nutmeg, cinnamon, salt, flour, and butter together until they form pea-size crumbs. Sprinkle the mixture over the fruit and cover with foil.

Bake for 30 minutes. Remove the foil and bake for 30 minutes longer, until the apples are tender and the crust is a dark golden brown. Serve warm or at room temperature with vanilla ice cream.

# CAKES

Cakes are especially good with berries because their billowy texture is just right for soaking up the fruits' luscious juices. Some recipes—The Perfect Strawberry Shortcake, Blue-Ribbon Sponge Cake with Boysenberry Curd, Pavlova, and the Chocolate-Espresso Hazelnut Cake—should be made only with fresh berries at the peak of the season to showcase the fruit. And the Upside-Down Cranberry-Pumpkin Polenta Cake needs to be made with fresh cranberries since frozen berries give off steam that alters the cake's texture. For the remaining cakes with sauces, use either fresh or high-quality frozen berries.

All of the cake recipes are versatile and can be adapted for a variety of berries or berry toppings. Try a slice of sponge cake with a scoop of Loganberry-Buttermilk Ice Cream (page 183) or Blood Orange Vodka Berry Sorbet (page 188) or make a raspberry shortcake instead of a strawberry shortcake and add a splash of framboise to the sauce. The choices are limitless, so let your imagination be your guide.

## *The Perfect Strawberry Shortcake*

Recipes that are good, like this one from the 1963 *McCall's Cookbook,* live forever. It's impossible to improve on perfection—it's tender and exceptionally moist and so tasty the shortcake can be eaten by itself. And when it's smothered in sweet, juicy strawberries and whipped cream, it's beyond words. Use blueberries and strawberries for the Fourth of July.

**MAKES 6 SERVINGS**

**2 pints (4 cups) high-quality fresh strawberries, sliced, a few whole ones reserved for garnish**

**½ cup granulated sugar**

**2 cups all-purpose flour**

**1 tablespoon baking powder**

**½ teaspoon coarse salt**

**¼ pound (1 stick) unsalted butter, softened**

**¾ cup milk**

**1 cup heavy cream**

**2 to 4 tablespoons confectioners' sugar, to taste**

**½ teaspoon vanilla extract**

Preheat the oven to 450°F. Grease an 8-inch square pan.

Slice half of the strawberries and sprinkle them with ¼ cup of the granulated sugar to release the juices. Mash them lightly with a potato masher.

Sift together the flour, the remaining granulated sugar, the baking powder, and the salt in a medium bowl. Stir in the butter and milk and mix. It should still be lumpy.

Spoon into the pan and spread as evenly as possible with the back of a spoon. Don't worry if it's not perfect.

Bake for 12 to 15 minutes, until a toothpick comes out clean. Let cool and cut into 6 pieces.

Whip the cream with the confectioners' sugar and vanilla until stiff.

Split a piece of shortcake horizontally and place the bottom, cut side up, on a dessert plate. Ladle on a spoonful of the mashed berries and cover with the top. Put another spoonful of the mashed berries on top and finish with a dollop of whipped cream. Repeat for the other 5 shortcakes. Serve immediately and savor every morsel.

### The Heritage of the Oregon Strawberry

When Dr. William Popenoe of the U.S. Department of Agriculture traveled to South America in 1921 to evaluate and collect fruit, he went to Huachi Grande, a village high (10,000 feet) in the Ecuadorian Andes known for centuries as a center for strawberry production.

"What sorts have we, may I ask, which could be thrown into boxes holding 30 to 35 quarts, carried seven or eight miles on mule back, worked over by hand and packed in two- to six-quart baskets, and then shipped down to a tropical seaport, there to be kept in a market for two or three dates [sic] at temperatures of 70 to 85 degrees? Even with such treatment as this, the Huachi strawberry holds up well, retaining its shape and texture to an extent altogether unknown among northern strawberries."

Years later, in the mid-1950s, Dr. George Darrow, noted Maryland strawberry authority, made three trips to Huachi for the USDA to learn about this legendary strawberry. He was impressed with the ability of the Huachi to thrive on the dry volcanic soils and produce large firm fruit with superior flavor.

Scientists speculate that when Popenoe visited Ecuador in 1921 he must have brought plants back to North America even though there is no written record of it. In the 1930s at the USDA Research Center at Oregon State University, plant breeder Dr. George Waldo used a USDA selection that had Huachi as a parent for strawberry breeding. Today most of the cultivars released by the USDA in Oregon have Huachi in their germplasm, although it is not found to any degree in Europe or on the East Coast or in California strawberries.

## *Shortbread with Warm Berry Port Sauce*

If you like shortbread, you'll love this recipe from the Porto Wine Institute in New York. Although it is simple to make, it's a sophisticated dessert that could be served for any occasion from a casual get-together to a formal dinner party. Heating the berries in the port creates a remarkably intense berry sauce that can also be spooned over slices of sponge cake (page 224) or mounds of vanilla ice cream.

**MAKES 4 SERVINGS**

**SHORTBREAD**

**1 cup self-rising flour**
**2 tablespoons medium-ground cornmeal**
**Grated zest of 1 lemon**

**¼ cup packed light brown sugar**

**9 tablespoons cold unsalted butter, cut into 6 or 7 pieces**

SAUCE

**3 cup mixed fresh berries, such as blackberries, raspberries, strawberries, and blueberries, rinsed and drained, or frozen berries, thawed with juice**

**¼ cup granulated sugar**

**1 vanilla bean, split lengthwise**

**¼ pint ruby port (late bottle vintage, if possible, see Note)**

Preheat the oven to 375°F. Lightly grease an 8-inch square pan.

Put the flour, cornmeal, lemon zest, brown sugar, and butter in a food processor and pulse 3 or 4 times. Process until the dough almost forms a ball. (Or cut the butter into the dry ingredients with 2 knives or a pastry cutter.) Remove the dough and, using your fingers, pat it into the pan. Bake for 17 to 20 minutes, until a toothpick comes out clean. It will be golden brown and slightly darker brown around the edges.

Put the berries, granulated sugar, vanilla bean, and port in a small saucepan. Cook over medium heat for 3 minutes, stirring at first to dissolve the sugar. Remove the fruit with a slotted spoon and gently cook the sauce until it thickens slightly, about 5 more minutes (slightly longer if you are using frozen berries). Put the fruit back into the sauce and serve warm, ladled over the shortbread and accompanied by a glass of port.

*Note:* Late bottle vintage (LBV) refers to a specific year of port, aged in wood 4 to 6 years with characteristic berry, chocolate, and spice flavors.

### Real Strawberries in Cream

"Take a deep cold bowl half full of cream (an old punch-bowl is excellent for this purpose). Whip the cream slightly, but do not make it too stiff. Then drop into it as many strawberries as it will hold, the smaller ones being put in whole, while the larger cut up. Stir as you go, mashing slightly, and when the cream really won't cover another strawberry, leave it to stand for an hour. It will then be a cold level pale-pink cream. Crust it over with dredged white sugar and serve forth, in June, on a green lawn, under shady trees by the river."

—From *Food in England* by Dorothy Hartley

## *Blue-Ribbon Sponge Cake with Boysenberry Curd*

All berries deserve a good, simple, homemade cake. The superb flavor and texture of a homemade sponge cake are so outstanding that it's worth the extra effort it takes to make one from scratch. (And you are not getting all those additives either.) Here the cake is sliced into three layers and filled with boysenberry curd, fresh boysenberries, and whipped cream.

**MAKES 8 TO 10 SERVINGS**

**1½ cups cake flour**
**¼ teaspoon baking powder**
**¼ teaspoon coarse salt**
**5 large eggs, separated**
**½ teaspoon almond extract**
**1½ cups sugar**
**¾ teaspoon cream of tartar**
**Boysenberry Curd (recipe follows)**
**2 heaping pints (5 cups) fresh boysenberries, rinsed and drained**
**1 cup heavy cream**

Preheat the oven to 325°F. Place a rack in the bottom third of the oven.

Sift the flour, baking powder, and salt together and set aside.

Put the egg yolks in a mixing bowl and beat for 45 seconds, until light and lemon colored. Add ½ cup ice water and ½ teaspoon of the almond extract and beat until the mixture turns pale yellow and is foamy on top. With the mixer still running, gradually beat in the sugar and continue beating until all the sugar is dissolved. Fold the dry ingredients into the yolk mixture.

Beat the whites with the cream of tartar until stiff but not dry. Carefully fold the whites into the flour-yolk mix. Gently pour the batter into an ungreased angel food cake pan. Bake for 1 hour, or until a toothpick inserted in the center comes out clean. Invert the cake over a long-necked bottle to cool.

Remove the cake from the pan by running a knife around the edge of the cake and around the tube to loosen it.

Using a serrated knife, cut the cake into 3 horizontal layers. Spread ½ cup berry curd over the top of the bottom layer and sprinkle with 1 cup fresh boysenberries. Repeat for the second layer. Cover with the third layer. Whip the cream until almost stiff and fold in the remaining ¾ cup curd. Frost the cake and cover the top with the remaining fresh boysenberries. Keep the cake chilled and serve within 4 to 6 hours.

*Variation:* Serve the cake cut into wedges, accompanied by a bowl of sweetened whipped cream (3 cups heavy cream whipped with ⅓ to ½ cup confectioners' sugar and 1 teaspoon vanilla extract) and 2 pints fresh berries sprinkled with a little sugar. (If you are using strawberries, slice them first.) Once the berries are sprinkled with sugar, let them sit at room temperature for 1 to 2 hours to allow their juices to start running.

## *Boysenberry Curd*

Berry curds are sinfully delicious and perfect for special occasions when it's okay to be a little decadent. You can also use them as spreads on biscuits or scones, folded into whipped cream and served in parfait glasses, or as the bottom layer of a tart, such as the one on page 209. Other berries can be substituted for the boysenberries.

**MAKES 1¾ CUPS**

**2 pints (4 cups) fresh boysenberries, rinsed and drained, or frozen boysenberries, thawed with juice, pureed, and seeded (see page 70)**

¼ pound (1 stick) unsalted butter, melted and slightly cooled
3 large eggs, beaten
¾ cup sugar
1 tablespoon fresh lemon juice

Combine all the ingredients in a saucepan over medium heat, stirring constantly until the mixture thickens to the consistency of hot pudding, about 15 minutes. It will thicken further as it cools. Store covered in the refrigerator for up to 1 week.

## *Cinnamon-Custard Sponge Cake with Wild Blackberries*

Imagine a cake so moist and perfectly tender that it's almost like eating a delicate bread pudding. This Basque cake comes from a small collection of recipes from the Basque Museum and Cultural Center in Boise, Idaho. It's a rolled sponge cake with a delicate cinnamon-flavored custard filling that is barely thickened. The custard is used as both the filling and the topping, which makes this cake exceptionally moist. I have also added fresh blackberries to the original recipe because they add a contrasting spark of flavor.

**MAKES 8 TO 10 SERVINGS**

**SPONGE CAKE**

**Confectioners' sugar for sprinkling**
**6 large eggs, separated into 2 mixing bowls**
**6 tablespoons sugar**
**6 tablespoons all-purpose flour**
**1 teaspoon baking powder**
**1 teaspoon vanilla extract**
**Pinch of coarse salt**

**FILLING**

**3¾ cups milk**
**¾ cup granulated sugar**
**Pinch of coarse salt**
**Two 2- to 3-inch cinnamon sticks**
**3 large eggs**
**2 tablespoons all-purpose flour**

**½ teaspoon vanilla extract**

**1 pint (2 cups) fresh wild blackberries or other blackberries or raspberries, rinsed and drained**

Preheat the oven to 325°F. Line a jelly roll pan (11 × 16 inches) with wax or parchment paper; lightly grease the paper. Alternatively, grease and flour the bottom and sides of the pan. Spread a clean dish towel out on the counter and sprinkle generously with confectioners' sugar.

Combine the egg yolks, sugar, flour, baking powder, and vanilla in a bowl and beat on high speed until thick and pale yellow, 2 to 3 minutes. Set aside.

Beat the egg whites and salt until stiff but not dry peaks form.

Gently fold the yolk mixture into the egg whites and spread the mixture evenly in the jelly roll pan.

Bake for 20 to 25 minutes, until the top springs back when lightly touched or a cake tester inserted in the center comes out clean. Remove the cake from the pan and invert onto the dish towel. Carefully pull off the paper and roll the cake lengthwise in the towel. Let cool on a cake rack.

For the filling, put 3 cups of the milk, the sugar, salt, and cinnamon sticks together in a pan over medium heat and bring almost to a boil. Remove from the heat and allow to cool in the refrigerator.

Beat the eggs, flour, vanilla, and remaining ¾ cup milk together until smooth, then slowly whisk the mixture into the hot milk. Put the pan back over medium heat and cook until the filling thickens slightly and coats the back of a spoon. Remove from the heat and allow to cool.

Remove the towel from the cake and lay the cake open on a platter with raised sides. Pour two-thirds of the custard on the cake and spread to within ½ inch of the edges on the side. Sprinkle with 1½ cups of the berries and roll it up. Trim ½ inch off the ends of the cake if they are dry and cracked. Pour the remaining filling over the top and sprinkle with the other ½ cup berries. Refrigerate until serving time.

## *Chocolate-Espresso Hazelnut Cake with Raspberry Glaze*

Many years ago Portland artist Carol Adams won first place in a local fundraiser with this cake, a variation of the classic Reine de Saba, or chocolate almond cake. I take it one step further and garnish the top with a single layer of plump fresh raspberries.

This cake is so dense and moist it can be made several days in advance if it is tightly wrapped first in plastic, then in foil. Garnish with the berries just before serving. It can also be frozen, without the berry garnish, for up to 1 month.

**MAKES 8 TO 10 SERVINGS**

**CAKE**

**12 tablespoons (1½ sticks) unsalted butter**

**½ pound bittersweet chocolate**

**4 large eggs, separated**

**½ cup sugar, plus a pinch for the whipped cream**

**⅓ cup potato starch**

**5 ounces (¾ cup plus 2 tablespoons) toasted hazelnuts (see page 73), ground in a blender or food processor**

**Pinch of coarse salt**

**2 tablespoons instant espresso powder, dissolved in ⅓ cup warm water, or ⅓ cup brewed espresso**

**GLAZE**

**3 ounces bittersweet chocolate**

**12 tablespoons (1½ sticks) unsalted butter**

**1 tablespoon framboise**

**1 pint (2 cups) fresh raspberries, rinsed and drained**

**1 cup heavy cream, whipped and sweetened with a pinch of sugar**

Preheat the oven to 325°F. Butter and line an 8-inch round cake pan with parchment paper.

Slowly melt the butter and chocolate together in the top of a double boiler or in a heavy saucepan. Put the egg whites in a deep bowl and beat until foamy, then gradually beat in ¼ cup of the sugar until stiff but not dry.

In a separate bowl, beat the egg yolks until lemon colored, then gradually beat in the remaining ¼ cup sugar until the mixture thickens and turns pale yellow. With the mixer on low, gradually add the potato starch, ground hazelnuts, salt, melted chocolate, and espresso. Blend until smooth. Carefully fold in the beaten egg whites. Pour the batter into the prepared cake pan and run a table knife through it to release any air bubbles. Bake for 25 minutes. It will look firm around the edges and jiggly in the center. The center of the cake should be slightly undercooked.

Allow the cake to cool for 8 to 10 minutes. Run a knife around the edge of the pan and turn it out onto a cake rack. Let cool completely before glazing.

To make the glaze, melt the chocolate and butter together in the top of a double boiler or in a heavy saucepan. Stir in the raspberry liqueur and pour the entire glaze onto the cake, spreading it evenly around the sides with a spatula.

When the glaze has set, arrange the raspberries in a single layer, stem ends down, on top.

Serve with a dollop of whipped cream on the side.

### Grandma's Raspberry Sandwiches

The kids will love this one:
you'll need bread, fresh berries, cream cheese—
apply a thin spread of cream cheese to the bread
add a handful of fresh picked raspberries
& press the sandwich together
for a lunch that will make you laugh.

—From *Earth Temples, Fires & Mandolins* by Stefano Resta

## *Fallen Lemon Cake with Melba Sauce*

This lemony cake has a slightly sunken center and cracked top, but don't let appearances fool you. One bite and you'll think you've eaten the lemon version of Chocolate Decadence. When I'm serving a big meal, I bake this in individual 4-inch cheesecake pans and serve bite-size wedges on a platter—like cookies—to accompany bowls of fresh berries. This cake is also good served with the Melba Sauce, strawberry coulis (see page 151), or lemon sherbet (page 189).

**MAKES 8 SERVINGS**

**4 tablespoons (½ stick) unsalted butter, softened**
**4 tablespoons vegetable shortening**
**1 cup sugar**

**2 large eggs, beaten**
**Zest of 1 large lemon**
**2 teaspoons fresh lemon juice**
**1¼ cups all-purpose flour**
**1 teaspoon baking powder**
**½ teaspoon coarse salt**
**Melba Sauce (recipe follows)**

Preheat the oven to 350°F. Grease and flour four 4-inch or one 8-inch springform pan.

With an electric beater, cream the butter and shortening with the sugar, then beat in the eggs, lemon zest, and lemon juice.

Sift together the flour, baking powder, and salt. Fold the dry ingredients into the creamed mixture.

Divide the batter among the prepared 4-inch pans or pour it into the 8-inch pan. Bake for 23 minutes (4-inch pans) or 30 minutes (8-inch pan), until the cake is golden brown around the edges and a cake tester inserted in the center comes out clean.

Let the cakes cool on a rack in the pans for 5 minutes before releasing. They will keep, wrapped in plastic wrap and then foil, at room temperature for 2 to 3 days.

## *Melba Sauce*

Melba sauce is a raspberry sauce flavored with kirsch, created by Auguste Escoffier for Australian opera singer Nellie Melba. She was living at the Savoy Hotel in London from 1892 to 1893 while performing at the Covent Garden Opera House. Escoffier, the chef at the hotel at the time, created this dish in her honor—vanilla ice cream with poached peaches and "Melba" sauce.

I freeze fresh raspberries in the summer in ½-pint self-sealing plastic freezer bags to have them on hand throughout the winter just for this sauce.

**MAKES ¾ TO 1 CUP**

**1 pint (2 cups) fresh raspberries, rinsed and drained, or frozen raspberries, thawed with juice**
**1 tablespoon kirsch or framboise**
**½ to 1 tablespoon sugar, to taste**

Put the raspberries, kirsch, and sugar in a food processor and puree until smooth. Strain to remove the seeds.

### *Lemon Curd Cake*

I can't have this cake in the house unless company is coming. It's so good I'd eat the whole thing myself. The recipe came from an article in *Cuisine*, New Zealand's top cooking magazine, written by Auckland cookbook author Jo Seagar, who also has her own television cooking show and Web site (www.joseagar.com). Her recipe is surprisingly simple to make, especially if you buy the lemon curd, of which several good commercial brands are available. Try Stonewall Kitchen, 2 Stonewall Lane, York, ME 03909; 800-207-JAMS; www.stonewallkitchen.com (jams, berry curds, lemon curd).

Serve this divine cake for breakfast as a coffee cake accompanied by a bowl of fresh berries or drizzled with a berry coulis and cloaked with whipped cream for dessert. I particularly like it with raspberries, but blackberries, blueberries, or strawberries can be substituted.

**MAKES 8 TO 10 SERVINGS**

**2 cups self-rising flour**

**1 cup sugar**

**7 tablespoons unsalted butter, cut into cubes**

**2 large eggs**

**1½ cups Lemon Curd, commercial or homemade (recipe follows)**

**Confectioners' sugar for sprinkling**

**1 pint (2 cups) fresh raspberries, rinsed, drained, pureed, and pressed through a strainer (see page 74) plus a handful for garnish**

**Whipped cream**

Preheat the oven to 350°F. Grease an 11-inch springform pan and line the bottom with parchment paper.

Put the flour, sugar, and butter in a food processor and pulse until the mixture resembles bread crumbs. Add the eggs and process until the mixture forms a soft dough.

Press two-thirds of the dough into the bottom of the pan. Spread with the lemon curd and then crumble the remaining dough over the curd layer. Bake for 35 to 40 minutes, until golden brown. Let cool in the pan. Release the sides and remove the cake from the pan—discard the parchment paper. Put the cake on a platter and sprinkle with confectioners' sugar.

To serve, ladle some raspberry puree into the center of a dessert plate. Set a piece of the cake on top, put a dollop of whipped cream on the side, and garnish with a few raspberries.

*Note:* To make the cake by hand, combine the flour and sugar in a medium bowl. Cut in the butter with 2 table knives or a pastry blender until the mixture forms coarse crumbs. Beat the eggs together in a small bowl and pour them over the dry ingredients. Mix with a spatula until blended.

## *Lemon Curd*

**MAKES ABOUT 1½ CUPS**

**2 large, juicy lemons**
**1 cup sugar**
**3½ tablespoons unsalted butter**
**2 large eggs, beaten**

Finely grate the lemon zest and squeeze the juice. Put the zest and juice in a saucepan and add the sugar and butter. Gently heat over low heat until the butter has melted. Do not let the mixture come to a boil.

Remove the pan from the heat and stir the lemon mixture into the beaten eggs. Pour the mixture back into the saucepan and heat gently, stirring constantly, for 2 to 3 minutes, until the mixture thickens.

## *Maine Wild Blueberry Gateau*

The Packard House, a bed-and-breakfast in Bath, Maine, serves this lovely cake to its guests year-round. In Portland, I buy frozen wild blueberries at Safeway, but I have also made this with commercial blueberries and a combination of blueberries and raspberries.

**MAKES 6 SERVINGS**

**1 cup plus 1 teaspoon all-purpose flour**
**1 teaspoon baking powder**
**½ teaspoon coarse salt**
**¼ pound (1 stick) unsalted butter, softened**
**1 cup sugar**
**2 large eggs**

**1½ pints (3 cups) fresh Maine blueberries or huckleberries, rinsed and drained, or frozen wild blueberries**
**1 teaspoon fresh lemon juice**
**Confectioners' sugar**

Preheat the oven to 350°F degrees. Lightly grease a 9-inch springform pan and dust with flour. (I have also made this cake in a 9-inch cake pan dusted with flour, the bottom lined with parchment paper.)

Sift 1 cup flour, baking powder, and salt together in a small bowl and set aside.

Using an electric beater, cream the butter and sugar until light and fluffy. Add the eggs one at a time and continue beating until well blended. Reduce the speed to low and gradually add the flour mixture. Beat until smooth. Pour the batter into the prepared pan. Toss the blueberries with the remaining teaspoon flour and the lemon juice. Spoon the berry mixture over the batter.

Bake for about 1 hour, until a cake tester inserted in the center comes out clean. Let cool in the pan for 10 minutes. Slide a thin knife around the edges of the cake to release the pan. Remove the sides. (If you used a cake pan, invert it onto a cookie rack.) Transfer the cake to a cake platter, berry side up, and dust with confectioners' sugar.

## *Upside-Down Cranberry-Pumpkin Polenta Cake*

Several years ago Flo Braker, author of *The Simple Art of Perfect Baking* and the award-winning *Sweet Miniatures: The Art of Making Bite-Size Desserts,* ran a recipe for Pumpkin Polenta Cake in her baking column in the *San Francisco Chronicle.* I found that the recipe made a luscious upside-down cake with cranberries when cut in half.

**MAKES 10 SERVINGS**

**¼ pound (1 stick) plus 3 tablespoons unsalted butter**
**¾ cup packed dark brown sugar**
**10 ounces (2½ cups) fresh cranberries, rinsed and drained thoroughly**
**1¼ cups all-purpose flour**
**1 teaspoon pumpkin pie spice**
**½ teaspoon ground cinnamon**
**¾ teaspoon baking powder**
**⅛ teaspoon baking soda**
**⅛ teaspoon salt**

**½ cup light brown sugar**
**½ cup granulated sugar**
**2 large eggs, at room temperature**
**½ cup pumpkin puree (canned is fine)**
**½ cup medium-ground polenta**
**¼ cup milk**

Place a rack in the lower third of the oven; preheat the oven to 350°F.

Melt 3 tablespoons of the butter in a heavy ovenproof skillet and stir in the dark brown sugar. Add the cranberries and cook gently over low heat until the brown sugar dissolves, 3 to 5 minutes. Keep warm over low heat.

Sift together the flour, pumpkin pie spice, cinnamon, baking powder, baking soda, and salt; set aside.

Using an electric beater, beat the remaining stick of butter until creamy. Add the light brown sugar and granulated sugar and beat until light. Add the eggs one at a time, beating well. Reduce the speed and add the pumpkin and polenta. Add the flour mixture alternately with the milk and mix just until blended.

Pour the batter over the cranberries and bake for 30 to 40 minutes or until a toothpick inserted in the center comes out clean. As soon as the cake comes out of the oven, carefully release it onto a platter.

Serve it plain as a coffee cake with Triple Red Berry Sauce (page 159) or for dessert with whipped cream or vanilla ice cream. Keep wrapped tightly in plastic wrap and then foil and store at room temperature for up to 2 days.

### Edible versus Eatable

"There's a big difference between edible and eatable. There are a lot of edible berries, but do you want to eat them?"

—Dr. Chad Finn, research geneticist, Oregon State University

## *Pavlova with Four Variations*

Once you know how to make a good meringue, you can create numerous variations of wonderful berry desserts. The first recipe is for a Pavlova, a recipe from Down Under originally served with strawberries and kiwifruit. Meringue cakes were popular in the 1920s in New Zealand, but it wasn't until six years after the famous Russian ballerina Anna Pavlova visited Perth in 1929 that the meringue cake—"light as Pavlova"—was given its current name.

This dessert is a variation of a recipe featured in *Gourmet* magazine several years ago and makes the best meringue I have ever eaten. It's crispy on the outside and sticky-gooey in the middle.

**MAKES 8 SERVINGS**

**2 large egg whites**
**1½ cups superfine granulated sugar (or granulated sugar processed for 1 minute with the steel blade in a food processor or blender)**
**1½ teaspoons cornstarch**
**1 teaspoon white vinegar**
**½ teaspoon vanilla extract**
**1 cup heavy cream, whipped**
**1½ pints (3 cups) mixed fresh berries or berries and other fruit (such as peaches)**

Place a rack in the middle of the oven and preheat the oven to 350°F. Line a baking sheet with foil.

Beat the egg whites, sugar, cornstarch, vinegar, and vanilla on low speed until blended. Add ¼ cup boiling water all at once and beat on high speed for 15 minutes, until the mixture forms glossy, stiff peaks.

Spoon the mixture into a 10-inch circle on the baking sheet, making it deeper in the center so it will be able to hold the berries and whipped cream.

Bake for 10 minutes, then turn the heat down to 200°F and bake for 40 minutes longer. Turn the oven off (don't open the door) and leave the meringue in the oven for another hour to dry out.

Remove the foil from the meringue and cool completely on a rack.

Just before serving, spoon the whipped cream into the shell and top with the berries.

*Variation I:* My grandmother always called these individual meringues "kisses." Make eight 4-inch individual meringue shells. Use the back of a tablespoon to make them deeper in the center. Decrease the cooking time at 200°F from 40 minutes to 25 minutes. Sprinkle sugar over 2 pints fresh raspberries and let sit for 1 hour. Fill the cooled shells with a spoonful of berries and top with whipped cream. Makes 8 servings.

*Variation II:* In England this favorite dessert is called Eton Mess. Mash 2 pints fresh raspberries in the bottom of a large bowl. Crumble the entire meringue into 2- to 3-inch pieces over the berries. Whip the cream and fold it into the meringue and berries. Refrigerate for 1 to 2 hours before serving. Makes 10 servings.

*Variation III:* This Italian dessert is called Boccone Dolce, "sweet mouthful." Prepare the meringue and bake in twelve 4-inch flat circles. (If you draw the circles with a pencil on foil, then turn the foil over and line a baking sheet, you will have a ready-made template for the individual meringues.) Hull and slice 2 pints strawberries. Put half of the berries in a separate bowl and sprinkle with sugar to create juice. Whip 1 cup heavy cream. An hour before serving, melt 3 ounces semisweet chocolate in ¼ cup water and drizzle over the meringues. Let harden. To serve, put 1 chocolate-covered meringue on each dessert plate. Spread with a ¾-inch layer of whipped cream and top with the unsweetened sliced strawberries. Repeat for the second layer. Put the third layer on top, spread with whipped cream, and top with sweetened sliced strawberries and juice. Makes 4 servings.

*Variation IV:* Add 2 ounces roasted and coarsely chopped hazelnuts (see page 73) to the unbaked meringue for the Boccone Dolce.

# PASTRIES, PUDDINGS, AND OTHER SWEET TREATS

When I want to serve a little bite of something sweet after dinner, I often make small pastries, like the Lemon Shortbread Turnovers or the Sautéed Filo Pastry Stuffed with Blackberries and Mascarpone. They are rich and buttery and always satisfying. Or I make a batch of berries dipped in chocolate for tiny decadent nibbles.

I've included candy recipes made with dried berries in this chapter, too. These candies are easy to make and serve as especially nice gifts during the Christmas holidays. A wide variety of high-quality dried berries is now available on the market, including raspberries, strawberries, and blackberries. They will keep for up to a year, so stock up when you see them, and you'll be able to make these candies on a moment's notice.

Keep a bottle of balsamic vinegar on your shelf, too, for those times when you are stuck with a basket of marginal strawberries; see Sautéed Strawberries with Balsamic Vinegar. The heat and butter soften the fruit, while the balsamic vinegar adds sweetness and flavor.

And spirits are excellent for enhancing the flavors of berries. Simply macerate a quart of fresh berries in a cup of muscatel wine, late harvest Riesling, or Prosecco for at least one and up to eight hours, to soak up those good flavors, and serve them in a large glass bowl or double martini glasses. Or when the Charentais melons are ripe in August (I buy them at the Portland farmers' market), cut them in half, scoop out the seeds, and fill them with port and a mound of fresh berries. If you can't find the Charentais melons, substitute small cantaloupe halves instead.

### *Lemon Shortbread Turnovers*

If you want just a little nibble of something to satisfy your sweet tooth, these turnovers are a fine way to end a meal. Every bite has a tangy burst of lemon, strawberry, and butter flavors.

**MAKES 2 DOZEN TURNOVERS**

**1½ cups sifted confectioners' sugar**
**½ pound (2 sticks) unsalted butter, softened**
**1 large egg**
**1 teaspoon lemon oil or lemon extract**
**2 teaspoons grated lemon zest**
**2½ cups all-purpose flour**
**1 teaspoon baking soda**
**1 teaspoon cream of tartar**
**Strawberry–Sweet Plum Jam (page 164) or any berry jam**

Stir together the sugar and butter. Add the egg, lemon oil, lemon zest, flour, baking soda, and cream of tartar and mix well. Wrap the dough in a self-sealing plastic bag and chill in the refrigerator for at least 2 hours.

Preheat the oven to 375°F.

Divide the dough in half (put the other half back in the refrigerator). Roll the dough out to ¼-inch thickness on a greased cookie sheet (this helps the cookies keep their shape). Cut out the cookies with a 4-inch round biscuit cutter. Put 1 scant teaspoon jam in the center of each and fold in half. Pinch the edges to close. Repeat for the remaining dough on a second cookie sheet.

Bake for 10 minutes or until the edges of the cookies start to turn a light golden brown. Transfer to a cookie rack to cool. Store in a covered container for up to a week.

### *Petite Blackberry Turnovers*

I make these little turnovers for summer picnics because they travel well and you don't need a plate or a fork to eat them. If your kitchen is hot, refrigerate the turnovers for 15 minutes to chill the butter in the dough before baking them. This important step helps the cookies keep their shape while baking.

**MAKES 11 TURNOVERS**

**1 heaping pint (2 heaping cups) fresh marionberries or other blackberries, rinsed and drained, or frozen marionberries, thawed in a single layer on a paper towel for 20 minutes**

**1 tablespoon all-purpose flour**

**2 to 3 teaspoons sugar, to taste, plus sugar for sprinkling**

**½ recipe Favorite Tart and Cobbler Pastry (page 213)**

**Milk for glazing**

Preheat the oven to 400°F. Lightly grease 2 baking sheets.

Toss together the berries, flour, and 2 to 3 teaspoons sugar and set aside.

Roll out half of the pastry to ⅜-inch thickness and cut five 4½-inch circles. Transfer the pastry to a cookie sheet and repeat for the remaining pastry half. Place 1½ tablespoons of the blackberry filling spread out lengthwise down the center of the circle. Fold the pastry over and press the edges together with your fingers. Brush the turnovers with milk and sprinkle with sugar. Bake them for 20 to 25 minutes or until the turnovers are a rich, golden brown.

## *Sautéed Filo Pastry Stuffed with Blackberries and Mascarpone*

I learned how to make these buttery pastries one year in Provence from a young woman, Delphine Polon, who came to the house we were renting and cooked a meal for us. That night she served filo stuffed with goat cheese as appetizers. I use the same method to make this stellar dessert. Unlike with most filo recipes, these are sautéed in butter instead of being baked, just before serving.

**MAKES 12 PASTRIES, SERVING 4**

**¼ cup Marcona almonds, toasted (see page 73) and chopped**

**2 tablespoons sugar**

**Twelve 9 × 13-inch sheets filo pastry, thawed if frozen**

**4 tablespoons (½ stick) unsalted butter, melted, plus butter for sautéing**

**½ pint (1 cup) fresh blackberries or raspberries, rinsed and drained**

**¼ pound mascarpone**

Blend together the almonds and sugar and set aside.

Open the package and unfold the filo. Cover with a lightly moistened towel. Lay one sheet of filo out flat and brush with melted butter. Top with 2 more sheets of filo, buttering each between the layers. Cut the sheets lengthwise into three 3-inch-wide strips. Put 3 to 4 blackberries (depending on their size), ½ teaspoon mascarpone, and ½ teaspoon of the chopped almond mixture 1 inch from the left end of one filo strip.

Starting at the left end, fold the filo over the top of the filling, then fold up like a flag by rolling one corner diagonally across to the opposite edge to form a triangle. Continue to fold to the end of the strip and trim if necessary. Brush with butter and place seam side down on a plate. Repeat for the other 2 strips.

Repeat this entire process three more times until you have made 12 filo packets. You should end up with 4 triple layers of filo (in order to make 12 packets). (Roll remaining unused filo sheets tightly in plastic wrap. Refrigerate for up to 1 week or freeze for up to 2 months.)

Heat 1 tablespoon of butter in a nonstick skillet over low heat. Sauté the filo packets on both sides for 2 minutes until they are golden brown. Serve immediately.

## *Raspberry-Gooseberry Duff with Lemon Sauce*

A duff is defined in the dictionary as a "boiled or steamed flour pudding often containing dried fruits." It is a variation of a dessert brought to this country by the English settlers. Today duffs are baked in the oven, but they still have that wonderful dense, puddinglike texture. My mother-in-law gave me this favorite Hibler family recipe that was passed down from my husband's grandmother, Grace Hibler. While it is traditionally made with huckleberries, I have found this recipe works well with most berries.

**MAKES 6 TO 8 SERVINGS**

**DUFF**

**2 large eggs**
**About ¾ cup milk**
**1 cup all-purpose flour**
**½ to ⅔ cup sugar**
**1 teaspoon baking powder**
**Pinch of salt**
**3 tablespoons unsalted butter, melted (cool or warm but not hot)**
**½ cup fresh gooseberries, rinsed and drained, or frozen gooseberries,**

**½ cup fresh raspberries, rinsed and drained, or frozen raspberries**

**LEMON SAUCE**

**1½ tablespoons cornstarch**

**¼ cup sugar**

**Grated zest of 1 lemon**

**2 tablespoons fresh lemon juice (from 1 lemon)**

**3 tablespoons unsalted butter**

Preheat the oven to 350°F. Grease an 8-inch square cake pan.

Break the eggs into a 1-cup measuring cup. Whisk with a fork, then fill the cup to the top with milk. Combine the flour, sugar, baking powder, and salt in a bowl and stir in the milk mixture and butter until the batter is smooth. Gently fold in the gooseberries. Pour into the prepared pan and bake for 40 to 45 minutes or until the duff is a rich golden brown and a toothpick inserted in the center comes out clean.

To make the sauce, combine the cornstarch and sugar in a saucepan. Set the pan over medium heat and stir in 1½ cups water, the lemon zest, and the lemon juice. Continue stirring for 2 to 3 minutes, until the sauce clears and has thickened. Remove from the heat and stir in the butter.

Put a piece of duff on each plate. Ladle a spoonful of sauce over the top and garnish with a sprinkling of fresh raspberries.

## *Mocha Mousse with Fresh Strawberries*

Julia Child was the inspiration for this mocha mousse, which she makes in her famous cookbook *Mastering the Art of French Cooking*. It's decadently rich and creamy, besides being lovely to look at with a mound of strawberries piled high in the center. If you don't have an espresso machine, use instant espresso coffee, such as Medaglia D'Oro.

**MAKES 6 TO 8 SERVINGS**

**4 large eggs, separated**

**¾ cup superfine sugar**

**3 ounces bittersweet chocolate**

**5 tablespoons brewed espresso (decaffeinated or regular)**

**12 tablespoons (1½ sticks) unsalted butter, softened**
**Pinch of salt**
**1 tablespoon granulated sugar**
**1 pint (2 cups) fresh strawberries (I like to serve them unhulled, but you can do it either way)**

Rinse a 4½-cup ring mold with cold water (shake the water out, but don't dry it) and set aside.

Beat the egg yolks and superfine sugar together until the mixture is thick and pale lemon in color. It will form a ribbon when it falls from the beater. Put the bowl over a pan of hot water and beat for 3 to 4 minutes, until the mixture is foamy, then beat over a pan of ice for another 3 to 4 minutes, until it forms a ribbon and thickens.

Melt the chocolate in a double boiler or microwave with the coffee. Remove from the heat and whisk in the butter. Beat the chocolate mixture into the egg yolks and set aside.

Beat the egg whites with the salt until soft peaks form, then slowly beat in the granulated sugar until the mixture forms stiff peaks.

Stir one-third of the egg whites into the chocolate-egg mixture and then fold in the rest. Turn into the mold and refrigerate for 2 to 3 hours or overnight.

To serve, put the pan in a sink filled with hot water for 10 seconds. Run a knife around the edges and turn upside down on a platter. Remove the mold and fill the center with the fresh strawberries. Serve immediately.

## *Key Lime Panna Cotta with Strawberry Sorbet*

I fell in love with this sumptuous dessert at a meeting in Minneapolis when Joan Ida, the pastry chef at Goodfellow's Restaurant, prepared it for a banquet one evening. Panna cotta originated in the Piedmont region of Italy and literally means "cooked cream." It's a molded creamy dessert that is traditionally served with fresh fruit. That night Joan served it with a fresh strawberry puree and a small mound of strawberry sorbet.

Both the panna cotta and the sorbet can be made days in advance, making this an ideal dessert for entertaining.

**MAKES 8 SERVINGS**

**Panna Cotta**

**One and a half ¼-ounce envelopes (1⅓ teaspoons) unflavored gelatin**

**¾ cup fresh lime juice (from about 10 limes)**

**⅔ cup sugar**

**1 cup heavy cream**

**⅔ cup milk (whole or 2 percent)**

**2 teaspoons dark rum**

**Zest of 1 lime, minced**

**MAKES 4 CUPS, SERVING 8**

**Strawberry Sorbet**

**2 pints (4 cups) fresh strawberries, quartered if large, rinsed and drained**

**¾ cup fresh lemon juice (from 4 to 5 lemons)**

**½ cup sugar**

**Strawberry Coulis (page 151)**

Lightly oil eight 4-ounce ramekins.

Sprinkle the gelatin over the lime juice in a small bowl. Let stand for 5 minutes to soften.

Put the sugar, cream, and milk in a nonreactive saucepan and bring to a boil over medium-high heat. Remove from the heat and add the gelatin mixture, rum, and minced lime zest. Stir until blended, then divide the mixture among the ramekins and refrigerate until firm, about 3 hours. Once set, cover with plastic wrap.

To make the sorbet, puree the strawberries with the lemon juice in a food processor or blender. Dissolve the sugar in 1¼ cups tepid water and blend with the strawberry puree.

Pour into an ice cream freezer and freeze according to the manufacturer's instructions or use the still-freeze method (see page188). It will keep tightly sealed in the freezer for up to 1 week.

To serve, ladle a spoonful of strawberry coulis onto 8 dessert plates and spread it into a wide circle. Unmold the panna cottas by dipping each individual ramekin into a small bowl of hot water for a few seconds. Give it a good shake and turn it upside down on a dessert plate. (You might have to run a knife around the edge of the mold first to help release it.) Put a scoop of sorbet on each plate and serve immediately.

*Variation:* Serve panna cotta accompanied by peak-of-the-season summer fruits cloaked in a raspberry or strawberry puree sweetened with a little sugar.

## *Gooseberry Fool*

Fools most likely get their name from the French word *foulé*, meaning "crushed or pressed." They are a sacred combination of pureed fruit, whipped cream, and a pinch of sugar, and the easiest of all berry desserts to make. Elizabeth David, in *An Omelette and a Glass of Wine*, says, "To me it is essential to serve fruit fools in glasses or in simple white cups, with shortbread or other such biscuits to go with them." In this recipe, unlike gooseberry pie, you do not need to tip and tail the berries because after they are stewed, the mixture is pureed before being added to the whipped cream.

**MAKES 4 SERVINGS**

**2 pounds fresh gooseberries, rinsed and drained, or frozen berries, thawed**
**¼ cup sugar, plus 1 tablespoon**
**1 cup heavy cream, whipped**

Combine the berries and sugar in a saucepan over low heat and slowly heat, stirring often, until the berries are soft. Drain off excess liquid, which would make the fool watery, then pass through a food mill. Refrigerate until cool. Fold in the cream and add more sugar if necessary.

*Variation:* For blackberries, raspberries, or strawberries, crush 1 pint of fruit and fold into the whipped cream with 2 to 3 tablespoons sugar. Or combine 1 cup stewed rhubarb and 1 cup crushed strawberries with the whipped cream; add sugar to taste.

## *Chocolate, Macadamia Nut, and Cranberry Nuggets*

Beware: these candies are addictive! Slightly sweet dried berries with chopped macadamia nuts and semisweet chocolate would be good just by themselves, but I've also added cacao nibs—crushed roasted cocoa beans separated from their husks—to add a crunchy texture and a more intense chocolate flavor. If you can't find them, simply replace them with ¼ cup more macadamia nuts.

**MAKES ABOUT 1 POUND**

**½ pound high-quality semisweet chocolate (such as Scharffen Berger), coarsely chopped**
**1½ ounces (about ⅓ cup) lightly roasted and salted whole macadamia nuts (see page 73)**

⅔ cup dried sweetened cranberries, raspberries, or other dried berries
¼ cup cacao nibs

Put the chocolate in the top of a double boiler over simmering water or use a microwave. When the chocolate is completely melted, stir in the remaining ingredients until they are well coated. Remove from the heat.

Using 2 spoons, scoop up about 1 teaspoon of the mixture and drop it onto wax paper. Repeat this step to make the remaining candies. Set aside to harden, about an hour. Store between layers of wax paper in a tin or tightly wrapped in foil for up to 1 week.

## *White Chocolate, Cranberry, and Pistachio Bark*

Chris Christensen, food editor of FOODday, the *Oregonian*'s food pages, has made this effortless candy for more than a decade to the delight of her friends. She gives it as Christmas gifts in little rectangular cellophane bags tied with ribbon. I was a lucky recipient several years ago and loved nibbling on the chocolate with its jumble of flavors—sweet and salty—and soft and crunchy textures. The red cranberries and toasted green pistachios make this candy a kaleidoscope of colors, too.

Chris says, "Since there are only three ingredients, I use the best I can find. I buy Ghirardelli white chocolate and salted pistachios, both from Trader Joe's, and really high-quality dried cranberries."

**MAKES ABOUT 1 POUND**

**¾ pound good-quality white chocolate, coarsely chopped**
**⅓ cup salted pistachios, toasted (see Note)**
**⅓ cup good-quality sweetened cranberries**

Butter a large cookie sheet and line with wax paper.

Melt about half the white chocolate in the top of a double boiler set over lightly simmering hot water (or place the chocolate in a bowl that fits snugly over a pot of simmering water, or microwave). Be careful not to splash water or drip steam into the chocolate. Stir occasionally until the chocolate has fully melted. Add the remaining chocolate and stir. Remove the pan from the heat and continue to stir until the chocolate is fully melted and smooth.

Add the nuts and fruits, quickly and gently folding them into the chocolate with a rubber spatula. Pour the mixture into the center of the cookie sheet and spread with spatula into a free-form shape about ½-inch thick.

Let the bark harden in a cool spot for at least 4 hours. Do not refrigerate.

With a heavy knife, cut the bark into odd rectangular shapes. Store the candy in an airtight container or divide among clear cellophane bags and tie with a colorful ribbon for gift giving. Stored in a cool spot, the candy will keep for at least a month.

*Note:* To toast nuts, heat in a dry skillet over medium heat until they start to brown, about 2 to 3 minutes.

## *Raspberry Russian Cream*

Albertina's luncheon restaurant in Portland, Oregon, serves this old favorite, also known as *Swedish cream and panna cotta.* I have incorporated raspberry puree into the recipe, and it works beautifully with other berry purees, too. Molded raspberry cream is a delicate-flavored dessert that is rich and satisfying. Make it either in stemmed glasses, for an elegant look, or in molds. Use six ½-cup individual molds or one 3-cup mold.

**MAKES 6 SERVINGS**

- **1¼ cups heavy cream**
- **⅓ cup sugar**
- **1¾ teaspoons unflavored gelatin**
- **½ cup sour cream**
- **½ cup plain nonfat yogurt**
- **1 teaspoon vanilla extract**
- **2 tablespoons framboise**
- **½ pint (1 cup) fresh raspberries, rinsed and drained, or frozen raspberries, thawed with juice, pureed and seeded (see page 70)**

Combine the cream, sugar, and gelatin in a small saucepan and heat gently until the gelatin is thoroughly dissolved. Cool until slightly thickened. Fold in the sour cream, yogurt, vanilla, framboise, and raspberry puree and whisk until smooth. Pour into stemmed glasses or molds and refrigerate, covered with plastic wrap, for 1 hour or up to 2 days. To unmold, dip the container in hot water until the edges just begin to liquefy. Invert onto a serving plate. Serve with fresh berries or a little Melba Sauce (page 230).

*Note:* Albertina's is located in the Kerr Nursery, a Portland building that served as an orphanage and nursery founded by Alexander Kerr, the creator of the Kerr canning jar, at the turn of the century. (This was at one time his home, and the restaurant is named after his wife, Albertina.) All the cooking and serving at the restaurant are done entirely by volunteers, and proceeds go to community programs for youth.

### *Berries in Bittersweet Chocolate*

You can buy chocolate-covered berries from Bissinger's French Confections in St. Louis, but if you have the time, these confections are simple to make and decadently delicious. Or have a chocolate fondue party and let your guests have the pleasure of dunking the berries in warm chocolate and putting them right into their mouths. It is instant gratification. You can buy chocolate-covered berries from Bissinger's French Confections, 3983 Gratiot Street, St. Louis, MO 63110-1176; 800-325-8881; www.bissingers.com.

**MAKES 8 TO 10 SERVINGS**

**1 pint (2 cups) fresh medium strawberries with stems, rinsed, drained, and thoroughly dry**

**½ pint (1 cup) fresh blueberries, rinsed, drained, and thoroughly dry**

**½ pint (1 cup) fresh raspberries, rinsed, drained, and thoroughly dry**

**10 ounces high-quality bittersweet or semisweet chocolate**

Lay a long piece of wax paper on a flat surface.

Rinse and drain the berries and thoroughly dry with paper towels. (The berries must be perfectly dry—any water on the fruit will cause the chocolate to tighten up.)

Slowly melt the chocolate in the top of a double boiler over simmering water, in a microwave, or in a small heavy pan over low heat. Remove the pan from the heat. Use a fork to dip the berries individually in the chocolate. Gently tap off the excess chocolate and put them on the wax paper to set; don't let the fruits touch each other, or they will stick together when the chocolate hardens. It will take about an hour for the chocolate to set. Transfer the berries to a platter and cover with wax paper until serving time. (Don't put them in an airtight container, or they will sweat.) Store in the refrigerator, but bring them to room temperature before serving. Serve within 1 to 2 days.

*Note:* I don't temper the chocolate for this recipe because I serve the berries the day or the day after I make them—it's not enough time for a bloom to develop.

### *Sautéed Strawberries with Balsamic Vinegar*

Chef Lucia Watson, proprietor of the highly regarded Lucia's restaurant in Minneapolis, likes to serve these sautéed strawberries—seasoned with a splash of balsamic vinegar and a pinch of freshly ground pepper—over rich vanilla ice cream. "A drizzle of Grand Marnier would be good here, too," she says. "I often make this recipe early in the strawberry season, when the strawberries are not quite at their peak of sweetness."

**MAKES 4 SERVINGS**

**1½ to 2 tablespoons unsalted butter**
**1 pint (2 cups) fresh strawberries, rinsed, drained, and sliced**
**Balsamic vinegar**
**Freshly ground pepper**
**Grand Marnier (optional)**
**1 pint vanilla ice cream**
**1 small plate of butter cookies**

Melt the butter in a medium sauté pan and add the strawberries. Sauté the berries over medium-low heat for 2 to 3 minutes, until they start to soften. Sprinkle them with balsamic vinegar and season with freshly ground black pepper. Toss and remove from the heat. Sprinkle with the Grand Marnier, if you are using it, and toss the berries again.

Put a large scoop of ice cream in each of 4 dessert bowls and top with the warm strawberries. Serve immediately accompanied by the butter cookies.

### *Blueberry-Raspberry Coconut Custard*

Fresh blueberries and raspberries add a refreshing burst of flavor paired with shredded coconut in this rich and creamy vanilla custard. Other firm berries work equally well, such as wild blueberries or blackberries. Don't make it with frozen berries—their soft texture will not hold up as well as the fresh berries.

**MAKES 8 SERVINGS**

**1 cup milk**
**1 cup heavy cream**
**3 large eggs**
**2 large eggs yolks**
**¼ teaspoon coarse salt**
**½ cup sugar**

**1 teaspoon vanilla extract**
**Heaping ¾ cup flaked or sweetened shredded coconut**
**½ pint (1 cup) fresh blueberries, rinsed and drained**
**½ pint (1 cup) fresh raspberries, rinsed and drained**

Preheat the oven to 325°F. Lightly grease a 1-quart baking dish. Fill a pan large enough to hold the baking dish or ramekins with about an inch of hot water (the water should come halfway up the sides of the baking dish) and put it in the oven.

Heat the milk and cream until hot, about 3 minutes on high in the microwave. While the milk mixture is heating, whisk together the eggs, egg yolks, salt, and sugar. Skim off any film that may have formed on top of the milk mixture with a slotted spoon or strain. Gradually whisk the milk mixture into the whisked sugar and egg and stir in the vanilla, coconut, and blueberries. Pour into the prepared baking dish and carefully set the dish in the hot water bath in the oven. At the end of 30 minutes, sprinkle the raspberries over the custard and poke them down into the custard with the tip of a knife.

Bake for 20 more minutes, until a knife inserted in the center of the dish comes out clean. (It should be lightly browned around the edges but loose in the center when jiggled. It will firm up as it cools.) Chill for 2 hours before serving. It's best eaten within 2 days.

## *Strawberry Coeur à la Crème*

Coeur à la crème ("heart of cream") is the name of a classic molded French dessert made in either a 3-inch or a 6-inch heart-shaped mold with sweetened cream cheese, and I have added strawberry puree, too, for more berry flavor. After it is chilled in the refrigerator, the mixture is unmolded, surrounded by fresh berries, and served accompanied by chocolate wafers to spread it on. It is the perfect dessert for Valentine's Day if you can find good, fresh berries to go with it.

**MAKES 6 SERVINGS**

**½ pound cream cheese, softened**
**2 tablespoons confectioners' sugar**
**½ cup fresh strawberries, rinsed and drained, or frozen strawberries, thawed with juice, pureed (see page 70)**
**½ teaspoon vanilla extract**
**1 pint (2 cups) fresh strawberries, rinsed and drained**
**One 8½-ounce package chocolate wafers**

Dampen a piece of cheesecloth and line a 6-inch coeur à la crème mold, leaving a 2-inch overhang. Using an electric beater, beat the cream cheese, sugar, puree, and vanilla together in a medium mixing bowl until smooth. Pack the mixture into the mold with the back of a spatula. Fold the overhanging cheesecloth back over the top of the cream cheese mixture. Set the mold on a plate and chill in the refrigerator for 3 hours.

Unmold onto a platter and remove the cheesecloth. Surround the molded cream cheese with the remaining strawberries and tuck a small cheese knife on one side of the plate between the mold and the strawberries. Serve accompanied by the chocolate cookies for spreading.

## *Charentais Melon with Port and Mixed Berries*

Charentais melons are named after the town in France where they are grown. These highly perfumed globe-shaped melons are small, 3½ to 4 inches wide, with sweet orange flesh. Once the seeds are removed, the cavity is a ready-made dessert bowl.

**MAKES 4 SERVINGS**

**2 Charentais melons**

**½ pint (1 cup) mixed berries, such as strawberries, blueberries, raspberries, and blackberries, rinsed and drained**

**Mild honey or a pinch of sugar**

**About ¼ cup tawny port**

Cut the melons in half horizontally and scoop out the seeds—a grapefruit spoon works well for this. Place each melon half in a small bowl and fill the melon cavity with ¼ cup fresh berries. Drizzle with honey and top off with the port. Serve immediately.

*Variation:* Replace the port in each melon with a scoop of vanilla ice cream.

# ABOUT THE AUTHOR

Janie Hibler is a contributing writer to *Gourmet, Food & Wine,* and *Bon Appétit* magazines. She is the past president of the International Association of Culinary Professionals and the author of five books, including the bestselling *Dungeness Crabs and Blackberry Cobblers,* and *Wild About Game,* winner of the 1999 James Beard Award for Best Book: Single Subject. She divides her time between her home in Portland, Oregon, and her cabin in the Cascade Mountains.

# WEB SITES

**www.agriculture.purdue.edu**
Web site sponsored by Purdue University School of Agriculture. Invaluable source of information on all berries, including lecture outlines, how to grow, and related links.

**www.albertafruit.com/html/links.html**
Research information, recipes, and links to many North American berry resource sites.

**www.ars.usda.gov/pwa/corvallis/ncgr**
Web site for the National Clonal Germplasm Repository in Corvallis, Oregon. Extensive berry information and links on berries.

**http://berrygrape.org**
The Northwest Berry and Grape Information Network is a cooperative organization on small fruit among Oregon State University, University of Idaho, Washington State University, and USDA-ARS. The Web site provides information on growing small fruit, the latest research, and links to other berry commissions, advisory boards, and councils in North America.

**www.nal.usda.gov/pgdic/Strawberry/darpubs.htm**
This Web site features the entire book *The Strawberry: History, Breeding and Physiology*, by strawberry expert George M. Darrow.

**www.oregon-berries.com**
Sponsored by the Oregon Raspberry and Blackberry Commission, this is the most thorough Web site on Oregon berries. There are photos of the individual berries, the latest information on health and nutrition, recipes, and links to berry products, including fresh berries for sale.

**http://plants.usda.gov**

The PLANTS database provides standardized information about the plants of the United States and its territories, including berries. It includes common and scientific names, distributional information, photos, and scientific classification.

**http://www.uga.edu/fruit/**

University of Georgia Web site featuring Dr. Mark Rieger, professor of agriculture. Includes taxonomy and history, folklore, medicinal properties, and food uses of the world's major fruit crops.

**www.whitesbog.org**

In-depth history and photos of Whitesbog, New Jersey, where the highbush blueberry was domesticated.

**www.wildblueberries.com**

Web site sponsored by the Wild Blueberry Association of North America, which includes growers and processors. Includes a map showing where the berries are grown, health and nutrition information, and recipes.

# SELECTED BIBLIOGRAPHY

*Alaska* magazine editors. *Alaska Wild Berry Guide and Cookbook.* Anchorage: Alaska Northwest Publishing Company, 1989.

Beck, Phineas (Samuel Chamberlain). *Clémentine in the Kitchen.* New York: Hastings House, 1943.

Bird, Richard, and Kate Whiteman. *Growing Berries and Currants.* New York: Lorenz Books, 2002.

Bowling, Barbara L. *The Berry Grower's Companion.* Portland, OR: Timber Press, 2000.

Brown, Catherine. *A Year in a Scots Kitchen.* Glasgow: Neil Wilson Publishing, 1996.

Dale, Adam, and James J. Luby, eds. *The Strawberry into the Twenty-First Century.* Portland, OR. Timber Press, 1991.

David, Elizabeth. *French Provincial Cooking.* Middlesex, England: Penguin, 1960.

_____. *An Omelette and a Glass of Wine.* Paris: Henri Jouquieres et Cie, 1928.

Eck, Paul. *The American Cranberry.* New Brunswick, NJ: Rutgers University Press, 1990.

Eck, Paul, and Norman Childers, eds. *Blueberry Culture.* New Brunswick, NJ: Rutgers University Press, 1966.

Finn, Chad. "Temperate Berry Crops." *In Perspectives on New Crops and New Uses,* edited by J. Janick, 324–34. Alexandria, VA: ASHS Press, 1999.

Finn, Chad, Jim Hancock, and Chris Heider. "Notes on the Strawberry of Ecuador: Ancient Land Races, the Community of Farmers, and Modern Production." *Journal of the American Society for Horticulture Science* 33 no. 4 (1998): 583–87.

Fuller, Andrew S. *The Small Fruit Culturist.* New York: Orange Judd & Company, 1867.

Gunther, Erna. *Ethnobotany of Western Washington.* Seattle: University of Washington Press, 1945.

Hancock, J. F. *Strawberries.* New York: CABI Publishing, 1999.

Hartley, Dorothy. *Food in England.* London: Macdonald & Co., 1954.

Heitz, Halina. *Container Plants.* New York: Barron's, 1992.

Herbst, Sharon Tyler. *Food Lover's Companion.* New York: Barron's, 1990.

Jennings, D. L. *Raspberries and Blackberries: Their Breeding, Diseases and Growth.* London: Academic Press, Harcourt Brace Jovanovich, 1988.

Joseph, James A., Daniel A. Nadeau, and Anne Underwood. *The Color Code.* New York: Hyperion, 2002.

Kozloff, Eugene N. *Plants and Animals of the Pacific Northwest.* Seattle: University of Washington Press, 1988.

Krumm, Bob. *The Rocky Mountain Berry Book.* Helena, MT: Falcon Publishing, 1991.

Long, Cheryl, and Heather Kibbey. *Classic Liqueurs.* Lake Oswego, OH: Culinary Arts, 1996.

Mackinnon, Andy, ed., and Jim Pojar, co-ed. *Plants of the Pacific Northwest Coast.* Vancouver: British Columbia Ministry of Forests and Lone Pine Publishing, 1994.

Mann, Gertrude. *Berry Cooking.* London: Andre Deutsch, 1954.

Mathews, Daniel. *Cascade Olympic Natural History.* Portland, OR: Haven Editions with the Portland Audubon Society, 1948.

Moerman, Daniel E. *Native American Ethnobotany.* Portland, OR: Timber Press, 1998.

Nichols, Nell B., ed. *Farm Journal's Complete Pie Cookbook.* New York: Doubleday, 1965.

Ostmann, Barbara Gibbs, and Jane L. Baker. *The Recipe Writer's Handbook.* New York: John Wiley & Sons, 2001.

Paston-Williams, Sara. *Jams, Preserves and Edible Gifts.* London: National Trust Enterprises, 1999.

Roach, F. A. *Cultivated Fruits of Britain: Their Origin and History.* Oxford, UK: Basil Blackwell, 1985.

Rombauer, Irma S., Marion Rombauer Becker, and Ethan Becker. *Joy of Cooking.* New York: Scribner, 1997.

Schneider, Elizabeth. *Uncommon Fruits and Vegetables.* New York: Harper & Row, 1986.

Speck, Frank G. *Penobscot Man: The Life History of a Forest Tribe in Maine.* Orono: University of Maine Press, 1997.

Sailhac, Alain, Jacques Pépin, André Soltner, Jacques Torres, and the Faculty of the French Culinary Institute. *Healthy Cooking.* New York: Rodale, 1994.

Sjulin, Thomas M. "The North American Small Fruit Industry, 1903–2003." Contributions of Public and Private Research in the Past 25 Years, and a View to the Future. *Journal of the American Society for Horticulture Science* 38 no. 5 (forthcoming).

St.-Pierre, R. G. 1999. History, use and economic importance. *Growing Saskatoons: A Manual for Orchardists.* Saskatoon, SK, Canada: Native Fruit Development Program, Department of Plant Science, University of Saskatchewan.

St.-Pierre, R. *History, Use and Economic Importance of the Saskatoon.* Native Fruit Development Program, Dept. of Horticulture Science, University of Saskatchewan, March 1997.

Tannahill, Reay. *Food in History.* New York: Stein and Day, 1973.

Traunfeld, Jerry. *The Herb Farm Cookbook.* New York: Scribner, 2000.

Turner, Nancy J. *Food Plants of Coastal First Peoples.* Vancouver: University of British Columbia Press with Royal British Museum, 1995.

Ukrainian Women's Association of Canada. *Ukrainian Daughters' Cookbook.* Regina, SK: Centax Books, 2001.

Vitale, Alice Thoms. *Leaves in Myth, Magic and Medicine.* New York: Stewart, Tabori & Chang, 1997.

Weatherford, Jack. *Indian Givers.* New York: Ballantine Books, 1988.

Wilhelm, Stephen, and James E. Sagen. *A History of the Strawberry.* Berkeley: University of California Press, 1972.

# INDEX